# Before Our Eyes

Also by Carol Hunter and Tim Rouse

*Reflections on Russia*

## Advance Praise for *Before Our Eyes*

*"Before Our Eyes* is a beautifully written memoir of two people who transform lives as they journey around the world. Their impact begins with women's emerging roles in the USA, to changing politics in Russia and China, to learning about sexual slavery in India. Carol Hunter and Tim Rouse, audacious, passionate learners, provide us with a wider lens of our new world. Their analysis and descriptions of events from 1979 to 2014 is fused with engaging stories, thoughtful reflections, and purposeful deeds. Based on their descriptions, if you are ready, they will become your mentors for future actions."

Geil M. Browning, Ph.D., Founder
Emergenetics International, Denver, Colorado

"The sharing of Carol and Tim's life experiences has added richness to the lives of everyone that they have touched over the years, including myself. I thank them for all that they have done for all of us."

Steve Grandfield, Executive Vice President
Blue Cross Blue Shield Nebraska, Omaha

*"Before Our Eyes* shares deep wisdom, unbounded love and warm human care. It is meant to change one's prejudices and perceptions and help develop leadership in many ways. I believe it will be an interesting reading for any thinking, open-minded personality, seeking for holistic routes in life and work."

Olga Bantsekina, Chief Representative
Coleman Services UK Ltd., Moscow, Russia

"The success of CBSD must be shared with Carol and Tim as partners in a vision and not simply trainers or consultants. As mentors and friends they kept me going when life was difficult in Russia, invited me to share in so many exciting projects and lead by example in the classroom. Carol and Tim give all their energy and expertise to really impact the lives they touch. This memoir is about embracing change and loving the opportunity to grow.

From teachers to mentors to partners and life-long friends Carol and Tim embrace life with a rare passion to touch people much deeper than intellectually transferring knowledge and skills. They pour every ounce of energy and emotion into each program and give something special to every participant. The love and passion for their work are obvious in this book."

Dennis Hopple, President
Center for Business Skills Development, Moscow, Ret.
Vice President, Thunderbird Worldwide, Thunderbird
School of Global Management, Glendale, Arizona, Ret.

"Even though we have been working together for 13 years, I've actually never had a chance to step back to see a larger picture of Carol and Tim as well as FGI. Now this book provides me such an opportunity. I realize in my life up to the present, I have never met anyone else like them. They live up to what they deeply believe, what they teach, what they work on in their lives. It's very very rare for me to see this. It's rare for others to also. Thus this sharing is precious and invaluable."

Rui Shujie, Management Consultant
Shanghai, China

# Before Our Eyes:

## Reflections on This Changing World

*A Memoir*

*Dear Barb,*
*We have so*
*appreciated your's*
*and Cliff's love for*
*so many years.*
*Love,*
*Carol & Tim*

Carol Hunter    Tim Rouse

A FGISpirit Publication

# ACKNOWLEDGEMENTS

*Before Our Eyes* is a labor of love for the two of us. It would have been an impossible task without the counsel, advice and hard work of a number of individuals. It is simply impossible to acknowledge all those who have been with us as these stories unfolded.

Those whose efforts have allowed us to actually write the book and move it into print are forever in our hearts. Though we may miss someone, we wish to thank and acknowledge the following:

- Rebecca Blair who worked tirelessly on the book for over two years, reading and editing our work, advising us on style and language, and then doing all the hard work necessary to get the book into print. Without Rebecca, there would be no book.

- Denny Aron, our friend and colleague for over forty years, who was the first to read the entire book and give us his wisdom and guidance in turning it into the final draft.

- Jeffrie Story who helped us in the early days clarify our purpose for writing and the organization of the book. She also read drafts of the early chapters and gave us excellent advice on style.

- Tim Hunter, Annie King, Tom Rouse, Lori Zahm and Karen Tompsett, each of whom worked with us for many years. Without them many of the experiences we describe would never have happened. They, along with Rebecca, are the ones who organized us, supported our every effort and ensured the quality of our work.

- Rui Shujie, our dear friend and colleague, who represented us as FGI International Asia, who made all of our China work possible and who is like a sister to each of us.

- Dennis Hopple, our friend, colleague and client, who as President of CBSD/Russia, invited us to teach and help build the organization over 15 years in Moscow.

- Our colleagues, clients and friends over many years, who were generously willing to offer their support and comments on the finished book.

- The colleagues, clients and friends who allowed us to use their names and/or images to illustrate the book.

- The hundred plus organizations in many countries who trusted us and allowed us to serve their organization as business consultants and friends.

- The thousands of women and men from over forty countries who have participated in our programs in the United States, Russia, China, New Zealand and India. Without them there would be no stories.

### And Most Important

- Carol wishes to thank her loving, patient, amazing husband, Terry Hunter, for understanding and always supporting her, the FGI work, travel and now the book time.

- Tim wishes to thank Maryanne, his loving, supportive wife. She sacrificed a lot and gave even more to make it possible for him to have the experiences and adventures described in this book.

# TABLE OF CONTENTS

# FORWARD

Sometimes as life unfolds, it's easy to see that Something Greater is providing learning moments meant to be shared with others.

We were riding the wave of a changing America and then, suddenly, the reconfiguring of World economies. Life was dynamic! We were learning and growing. We had insights, understanding and real life experiences that put history before our eyes, onto our calendars!

The phone calls and email invitations to serve continued to come – there was little time to stop, to write, to share at any deep level.

That time has come. The reader decides the message for her or him. Let the Magic we experienced be shared.

# INTRODUCTION

We sit for a few minutes, deciding where to begin. Stories push themselves into our minds, fighting to be first, juggling for attention. The many years of adventures and work have given us treasures we wish to share. It would have been impossible to even imagine how things would unfold when we began The Futures Group in a tiny office at 15ᵗʰ and Farnam, Omaha, Nebraska, March 1, 1983.

We are just two Americans who, through a bountiful Universe, have now experienced over thirty years of building a business full of travel, incredible work and life events, marvelous clients and friends, plus never-ending learning.

There are many ways to approach this book as a reader. You know your preferred style. Some will start as learners, looking for new understanding about various world experiences and work situations. Others may prefer the expanse of over thirty years, during which the two of us grew, matured and learned while the world changed and reconfigured itself before our eyes.

We've had a series of eyewitness encounters to the fast-changing world which allows us to share what we've learned and experienced. May the stories have relevance or at least add to your own views of how the world has changed over the past thirty years. Not intended to be a diary or travelogue, the pages that follow are more about the world changing before our eyes and what we've learned in response.

These are our personal experiences as business people. However, the larger world set the stage as we traveled and worked with people from over forty countries. The old saying is true: we are truly each other's teachers.

One never knows when the teacher will appear, but we were blessed by many teachers in many countries. Just one example here, about a precious lunch spent in a tiny apartment in Beijing.

Our long time friend and driver in Beijing invited us to lunch. His wife was at work and their tiny baby boy was asleep on the bed. Mr. Rao decided to make us lunch himself as a way to thank us for all of the opportunities he felt we provided him. The lunch group was Rui Shujie, Denny Aron, Carol and Tim, plus Mr. Rao.

Mr. Rao set about preparing lunch and marvelous smells began to fill the space. Whatever he was making was boiling in a ferocious hot pot of oil. Carol and Rui took turns tiptoeing in to peek at the tiny baby boy. Tim, Denny and Mr. Rao somehow kept up their conversation, though Mr. Rao had only a few words of English. After about four years of being our driver, we all developed a sweet friendship with a common language, just not a spoken one.

Finally, it was time to sit down to lunch. We were all eager to dive into the delicious smelling food. Although it was simply rice and meat, it was more than enough. It tasted as good as it smelled. The three of us, Denny, Carol and Tim, imagined what meat we were eating. We decided it was most likely goat or lamb.

At the end of the meal, we were stuffed and happy. We had some good conversations and confirmed the joys of such a lovely friendship. As often happens, Carol could contain herself no longer and as she said again how delicious the meal had been, also asked what the meat was.

Mr. Rao said in Mandarin, "Ah, horse intestines." Rui looked at us quickly to see our responses. We all smiled and said again how delicious it had been! We could never have imagined three people from Nebraska sitting in a tiny high-rise apartment in Beijing, playing with our friend's baby and eating horse intestines. It was a lovely day and we remember it fondly!

Had we measured every opportunity and known in advance every outcome, we would have missed so much. Thank goodness, we trusted the Universe and ourselves to be okay and allowed life to unfold before our eyes.

# The Discovery Years

## 1979 - 1990

*What our eyes saw was continually influenced by key events in the world. Each decade of our experiences will be preceded by a summary of major events.*

CONTEXT

# 1979 - 1990

## 1979

Iranian Revolution overthrows the Shah, prompts the hostage crisis with US.

The Soviet Union invades Afghanistan.

Deng Xiaoping begins economic reform in China.

Pope John Paul II visits Poland, accelerating freedom movement.

The Moral Majority begins in the US.

Inflation peaks at 13.3% in US.

## 1980

Southern Bell consent decree by US Fourth Circuit Court of Appeals finds Bell Companies guilty of discrimination against women. Remediation required.

Staggers Rail Act passed by Congress allowing deregulation of railroads.

## 1981

President Reagan begins expansion of US military.

Spring recession, GDP drops 2.9%.

Betty Friedan's book, *The Second Stage,* is published. It focused the Women's Movement.

## 1982

Recession continues.

Union Pacific/Missouri Pacific/Western Pacific merger

## 1983

Inflation drops.

Bombing of US Marines in Beirut, Lebanon

South Korea Flight 7 shot down by USSR.

Banks deregulated.

Rise of Japanese economy concerns US.

America on Line (AOL) begins.

## 1984

AT&T Divestiture

First Apple Macintosh computer sold.

Indira Gandhi assassinated.

Ronald Reagan reelected.

## 1985

Mikhail Gorbachev assumes leadership in USSR – Glasnost and Perestroika begin.

## 1986

Chernobyl disaster

## 1989

George H.W. Bush becomes President.

Berlin Wall falls.

Tiananmen Square

Average growth of GDP in '80s = 4%.

Sony purchases Rockefeller Center and other US landmarks increasing the perceived threat from Japan.

## 1990

Robert Bly publishes *Iron John: A Book About Men*, beginning the "Men's Movement" of the '90s.

## CHAPTER ONE

# Where It All Started

Two agendas were being put into place at exactly the same time. Tim was busy searching for the right woman to come into the Union Pacific Railroad to take on one of the most difficult assignments in business at that time.

Carol completed her Master's Degree and settled in happily at the University of Nebraska at Omaha (UNO). The UNO work managing corporate contracts and recruiting for the on and off-campus credit classes was fulfilling. Being able to teach a class now and then added challenge and satisfaction. Occasional time spent in life/educational coaching or counseling with students in the University Counseling Center added great meaning and important experience. Additional duties on various campus committees were stimulating and felt useful. Later, she would learn these had been excellent early examples of organizational politics.

It was easy to decide the next step would be to begin her Ph.D.; plans were eagerly set in place. And then in 1979, "The Call" came. Thoughts swirled and shouted in Carol's head.

"Who was this guy? What would make him think I would leave Academia? A Railroad, really? Okay, I'll see what he wants and have a short meeting with him. But, he'll have to come to me."

Prior to this, the "guy," Tim Rouse, had worked inside the Union Pacific Railroad for nearly ten years with the multiple responsibilities of creating and designing the Company's Human Resources Development work such as the Management

Recruiting, Management and Organizational Development. This was now to include the most recent initiative, Affirmative Action.

Tim's goal was to contribute to the Company's progress in Diversity as well as to continue the excellent work in the many other areas of his accountability. Some executives above him supported this Affirmative Action work. Others found the level of his personal commitment surprising and even curious.

Before joining the Union Pacific Railroad, Tim dedicated his early career years to working and teaching in secondary and higher education, plus serving in two political offices.

The time for the short meeting came. Tim agreed to meet Carol in the Campus Café. The short meeting lasted over two hours. The conversation covered a myriad of topics; all seemed interesting and relevant.

Life so far, plus work at UNO in the Women's Support Area, provided Carol with important experience and knowledge regarding the dynamics of Institutional Racism and Sexism. The so-called "Glass Ceiling" was real. Carol understood this prior to meeting Tim. There were marches around the State Capitol, organized gatherings on the UNO campus and meetings among the few women professionals in Omaha business and education to gather for conversation and support.

Tim returned to the Union Pacific and reported he found the "Right Person." The voice in Tim's head was very active and he remembers it today. "At last, a person I believe has what it takes to make some real progress in Affirmative Action for the Railroad. I've worked for six years to gain permission to really work these issues. Now, this is possible!"

Following the meeting in the Campus Café, Carol was energized and curious to learn more. The excitement of continuing the work begun at UNO was inspiring and challenging for Carol. Both Tim and Carol knew at the time this new work would also be very challenging. However, the promise and excitement of bringing the issues of societal inequity into the actual realm of corporate life took root in Carol's brain. Soon, it became a tangible, daily intention.

After long talks and much consideration with her husband, Terry, Carol accepted the Union Pacific offer. Life was forever changed. Tim and Carol agreed from the initial conversation it would be difficult, yet it was the excitement and challenge that called Carol forward. It was one thing to focus on this at the University level and an entirely different thing to put it into action. The new "laboratory" was to be The Union Pacific Railroad.

Both were correct in that first conversation. The work was a challenging assignment worth taking on, but also a life changing experience for both.

However, life for Carol had put some of the building blocks for this work into place over the past thirty years. It had been much too early for the outcome to become anywhere close to clear. Only in retrospect could she see how these building blocks had emerged from early girlhood into womanhood.

Earlier, high school teachers and counselors strongly encouraged Carol to enter Mathematics as a major field of study. Those early days as the only girl in Mechanical Drafting, Calculus, Trig and other classes, caused grief and even what would become known today as bullying or harassment.

One male high school teacher even suggested to the rest of the class, all boys, "We all know why Carol is here. She wants some dates. Ha Ha."

Never one to be shy, the angry response flew out of her mouth without thinking, " Oh believe me, I have plenty of dates!" The stomachaches began and continued through her college years as a math major.

College was much the same for Carol in terms of being one of only two women students in the Math classes.  Her first real teaching job was for the US Department of Defense. Carol was to teach a college credit math class for American military men at Incirlik Air Base, Adana, Turkey. This offered an excellent challenge, though initially it felt frightening. Walking into the classroom on her first day, the seasoned Airmen in their work fatigues simply stared at Carol.

"Hello gentlemen!" she said.

"Oh #xb%!" shouted the ranking Chief Master Sergeant among them, "They've sent us a "#fm!@H# GIRL to teach us Math. Let's go!" They stood up to leave. Carol felt the energy surge and spoke out.

"Please, sit down, gentlemen! My name is Carol Hunter. I am a mathematics teacher. We have work to do. I know Math and you want or need to learn Math. Let's get started." Carol breathed a sign of relief as the Chief sat down and the other men muttered "Okay." Things went exceedingly well from that point on.

The final exam was a standardized test from Detachment 10, United States Air Force/Europe. Apparently, hundreds of Air Force personnel took this test in order to gain mathematics college credits toward their college diploma. No one was more amazed than Carol when she received the official Commendation Certificate from Frankfurt! This first class of hers scored the highest scores in the entire European Command's Detachment!

These bright, strong men became her best recruiters. What is it like to be "one of the few among many?" In this case, a young woman teaching mathematics to seasoned military men. The learnings turned out to be essential for the years ahead. Carol learned this time and again. She learned to be strong in a new way.

Now another large laboratory, the Union Pacific Railroad, and most other corporations of the 1970s/80s, offered new opportunities for truly understanding how to begin creating a world that works for all. Does it exist yet? No. Do we both continue to hold and work toward this goal today, over 30 years later? Yes.

Due to the impact of Federal Legislation finally being enforced after fifteen years on the Books, large organizations now were painfully aware of and required to provide Equal Opportunity and Affirmative Action. Examples such as the AT&T Consent Decree frightened US CEOs and their organizations. The assignment Tim Rouse was offering Carol was to enter one of the United States' largest Railroads to work on this challenge. Carol believed she was ready, but there were to be new challenges and great learning ahead for both.

Today the Union Pacific Railroad employees number over 45,000 with Rails linking twenty-three states and is the largest American Railroad. The pride we felt in having worked at Union Pacific remains.

The Union Pacific consistently receives awards and recognition for the many ways it ensures a healthy, productive and diverse workforce. Recently, for example, *Diversity Careers In Engineering and Information Technology* named Union Pacific a Best Diversity Company for the third consecutive year. The award was based on the level of support of women, minorities, and on efforts to support work/life balance and supplier diversity.

Additionally, *Corporate Responsibility* identified Union Pacific one of its 100 Best Corporate Citizens for the second year in a row. This acknowledgement was based on seven categories: climate change, employee relations, environment, financial, governance, human rights and philanthropy.[1]

Thousands of women and men throughout the past thirty-plus years have worked with conscience and clear intention to create such a work environment. This did not and could not have happened overnight. Though few today remember the beginning of the work, we do. We were there.

It was late September, 1979, Carol's decision was made. She accepted Tim Rouse's offer to join the Union Pacific Railroad. Her life would be changed forever. Carol found it difficult as she left her many friends and meaningful work at the University of Nebraska at Omaha. Little did she know within a short time, Carol would recruit a handful of those UNO friends to join her at UPRR.

As Carol walked into the Union Pacific Railroad building on October 1, 1979, she carried with her the Betty Friedan quote, "Women and men, working together, without anger, toward a new society." It inspired Carol and to her, explained so much. This was to be a significant part of the Union Pacific work.

The early days at the Railroad were both exciting and overwhelming for Carol. The entire Railroad was advised this new person had been hired. The new role was to be called Manager, Affirmative Action and Human Resources. Carol believed everyone understood that if successful, the "face" of the Railroad would change forever. No one person could do this alone. It would take everyone. However, it was the key leaders, all of whom were White men, who would actually make the final decisions and support changes to bring additional women and men of Color and White women into the Railroad at all levels. Carol, ever the optimist, believed these key leaders understood and were all on board.

Having come from an educational background, there was little in Carol's prior work experience to help her understand what a very successful, one hundred-plus year old railroad had as its history and values. However, what she did know was that there were bright, kind, good men who interviewed and met her during those first weeks.

Tim worked the system prior to hiring Carol. He shared with all key stakeholders the benefits of increasing the numbers of women and men of Color and well as the number of White women. While there was a Director of Equal Opportunity, his primary role was to ensure compliance and keep the Railroad advised of progress or lack thereof. Tim designed the job Carol accepted to one day include a variety of strong programs and HR interventions as key components to the Affirmation Action work. Carol was to develop and provide those through her own staff, outside consultants, plus those who worked for Tim in Organization Development and other areas.

The one person who had the role prior to this was a White man. For a variety of reasons, this person left the Company. Eager to make a difference, a strong advocate for doing the right thing and certainly a risk taker, Tim somehow convinced those above him that perhaps a White woman would or could be more successful. Perhaps others also believed she would be less threatening. Who really knew what would happen at that time in history, within a strong, successful, male-oriented railroad?

Early in the morning on October 1, 1979, Tim met Carol at the front door of the Union Pacific Railroad building. How both of their lives would change!

Tim's quick intro of Carol to her office was the first surprise. Tim was not on the same floor, but three floors above. Carol's so-called "direct reports," Richard Gregory and the late Kay Peterson, were located on the same floor as Carol. Kay, however, was traveling on business that day and would be back soon.

Tim handed Carol off to Richard Gregory. Carol began to wonder: "Where's the orientation? Is he just leaving me here like this? Is anyone going to really tell me what I DO on this job? What are my goals? Who are all of these men sitting in every office up and down this hallway? Ah, I see it's true. There aren't many women here! How very different this feels from the University . . . What am I supposed to do now?"

Richard Gregory gave Carol a few minutes alone to see her new office. Once more, Carol felt a strong reaction: "What now? Is this how it goes? No real conversations? No real information? Just 'Welcome, here's your office?' Is this about the difference between a University and a Railroad?"

Within fifteen minutes, Richard was back. What a welcome relief for Carol. It seemed as if an hour passed.

Richard sat down and told Carol "My friends call me Greg. Most people here call me Richard or Rich." Carol easily responded, "Seems good to me if we imagine the best. It's nice to meet you, Greg."

Greg, his tone accepting, welcoming and supportive, responded, "Good to meet you too, Carol. I hope you know what you are getting into. I am here to support you and work with you. I'll share all I have learned during these past years. I need to tell you though, I had not imagined a sign of progress to be having a White woman as my boss. I thought it would be the day when I was the Boss with White men and women who reported to me."

Carol responded, "I totally understand. Someday, no doubt you will be the Boss, but we'll see how all of this unfolds." That day came within two years. However, Greg and Carol learned much together, handled challenging projects together along with their colleague and good friend, Kay. There was never a day without trust as they worked together. The two became great friends and valued teachers.

Carol soon understood Tim's support, counsel and behind-the-scenes work in opening doors and minds for her arrival. This all seemed to have made a positive difference.

The work and job were definitely what anyone at that time, and since, would have to admit were certainly like "paddling upstream" every day, day in and day out for those first 18 months. The issues of equity among races and genders were something no one in the System had ever had to seriously deal with during the first 100+ years of the Railroad. The Betty Friedan quote became more and more relevant for Carol.

In every Railroad in the world until at least that time, the

Operating Department was the main event. Most Railroad Presidents came from the Operating side of the business: running trains, fixing trains and maintaining track. They were good men; hard-working, loyal men. Many came from generations of railroading families. There was enormous pride in being a part of this great big rolling railroad. Carol began to feel it within weeks. Even the history of our country was wrapped up in the Union Pacific Railroad. Carol soon felt pride in being a part of the Union Pacific Railroad.

These were different times when it came to composition of the workforce, safety issues and regulations. Without the understanding time now gives, it was impossible for most railroad employees to understand nearly everything would change within the coming years.

The work at hand for Carol Hunter, Richard Gregory and Kay Peterson, with their boss, Tim Rouse, was work most Union Pacific employees were not keen to embrace. The Railroad took a giant step in the early 1980s by hiring the first woman in the Operating Department with plans to eventually train her as an Engineer. However, things could not and would not be rushed. Nor was there any work manual for how this new workforce would all unfold.

This in no way infers there was general systemic, conscious opposition. The reality of every new era or time in history is people generally become used to how things were. It was easier just to keep on doing what they were doing. Perhaps as many as 50% of the Union Pacific employees in 1979 had come from previous generations of railroad families. An example was Tim's family. His father had worked for the Railroad for 52 years. The family felt a great pride, which continues today.

In all of the major and even smaller traditions and work routines, the way things were was simply the way things had been. This was nothing consciously resistant. It was simply a proud history. It had worked fine up until now.

Change is never easy. Organizational theory suggests the older the system, the more difficult the change. The first, recent big driver of change for railroads was the automated information systems in 1971. In the late 1980s, even larger changes were to come.

Tim's plan for orientation was to introduce Carol to the main "movers and shakers" of the Railroad. Carol, as a new "30-something" woman in the Railroad, was now only the third woman manager at Union Pacific Railroad. She was soon introduced to the key Operating Officers as well as all of the Vice Presidents and others who made things happen. Within weeks of her first day, Tim put Carol on a train to North Platte. Certainly each "Railroader" had to ride the Cab to North Platte at least once!

The friendly Engineer did his best to give a great orientation and encouraged Carol to hold the Throttle plus understand each Throttle Notch. With the bell ringing and the air horns sounding, Carol felt the thrill of the Railroad for real! The excitement of learning new things and understanding all that was possible before her gave Carol great hope for what could be achieved.

However, Carol soon began to understand some of what may have been going on behind the scenes relevant to her Role. The telephone calls came first. Soft, emotionally-stressed voices, barely whispered into the phone:

"Is this the new lady in Affirmative Action? I need to tell you what's been going on out here in Western Nebraska. I am a Black employee of the Railroad. Last night a huge cross was burned in my front yard. I know it was people from work. Can you help me?"

"Hello, is this Carol Hunter? I want to tell you about the pin-up pictures in my work area. They are very suggestive and I'm the only woman here. I've told my boss they are offensive to me. He asked me if I still wanted my job. What should I do?"

"I want to speak with Carol Hunter please. Be very careful, Carol. There are people here who do not want you to be successful. Your life may be in danger."

Carol was learning that Railroads, and other heavy industry in general, were historically thought to belong to men. The things she was hearing, learning and seeing were not unique to this Railroad nor to Railroads in general. This was the historic reality of US business up until this time.

So, this was her job. It was about CHANGE. Change for the better, change to serve all, including those many companies with such proud heritage and history as Union Pacific Railroad.

As the time went on, new encounters escalated. Carol never imagined just how uncomfortable an elevator ride could be. One day, riding alone to an upper floor, the elevator stopped, the door opened and in walked a very charming officer Carol had been introduced to weeks before.

"Well, hello there! I was hoping we might meet again like this," he said. Suddenly, without warning, his arms were against the walls of the elevator, one on either side of Carol, her back against the wall.

"How in the world did this happen? I'm trapped!" Carol thought to herself.

"Better fix this now, Carol," she replied to Self.

"Please step away now, Mr. X!" Carol said in her best strong, assertive voice.

"Who's going to believe your word over mine?" he said.

Holding onto courage and composure, Carol said in her strongest voice, "Step away now, Sir!"

"Oh, come on, Carol, have a little fun" he replied.

"Let me make myself clear. This is not fun. If you leave this elevator immediately, I will not report you. Otherwise, I will report you or you will have to kill me to keep me quiet. " Heart fluttering, with an even stronger voice, Carol somehow said these words with true conviction.

"Oh, you are really no fun!" He said as he pushed the elevator button for the next floor. He exited. There was never another such episode from this man, nor any other toward Carol. She did share this with Tim. Her own anger and understanding about what many women could have been encountering grew daily. She promised herself then, she would not give into fear. She would stay strong, even if it meant her job. The new Mantra started, "I am free of fear."

Tim responded simply and with confirmation, "Sounds as if you handled it well. Good work."

Later, as the first year of Carol's employment anniversary was near, Tim knocked softly and walked into Carol's office. Carol did not hear the knock because she held a sobbing woman in her arms. The woman had just shared story after story about her boss who was physically inappropriate with her, all the while threatening to take her job away if she told. This one demanded more aggressive action on behalf of the Company. Carol had vowed to bring it to the attention of others and ensure the woman's safety. Her feeling of being understood and feeling safe simply overwhelmed the woman.

Carol stepped quickly toward the door and quietly explained to Tim she was busy. The woman quickly gained composure. Tim asked Carol to give him a call and left immediately. This harassment issue was addressed promptly with professionalism and discretion. Carol and Tim met with the man to explain clearly what was at stake for him. The woman was able to retain her job with her boss having clearly understood what was required of him. Small changes began to take place.

Later, more employees began to understand the work of safety and equity was serious. As more situations began to come forward, the Railroad took strong and serious action to stop any and all kinds of harassment and discrimination. Until this time, People of Color and White women did not understand this Railroad intended to value them, to protect them and their excellent work.

Although Carol's life was threatened more than once during her years at Union Pacific, Mr. Cliff Shaffer, Union Pacific's Chief of Security, provided safety, protection, experience, expertise and friendship.

The Union Pacific area of Professional Recruitment and Employment also reported to Tim. With specific, focused recruiting programs, more and more People of Color and additional White women were brought into the Craft positions and professional roles. Today, the Union Pacific Railroad is a leader in diversity, inclusion, professionalism and excellence. Leaders of today work hard to continue and ensure this.

New opportunities for Training and Development also were designed. These programs challenged both senior and more recent employees to learn and grow, continuing their professional education and enhancing their leadership knowledge, skills and development. Equally greater changes were ahead within the Union Pacific Railroad. Carol and Tim, along with their colleague Denny Aron, were privileged and grateful to be a part of them.

The United States' Railroads were involved in a period of great change. The work was challenging, exciting and a great learning opportunity for all.

By early 1980s, the Union Pacific Railroad and all US railroads were actively responding as well as planning for their futures. Carol and Tim's relationship with C. Barry Schaefer, Executive Vice President, Union Pacific Railroad, grew stronger. Life was even more exciting as the external environment provided new opportunities for the UPRR to change and grow. First as internal

UP employees and later as outside business consultants, the two worked to support the changes Barry saw as important to take the Railroad into the next Century. His ability to see into the future and develop plans to keep the UPRR competitive and a leader among North American railroads did, in our opinion, shape the future.

Richard Gregory soon became "the Boss" of the Affirmative Action and Human Resources area of the Union Pacific Railroad. Carol accepted the role of Sr. Manager of Organizational Development, with Tim still as her direct boss.

Greg continued the work of Affirmative Action with excellence. Though Carol was officially given a new work responsibility with Organizational Development, the issues of justice and equity for all were in her heart and Soul. This continues to be true today. Union Pacific women called Carol for many years, even after Tim and Carol started FGI, to share issues and ask for guidance.

Behind Executives' doors, the conversations continued with regard to keeping the Union Pacific competitive. This was not about creating more track, but creating end-to-end lines with little to no overlap. The next step would be some kind of consolidation with other Roads. The goal was to create new opportunities that previously did not exist. The very excellent Planning and Analysis experts began their in-depth research and studies on behalf of the UP executives.

Across the United States, organizations were said to be experiencing "Merger Mania." Business magazines used this and other headlines to share the exciting and sometimes tragic stories of employees and previously proud companies. However, for the Union Pacific Railroad, it was to be good news.

Working inside the UP at this time provided incredible life/work experiences as well as learning for both Carol and Tim. No doubt, this was true for all employees at the Railroad. Tim was invited into those larger discussions, while Tim and Carol together began to meet regularly with C. Barry for planning meetings.

The Interstate Commerce Commission would not officially approve the Merger until 1982. However, there was agreement the key leaders of the potential merged companies would meet in 1980 to begin the familiarization process. Barry called upon Tim to work with him to design and bring together the top seventy-five Officers of the three Railroads to be merged. These were the Union Pacific Railroad, the Missouri Pacific Railroad and the Western Pacific Railroad - three proud railroads, each with very different histories, cultures and stories.

Those seventy-five railroaders came together for the first time, face-to-face, for food/drink and meetings at the Kansas City Club, MO. The three railroad's Presidents, Mr. Kenefick, Mr. Jenks and Mr. Flannery gave opening and closing remarks, with Barry leading the meeting and Tim managing the conversations and small group work at the tables. It was the first meeting for leaders of one of the most successful and significant railroad mergers in US History.

Multiple organizational development initiatives were underway continuously, as were the other initiatives and accountabilities undertaken by Tim and his HR group at UP. Little did Carol and Tim understand what they had learned with the UP-MP-WP merger work would become very important and valuable to them well into the next 10-15 years.

Without any conscious understanding at the moment, the early seeds of FGI International were being sown. The Universe was at work in mysterious ways. However, there was important work plus new experiences that had to come first. Perhaps it was best we did not understand at that time the huge challenge of it all?

Nor did we have any sense of our experiences yet to come beyond the Union Pacific Railroad. How could we have imagined such things as:

    &#x2766; Over sixteen years and more than fifty trips working back and forth from Omaha, Nebraska to Moscow, Russia?

- Climbing China's Great Wall at least five times over 12 years of working in China?

- Having Membership Cards from the Hungarian Airlines Malev Frequent Flyer Club, not to mention personal bottles of Hungary's best Paprika purchased in the Budapest Airport?

- Having Medallion Status or above in the three major US Airlines?

- Receiving Special Guest Status for each one of us for having accumulated over 150 nights in one Moscow Hotel? (This does not cover the many other Moscow Hotels we had as homes away from home.)

- Standing on the Embankment of the Moscow River watching as tanks shelled the Russian White House?

- Being the first-ever foreigners in 900 years granted permission by the Local Communist Cadre to enter the closed town of Bo Hai Suo, the Chinese village charged with protecting the Great Wall?

*FOOTNOTE: Though part of this story comes later, it feels important to state here that our Union Pacific colleague and dear friend, Denny Aron, also shared each one of the bulleted items above.*

Paddling upstream is seldom easy. It is often unpleasant and occasionally even dangerous. Life's unfolding can never be fully anticipated, nor fully appreciated in the moment. However, in hindsight, this unfolding becomes nothing short of a string of miracles.

## CHAPTER TWO

# Jumping Off the Train

Awakened to the dynamic, challenging world of business, Carol felt true gratitude for all she learned at Union Pacific Railroad. The excitement of a business environment was totally different from University life. For Carol, a different kind of positive energy and buzz seemed to fill her as a businesswoman in contrast to the good energy she had always felt in the academic environment. Not better, just different. A different clarity existed about what was important in life and what brought true meaning to work, along with dreams of the future.

Crazy thoughts began to enter Carol's mind: "If one company could be this dynamic, exciting, full of so much learning, such excellent people and opportunities for change, just imagine what's out there in the entire business environment!"

No thoughts of a global economy had yet begun. Little did she know what a true "BUZZ" was coming in her future!

During 1980-83, more and more local and national invitations and opportunities came for Tim and Carol to share their experiences and learning at conferences and various business associations. Union Pacific provided amazing friends, teachers, life experiences and incredible opportunities. While Carol had thought she might actually retire at the Union Pacific Railroad, new thoughts began to flow in the night. The Universe offered another Plan.

Several sleepless nights and long conversations with Carol's husband, Terry, allowed Carol to understand what was coming next. "Carol, I believe you have to do what you are called to do. You can make a difference. I am here for you as I have always been," said Terry after another late night of discussion. It was some years since their wedding with multiple Air Force assignments in the United States and abroad for over 20 years. The two experienced much together. The two years of life living in Adana, Turkey, provided a marvelous life of learning, service and world travel. Their children were young, bright and healthy. The two owned a lovely home and enjoyed a good life. It was soon time to jump off the train!

The recent years of Union Pacific work were full of excitement, camaraderie, constant positive stimulation and excellent challenges. The close working relationships with many Union Pacific colleagues and executives were very dear. Tim and Carol's friend and colleague, Denny Aron, and his wife Suzanne had just learned they would have their fourth child. It was an exciting time for them.

Tim, Carol and Denny were working more and more closely. The merger work utilized their different knowledge, skills and abilities. The three made a very effective team. Each knew she/he could count on the other two. They had many of the same areas of expertise, but enough different ones to complement and supplement each other. How could Carol leave Union Pacific alone and what would she do? The Call was coming with more and more strength and immediacy. What was this Call? There was always the one best way to "hear" the unspoken for Carol. Simply listen with mind, heart and Spirit. Listen and, most difficult of all, listen with patience.

Within weeks, Carol approached first Tim and then Denny with her plan: The idea of a team of external consultants to start a new business that could serve businesses all over the United States. "Merger Mania" was raging and the three had some of the most excellent and high-level experiences in a huge merger situation across multiple states.

While Carol's expectation was both would say "yes," exactly the opposite happened. Tim, with his UP heritage and nearly 14 years of service to this point, talked with his wife, Maryanne. They were hesitant to make this change. Denny, with a fourth child on the way, talked with his wife, Suzanne. It seemed irresponsible to leave a company with such excellent benefits, opportunities and satisfaction, while knowing their family would grow soon. Both Tim and Denny declined and promised they would support Carol in any way they could. Feeling somewhat alone, Carol moved forward with her planning.

Less than two weeks later, with Maryanne's support, Tim told Carol he changed his mind. The thrill and excitement of new learning and growing opportunities were something this man could not pass. The earlier stopping point had been his family would lack health care in the new small consulting company. However, Maryanne found a meaningful position with Catholic Charities while continuing her longtime dedication to serving in many community groups. Now she was also providing health care for the family. Carol and Terry did not face this challenge due to the benefits of Terry being an active duty Air Force Officer. Having always understood the value of his service to the Country, the Hunters gave thanks. Denny, his friendship and solidarity ever strong, kept to his decision, but promised support and assistance whenever asked. This commitment has been generously kept without hesitation over more than thirty years.

Things began to unfold.

Union Pacific friends and colleagues seemed amazed we were actually leaving. People didn't leave the Union Pacific Railroad!

Prior to leaving UP, Carol and Tim visited all those who were Union Pacific Railroad internal clients and friends. Many were speechless. Some suggested the work between the two of us and the Company could continue. What did this mean? How simply amazing it was for both Carol and Tim as new business owners.

The new Futures Group, Inc. offices were two blocks South of the Union Pacific Railroad Headquarters in Omaha. Flower arrangements and gifts were soon delivered to the new office. This was amazing and heart warming. We were not alone.

We had many goals for this new, very small business, The Futures Group. The primary experiment and a significant value of the two of us was to determine if a woman and man colleague, both married and each very committed to someone else in marriage, could share power equally in a business partnership. It sounded worth doing.

We set about finding a banker, a lawyer and an accountant. Things were becoming quite official. How had all of this unfolded so quickly? It seemed as if it were yesterday when Tim came to the University of Nebraska at Omaha to interview and recruit Carol for the job at Union Pacific.

The work with the Center for Creative Leadership (CCL) in Greensboro, North Carolina, began in 1981 as an earlier piece of work with UP. Originally founded as an internationally known center of research and leadership enterprise, CCL was one of the service providers to the Union Pacific. Once we advised we left the Railroad, the CCL people began to work directly with Denny as their contact. However, as a huge surprise to the newly formed Futures Group, CCL also asked both Carol and Tim to become Adjunct Faculty. The Universe was providing! The most amazing part of this CCL relationship was that it did not seem as if it was work. It was constantly exciting, always a learning opportunity for us. Could this be really true?

CCL paid our expenses plus stipends for teaching CCL programs. The work was enjoyable and meaningful. It also opened new doors for The Futures Group, in addition to the many new clients we were developing. These new colleagues and clients from all over the US began to fill our Futures Group database. Well, of course, it wasn't a "database" in those days! It was a paper file. The computer would not arrive for at least two more years. It's amazing to consider all our little office accomplished without our MacBooks and iMacs! It was the two of us and an electric typewriter.

We could never have imagined how incredibly important to us our work with the Center for Creative Leadership would become. With mixed emotions, we retired our CCL adjunct faculty roles in 2012 after 30 years. The many locations, the many open enrollment programs we were able to provide, plus the additional custom programs for individual corporate clients, offered different and varied experiences and a reputation for excellence. CCL gave us the gift of a new level of credentials and experience, plus bright, new colleagues and our first global experiences.

However, as always, it was the depth of friendships and shared colleague experiences that stay with us. Mike Lombardo, Bob Kaplan, Morgan McCall, David DeVries, Betty Williams, Russ Moxley, Dan Pryor, Jane Tucker, Nancy Pryor, Mignon Mazique, Bill Saunders, Jane Linnane and especially the late, brilliant Anne Faber taught us, shared life and exhilarating teaching experiences with us at the Center and as the Center on the road. Together in small teams, we served professionals from hundreds of corporations in the US, Europe and New Zealand.

New opportunities for The Futures Group continued. Our experiences multiplied. Our own expertise, understanding and growing depth of knowledge in organizational dynamics, management/leadership development and general organizational challenges became a part of the content of our daily lives.

Within the first year of our leaving the Railroad, Carol received a Registered Mail letter from a Law Firm in North Carolina. "Oh my! What was this?" The letter advised Carol that The Futures Group located in North Carolina, had begun receiving telephone calls for a "Carol Hunter from The Futures Group." Their lawyers were going to put a stop to this, now!

Ah, what brilliance Tim had in encouraging us early on to find a lawyer as our first act. The call went out to the late Mike Dugan, our business lawyer and an old friend of Tim's. Mike quickly came up with the solution: we would retain the official, legal name of The Futures Group, Inc., but move immediately to using and being called "FGI." Ah, how easy he made it for us. He wrote the letter explaining this to the company in question and our first corporate challenge was solved.

We set about marketing FGI with other organizations and corporations. It's one thing to work within a closed corporation with internal clients as colleagues. It's another altogether to market to corporations who may or may not need you and perhaps have never heard of you or your firm. Luckily, the two of us love challenge and love learning.

We used Carol's many positive relationships developed at the University of Nebraska at Omaha. She began to contact friends and colleagues from the corporations, businesses and government branches who were her students and contacts in the academic setting. These good people were happy to renew the friendship and work relationships! How fantastic! Carol was not forgotten during her years at UP.

Immediately, we began to practice what we believed in theory. What could it hurt? Using learning from the book, *Illusions*, Carol suggested we begin to visualize what we wished to have come into our lives as FGI. Previously, Carol tested the theory. In those earlier days, she began with something basic.

"I have a parking place." Parking places began to appear on the most crowded streets just when she needed one.

"I find money." Actual five-dollar bills and enough coins to fill jars were soon found lying on sidewalks or next to the curbs in a variety of cities. Why could this not work at FGI?

So, the two began. "The FGI phone is ringing. New clients are calling us now." The client phone calls began to come!

From Day One as FGI, we have practiced what we preach. Today's publications confirm this approach as Science. Many scientists, both physical and social, have found that positive present tense intentions, if clearly stated and acted upon, manifest in reality.

We continue to be grateful for the degree to which our conscious use of intention setting has served us. Without it we might never have worked overseas, never created FGISpirit, never developed many of the programs and processes which have been so central to our learning and feelings of satisfaction.

Just to be on the safe side, we began to supplement this first approach with regular written letters and the US Postal Service. This one-two approach was an amazing gift. Within the first 6-9 months, a variety of potential client organizations became our new FGI clients. Additionally, we received the gift of follow-up work from some of our former executive clients within the Union Pacific Railroad. The learning experience we had in the pre-merger and early merger days was valuable. They wanted continuity.

Suddenly, within the first year, we were learning how to manage our time and our own small business in new ways. Calendars, billing hours for consultation and program fees for tailored program designs aimed at specific Federal Agencies and new industries began to provide a revenue flow for our fledgling company.

It was nothing short of amazing for us to experience the keen differences between various government agencies. From the Department of Defense to the Department of Agriculture to the Corps of Engineers, people were basically committed, well educated, capable, bright and hard working. However, the organizations in which they worked had subtle differences. We were filled with "Ah Ha's" daily.

The UP-MP-WP merger became one of our most important opportunities for contributing while learning and growing. Much of the initial work was done in Planning and Analysis by John Rebensdorf, the late Jim Young, Jack Koraleski and Charley Eisele. Our opportunities for planning, designing and providing interventions took on a life of their own.

We were suddenly traveling even more than we had as full-time Union Pacific employees. This was no longer the former Union Pacific System of our previous UPRR workdays. We were now external consultants. This was the greatly enlarged, newly merged Union Pacific Railroad! Trips to Saint Louis, San Francisco and other UPRR offices became a regular part of our work life for 3-4 years. The difference in company cultures became clearly apparent as we traveled from location to location, from St. Louis to San Francisco to Dallas to Portland and other stops.

We now marvel at how much we learned about different corporate cultures and the challenges of bringing them together OR creating a new culture that reflects the needs of the marketplace.

When we worked in these different locations, we were often given an office for a couple of days. To make it easier, this office was often a conference room where both of us would have room to sit, work, have meetings with employees and so on. In one location in Texas, we were set up in the Conference Room of the Law Department. The building was a rather ornate, fine old building with many years of history held within its walls. In every location, people were very kind to us, very interested in what was happening and open to the work we all shared.

It was normal for a key leader to take us to lunch on the first day over nice conversations full of merger stories and local lore. However, you can only have consultants for so many days, so we often suggested the two of us could just bring food in and work over lunch. These times also included great conversations about what we were each learning in our interviews or research. However, on one day, Carol began to look more carefully around the room. How interesting all the memorabilia was!

An administrative person knocked on the open door and asked if she could bother us for a minute. She needed to get into a closet. We were amazed to see the lovely wall with its many decorative plaster art panels disguising an actual closet!

As she opened the huge door, a closet the size of a small room appeared. The closet was packed with office supplies, extra chairs and a variety of interesting, historical items. Several seemed to have been there for many years. As she looked for what she needed, Carol jumped up to help her move aside what she believed was an old sign.

"Oh, look at this!" exclaimed Carol. It was in fact a podium with a railroad three-dimensional insignia on it.

"Will you look at that," said Tim, his railroad history far superior to Carol's. Tim said, "It's an old T&P Railroad Podium! Wow! You won't find many of those."

Once the woman left, Tim shared with Carol what made this find so interesting. The majority share of the Texas Pacific Railroad was purchased by the Missouri Pacific Railroad in 1928. It was fully merged in 1976. The building in which we were sitting most likely witnessed this history. Those who were present at the time held onto their podium, though the name of the Railroad had been changed to Missouri Pacific.

Thousands of employees worked for the newly merged Union Pacific Railroad. As with any corporate merger, some were more involved than others due to their roles and/or locations. Change causes different reactions in different people. Additionally, the nature of the various changed conditions produce different reactions in people. This is natural.

As FGI consultants working specific projects for the Union Pacific Merger, our own educations were again enhanced. We came to deeply understand how personal a name change for a company could be to the employees who worked in one company for 20-40 years. The change in company identity caused stress for many who were bright, conscientious employees. Loyalty had always been a true asset for any railroad.

Our travel calendars happened to coincide with the particular day the external signage above the main entrance was to be changed in the previous San Francisco "headquarters" office of the Western Pacific – now Union Pacific Railroad. Hundreds of employees went out to lunch through the main entrance where they entered and departed over the many past years. The signage overhead was barely noticed because they knew what it said and how it looked.

About 45-60 minutes later, the same large number of employees returned from their lunch. As they approached their building, they stopped in their tracks, unable to move. Suddenly, reality struck them.

We, too, left those doors to go out for a quick lunch. It could only have been destiny that allowed us to return at exactly the moment these employees were stopped in their tracks, staring above the door. Staring, stopping, surprised. Then suddenly saddened, angry, hurt!

Certainly no one at any level ever intended disrespect or hurt. The task had to be accomplished. Someone simply called, most likely weeks or months ago, to schedule the old signage of the Western Pacific Railroad be taken down and the new signage of the Union Pacific Railroad be installed. It was innocent. It was a task to be accomplished. Inevitably, this had to be done.

As we walked the sidewalk toward the entrance, we felt a heaviness, a curiosity about the crowd standing around the front entrance steps. Suddenly, we noticed some were crying softly, others were speaking loudly with anger, others were just staring, looking unhappy or somehow speechless.

Carol looked at one group of women. Suddenly one of the

women said to her, "How could they do this without telling us when it would happen? Many of us planned to take a photo of the entrance before the sign came down. My father worked here for 45 years. I promised my Mother I would take the photo for her! Don't they have any feelings?" All she knew was that Carol was some new face. We both felt the depth of feeling this woman shared. There was no explaining it, as if we had answers. Only sharing that the woman's feelings had been heard seemed sufficient. Carol quietly said, "I understand."

Other employees were more angry than sad. They felt somehow not advised of what they felt they had the right to know.

This was no one's fault. This was a perfect example of the pain most company mergers often produce for longtime, loyal employees whose identity with their company is difficult to switch on a given date on the calendar. Finally, the reality of a human toll became more clear. Mergers are never intended to hurt those who are a part of the companies being brought together. They are intended to make the new company stronger, more able to serve, more likely to find healthy life into the future. However, as many authors have said, "There is often a human toll to mergers." Thank goodness, it is generally not human life, but sometimes it is human spirit wounded.

We immediately took note. From this day forward in any merger or acquisition work, we had new requirements for FGI. We must make very strong recommendations about the external changes, such as signage, logos, letterhead, pencils, publications, mugs and so on. All pre-merger signage, logos, etc., must disappear. The new name and logo must be the only one publically on display. Employees need to be advised when familiar old logos and signs will disappear. They need time for grieving, celebrating, capturing the old familiar images of their own histories.

In all three of the railroads merged into the Union Pacific Railroad, one thing remained the same. The pride of being a railroad employee, the love of railroading and the long family histories of thousands of employees were obvious and palpable in every location where we spent time with valued, meaningful merger work.

Thankfully, the feedback from our clients confirmed the level of work we were able to provide was at a much higher level of accomplishment with many positive downstream results. At certain times, we were staggered by the feedback we received and felt almost guilty because this work was so enjoyable and provided such enormous learning.

In all of our experiences working with change issues, we consistently urged leaders to be open and candid with employees about what was going on, why it was happening, and what tangible impacts on people could be expected. We know that those who took our advice had less turbulence in the change process than those who did not.

Unfortunately we were sometimes called upon to be part of teams that released former employees, beginning outplacement and job searches. Because there were a number of redundancies in key positions resulting from the Merger, there were more than a few executives who couldn't find appropriate positions in the new Company.

Within four years of "jumping off the train," we struck a balance between the Union Pacific and our non-UPRR clients. These clients provided us with totally different perspectives and new understanding about the differences in the service industry, transportation industry, banking and finance, government, manufacturing and so on. We were "going to school" while having the time of our working lives!

Within the coming few years, we would work with more industry categories than we may have even understood existed prior to FGI. As our dear colleague, Geil Browning, Ph.D., creator of Emergenetics, might say: We were "expanding our number of neuronal pathways."

## CHAPTER THREE

# When the Red Phone Rings

As the first years of the Futures Group unfolded, we realized again and again how differently we were seen by clients or potential clients. Some clients told us they really appreciated our creativity, out-of-the-box thinking and excellent business savvy. Others were uncomfortable with how we thought and with our freedom to express new ideas or ask questions.

As the years went by, life and business itself began to lighten up and allow for more creative and innovative approaches. Asking the unasked questions also became more acceptable.

As earlier said, March 1, 1983, officially began The Futures Group, Inc. It was a time of great excitement, planning and marketing, deciding who we were going to be and how we were going to share with potential clients what was the business of this new enterprise.

We began to develop marketing materials and experiment with sales calls. Our marketing lists contained many people we knew who were involved in local organizations. They were, of course, the easiest face-to-face marketing calls we made. Being active in organizations such as ASTD and the OD Network,[2] we began setting up our marketing visits.

Occasionally, we called on friends as well as friends of friends. This is how we ended up in the Kiewit Plaza, best known for housing the office of Omaha's most famous person, Warren Buffett.

However, it was not Warren with whom we were going to meet. This was a marketing call to the regional offices of one of the then Big Six accounting firms. Having done several years of consulting with the large Accounting Department of the Union Pacific Railroad, we felt it was not out of the question to call on this particular prospect.

The meeting began well, though more formal than most of our previous marketing calls. Then the questions became more pointed and clearly showed doubt about who we were. The biggest unstated question appeared to be this issue of a woman and man working together as equal partners in a new business. How would it work? Who would really be in charge? Which one of us had the most valid business experience? How would a woman consultant deal with a group of male accounting partners? We answered the many questions until it felt we must have been turning blue. The gentleman was clearly still very uneasy.

Finally exasperated and eager to get to the bottom of who was in charge, he blurted out, "Okay, here's my question: When the red phone rings, which one of you answers it?"

Ah, easy . . . Carol responded first saying simply, "Whoever is closer to the phone."

That was it! No clear prioritized business protocols.

He then asked Tim the same question. Tim responded the very same way as Carol had answered.

"This just won't work for my business. I need more discipline. Thank you for stopping by."

Ah ha! Our learning just would not stop! Suddenly, we were more and more clear about how we would be FGI and what we would stand for. This very uncomfortable but short meeting began to clarify our values, our identity and how we wanted to be a different kind of creative, empowering, enlightened business consulting company. It also became clear that we had to be somewhat choosy about the clients we would accept.

Rather odd for two business partners to decide with only a few clients to their names. Still, our belief in what was possible was tangible and real. Our clarity around our values grew sharper. Our commitment to a woman and man sharing equal power as business partners became rooted in the identity of what became FGI International.

During those first months as The Futures Group we had another similar experience.

We were with a group of executives from a famous Midwest-based railroad in 1983. One of us said something such as, "Have you ever considered the railroad going both East to West and also North to South?" The ranking executive said, "This just shows what you people know about the railroad. That's enough. Good-bye."

A few years later in 1988, we had had success with a number of clients. However, we were with a well-known, metal cap producer. One of us said, "Have you considered the option of plastic caps, especially for foreign countries such as China and India?" They answered with, "You people simply don't understand vacuum closures! No one would ever settle for plastic caps! We are not going to those countries. There will never be a market." We were excused again. Still this one was easier to take because not many years later, plastic caps became very common.

We enjoyed many years of work with telecommunications companies. For one particular organization in 1991, we had written a series of business scenarios to use with their managers in leadership development programs. During the program, we introduced a scenario for discussion by one of us saying, "We've written a scenario that suggests within 5-6 years some company will be offering a flat-fee program to cover unlimited local and long distance calling on a cell phone. People would eventually stop using line phones."

One of the men present seemed to shout, "This is ridiculous! This will never happen. The costs would be so great a flat-fee wouldn't cover it. People will always want the security of the wire line phones."

We said a few words about what we were seeing and thanked him for speaking up. With this example, we simply waited and watched. It wasn't long.

This is not to suggest we are able to predict the future. However, we have always followed business trends, growth of technology and increased readiness by consumers, especially the younger demographics. We never intend to shock our clients, but we have promised each other to keep our own minds open and informed. We share this with others as they are willing. Living with the knowledge of what's unfolding keeps minds stimulated and flexible. We strive for this ourselves.

CHAPTER FOUR

# The Story of Influence

*"In many ways, I feel* INFLUENCE *changed my professional life.*
*It gave me increased confidence and a better perspective on my*
*own self worth. My group was excellent – I am proud to know*
*all of them plus Carol, Tim and Geil."*

*–Director, MIS*

We were standing in Baggage Claim at the Portland Airport, waiting for our luggage when a woman approached us. She looked to be about our ages. She was dressed in the best example of a professional in those days – a stylish black and white suit, large organza bow and taupe colored pumps.

"Hi! I am Dr. Geil Browning from Omaha." A short conversation revealed she lived about a half mile from Tim's home and had been active in the Omaha community for many years. However, the three of us had never met. We promptly began a friendship and work partnership, which has only become richer with the passage of time.

It was 1980. The two of us were already in Oregon to give a presentation to a national women's conference at Portland State University. At the time, the two of us were both working for the Union Pacific Railroad. We always looked forward to opportunities to work with professional women from across the country. Over the years, the presentation and the specifics of our time at

Portland State University have dimmed in our minds. But memory of the trip still remains.

During her introduction, we learned Geil came to the Conference to get ideas for an institute for women she would create in Omaha. The two of us recruited and created classes and programs for talented women at Union Pacific. It was a perfect match.

Over the next several months, we consulted with Geil on the mission and structure of what became the Institute for Career Advancement Needs (ICAN). A little over a year later, ICAN held its first Women's Conference. We provided a keynote speech about how women and men could work together as colleagues in organizations. We suggested that by using the very special gifts women bring to the workplace, organizations would become more effective. At the time, our remarks were seen as quite radical. Today they would be very "ho hum."

As another result of the Portland meeting, the three of us, Carol, Tim and Geil, worked to create a more intense development experience for women leaders that would extend over some time. Several breakfast meetings at a Coco's restaurant, with elaborate notes taken on placemats and napkins, gave birth to the INFLUENCE program. The design concept was based on programs Carol provided previously at the University of Nebraska at Omaha and then at the Union Pacific Railroad.

The story that follows is the beginning of our thirty-plus years love affair with INFLUENCE.

The first group of INFLUENCE women met in September 1982. Very few women were being selected to participate in leadership development programs at that time. Most organizations were willing to invest in men as leaders and potential leaders. Believing that business would eventually recognize the potential of women to be leaders, we believed INFLUENCE would meet an important need for perhaps five years.

Who could have guessed thirty-two years later, this single gender program for women would still be over-subscribed? And who could imagine the results of this program for the women who participated? It's a story worth telling.

We initially recruited through the leaders of major Omaha corporations, encouraging them to let us work with their up and coming women. We told these leaders INFLUENCE was an experiment and invited them to see if it would have value for their corporations. Between Geil and the two of us, we knew enough corporate leaders that it was possible to recruit the first couple of classes. Then word of mouth took over.

One of the very pleasant surprises for us in the early years with INFLUENCE was the number of applications from USWest women. We didn't realize it immediately, but these applications were aided by a 1980 Consent Decree from the US Fourth Circuit Court of Appeals which spread to all of the Bell System.[3] It required remediation for systemic discrimination against women. As a result, USWest was looking for ways to accelerate the development of their female employees.

We were happy and proud they chose INFLUENCE as an important factor in that development. We were privileged over the years to work with well over a hundred bright, capable women from USWest.

Originally, INFLUENCE was structured as a nine-session program over nine months. The first session was a two-day retreat. Each of the other eight sessions was one day in length. The curriculum included psychological and leadership assessment tools, multiple presenters who had significant leadership roles in Omaha, a variety of relevant leadership content plus focus on global events.

The big differences between INFLUENCE and most other leadership development programs were two. The first was the learning process of "Reflection" and developing a Reflective Voice. It was during the periods of Reflection at each meeting we first heard the women's stories. Many women had huge guilt about their roles of mother and wife as their work took more and more of their time. It wasn't long before many INFLUENCE women were making more money than their husbands or partners. This often resulted in even more tension. Other women reflected on confidence issues and/or work challenges.

As women developed their Reflective Voices, they began to find ways to manage the issues of guilt or regret or conflict. Some also began to tune in to the larger world as a lot was happening in the '80s.

Second, the process of "coming and going" over nine months allowed a process of "learning – application – learning – application – learning – etc." Years later when we were working in New Zealand, the New Zealanders were quite fascinated with the concept and talked about it as "to-ing and fro-ing."

During the first several meetings of each INFLUENCE group, women would report their lives were so consuming that they forgot what they had learned at the previous session(s). As we passed the halfway point in the INFLUENCE year, we heard this less and less as participants internalized their learnings and began making real changes in their lives.

In the early years, emphasis was placed more on leadership skills, assertiveness, self-confidence, personal rights, dealing with rapid organization and societal changes. We believed it also important for us to deal with breaking the glass ceiling, dressing for success and understanding the changing global and national realities.

The women in the early years of INFLUENCE were bright, capable and curious. Most were born and raised within a hundred miles of Omaha. Many were the first women in their families to have had a significant career. About half of the first INFLUENCE group had children.

The vast majority were tired. Many were not used to imagining that as women they had rights. They were the first generation to experience the results of the Women's Rights movement of the '60s and '70s. They found in the INFLUENCE experience: confirmation, encouragement, information and tools they could use.

Tim's early career experience had been at all-girls high schools. He saw many of the girls as confident leaders. Then in the world of work, he saw them being "put back in their place." He learned that through INFLUENCE we could empower them to truly animate their potential. Carol's early experience was focused on women in the workforce. INFLUENCE provided the perfect opportunity to continue her work from UNO and Union Pacific. It also provided confirmation.

In the first INFLUENCE years, there was little knowledge or experience of the world beyond the United States. The '80s were the time of Betty Friedan's book *The Second Stage*, the Chernobyl disaster, Mikhail Gorbachev's efforts at Perestroika and Glasnost, the fall of the Berlin Wall and more. Most INFLUENCE women were too busy to be concerned. As a woman said at one meeting: "My reading of the newspaper each week is limited to the grocery store ads. I don't have time for any more." In the 1980s, despite our valiant efforts sharing world events, the "World" still seemed far away.

A favorite activity we use with INFLUENCE groups is to have each woman draw a picture of the organization where she works shown as an animal or vehicle. She shows in the picture how her organization is dealing with change. Those pictures in the '80s were often gruesome. We saw pictures of employees being run over by trucks and busses; employees being pushed out of busses or planes; CEOs with axes and dripping blood; huge animals devouring humans. Organizations were often pictured as vehicles with no wheels or as planes crashing.

What was going on? Listening to the stories women told us, it was clear the United States economy was rapidly shifting. Since the '50s, it was a given that good workers would be cared for by their companies, would receive promotions for good work plus have a good pension at the end of their careers. In the 1980s, INFLUENCE women were experiencing employers who were cutting thousands of jobs, re-organizing again and again, making long-term careers very tenuous.

The nature of jobs was changing. It would take another ten years or more before women and men could be clear about how the changing economy influenced job stability. We spoke with the women in the first INFLUENCE groups about the historic contract no longer existing. They refused to believe it. Now they were telling us stories about it. But these stories raised a bigger question: if the contract no longer existed, what did exist?

In our consulting work, we had been working with a number of organizations on deregulations, mergers, new technology and changing markets. As a result, we were very familiar with what seemed a shocking reality to many INFLUENCE women. Of course, the same was true for both genders.

Several women experienced their employers going out of business or changing direction so dramatically that the women were required to find new employers. These included historic Omaha firms such as Brandeis, Northwestern Bell, Enron, Peoples Natural Gas and Contemporary Industries. The familiar Omaha world was changing and unsettling for many people.

Our FGI experiences gave us much to share with the women in INFLUENCE. This information provided insights to provide both leadership tools and increased confidence so they could be more successful in times of major transitions.

From the women, we learned how different organizations were reacting to the rapid changes occurring in Midwestern companies. Over the years, INFLUENCE, along with the added program for men, FOCUS, provided a window for us into many organizations and their reactions to rapid changes in the business environment. This, in turn, allowed us to be more effective in our consulting to other organizations.

In retrospect, we probably picked the perfect time to begin INFLUENCE. It was a time when more and more women were ready. It was also a time when there was so much change beginning that it was the perfect time for great learning.

In 1988, we began a second INFLUENCE program – this one in Denver. While the content was the same as in Omaha, we were initially surprised to see how the culture of Denver made many elements different. First, a majority of the participants in Denver had not been born and raised there – unlike the life experience of those in Omaha. This made the two locations' groups somewhat different.

Many women had much larger jobs than those in Omaha. We found more of the Denver INFLUENCE women traveled overseas regularly for their work than did those in Omaha. It wasn't unusual for two or three women to come to a Denver INFLUENCE session and tell the group that they had returned the night before from Frankfurt, London or Sydney; or, for a woman to announce she had to leave early on the second day to catch a flight to Brazil or Paris. The Denver participants seemed confident, aware of world issues and far more open to risk-taking.[4]

In the Denver program, participants generally knew more about world and national events, were often more ambitious and frequently felt even less able to balance work and family and home than those in Omaha. Also, women came to the Denver program from all over the United States, so their regular life stories were quite different. Additionally, we had far more Women of Color in the Denver program. This combination of life stories and diversity resulted in groups being able to go "deeper" faster. Denver groups were not better, they had difference life experiences. Overtime these differences disappeared.

As we began our tenth year with INFLUENCE, we asked all previous graduates to tell us about the value of their experience.

The results of our request were amazing and humbling.

The three biggest messages from the survey were:

- Virtually all the women reported the experience was very valuable. A public relations consultant from Boston reflected, "Women in general and minority women in particular often are discounted in the corporate environment because they think and behave differently from white men. This program provides tools to counter that trend."

- 25% reported INFLUENCE had "life changing impact" on them. An Omaha hospital administrator told us, "I am not sure I can adequately convey my thanks for the change in me . . . It is a process and program of which I am so proud. It's that inner core plexus of strength, camaraderie and caring for all of us."

- Participants believed INFLUENCE had greater impact on them in the years following the program than during the program year. As a Denver insurance executive told us: "I believe the program gives you what you put into it. It took 3-4 years for me to see the value of the program."

This last finding was perhaps the most amazing. Learning from leadership development programs typically falls off very rapidly after the program has concluded. We sometimes see many of the women who participated in INFLUENCE in the '80s. They still believe INFLUENCE was a major contributor to their life success.

Our INFLUENCE program focused on subject matter and processes that were not mainstream until well into the '90s. We focused on the challenges facing our society and economy in order to remain competitive in a growing global environment. INFLUENCE became what author Peter Senge would later describe as a "learning organization."

In his quite popular 1990 book, *The Fifth Discipline,* Senge said "At the heart of a learning organization is a shift of mind – from seeing ourselves as separate from the world to connected to the world, from seeing problems as caused by someone or something 'out there' to seeing how our own actions create the problems we experience. A learning organization is a place where people are continually discovering how they create their reality. And how they can change it."5

In INFLUENCE, we were able to observe from the beginning how each person creates her own reality and only she can change that reality by seeing how she interfaces with the greater global reality. In the '80s, we were often surprised most participants seemed to not feel the importance of what was going on in the world. Looking back today, we understand it was simply too big a stretch for American society as a whole. The women often felt they were drinking from a fire hose. But this would change!

And indeed, as the '90s began we saw INFLUENCE women journeying to Europe, South America and Asia for work and for continuing development. We also saw an increase in participants who had been born in places such as Egypt, Russia, Iran, China, India, Brazil, Poland and many other countries.

INFLUENCE women confirmed their participation helped them build "from the inside out" by looking at their own roots, seeing how each one's character was created and thus creating a lens through which she could see the rest of the world. The process of discovery enhanced self-knowledge, allowed the participant to recognize herself within a global context, to see the importance of valuing differences and to prize learning through ensuring a growing community.

We began INFLUENCE as an experiment in non-traditional learning for high potential women in organizations. Nine years later, it was clear the "experiment" had been incredibly successful. Former participants had gone on to significant roles in organizations across the country and even abroad, had taken on ever-increasing responsibilities in their communities and within their homes and families.

We soon learned companies could see a very positive difference in their women professionals who completed INFLUENCE. As a result we no longer needed to do much selling in order to fill a class. Many years we had too many qualified applicants and actually had to turn qualified candidates away. We always promised them seats in the following year's INFLUENCE program.

In 1988, the American Society for Training and Development Women's Network recognized FGI's work in INFLUENCE with their National Professional Development Award. People all over the United States became more aware of the impact of INFLU-ENCE. This was confirming and motivating for us and our work.

## CHAPTER FIVE

# Learning With Men

After three very successful years of INFLUENCE, a member of the ICAN Board of Directors, General Manager of the Western Electric Works in Omaha, asked for a program like INFLUENCE to be offered for men.

There were many long discussions among the three of us on whether, or how to respond to the request. Our decision to begin INFLUENCE came because there was so little leadership development available for women. On the surface, therefore, we thought we had not believed there was a need to offer a program for men. However, we were wrong! We began the program for men in 1986, designed to be as close as possible to INFLUENCE. We called the men's program FOCUS.

After working with INFLUENCE, the early days of FOCUS felt quite different. Given the make-up of the Omaha corporate scene in the mid '80s, most of the first participants in FOCUS were White men. Of course, in the mid 1980s, Euro-American men controlled the US economy and most of the world economy – just as they had since the beginning of the 20th Century.

In other words, at the time, White men were psychologically – if not actually – in charge. We learned through the FOCUS experience how much change men would experience during the coming thirty years. As we went about our work with INFLUENCE and FOCUS, we continued to make our observations about this reality. We also enjoyed working with the FOCUS men.

As with INFLUENCE, FOCUS begins each year with a two-day overnight retreat. This serves to ground the group and begin forming a learning community. In the first years of FOCUS, Carol made the observation that men may or may not know any more about global events than the women in INFLUENCE, but appear more comfortable having the discussions. Geil thought men's jobs may have required them to read more about the world, so they really did know more. Tim agreed with both and said he thought it was about how boys are taught. He felt he was always taught to appear confident. He said boys were taught "be a man." He felt we were observing the "White Male" stereotype.

Many men learned much about themselves through the Reflection process. As with INFLUENCE, Reflection is the cornerstone for all the work. In the early sessions of the FOCUS program, the men often reflected on their work, the challenges of that work and how they were dealing with problems on the job. They would also reflect on issues related to support of their families. These subjects easily fit the stereotype of the time, which described the "ideal" for a White man. Men have been taught to be the strong, silent John Wayne, Clint Eastwood type of individual. This individual was responsible, supported his family, went to Church and was very patriotic.

This same confidence continued to show up in nearly every activity throughout the first several FOCUS years with the men, displaying this confidence more readily than their peers in INFLUENCE. Men often spoke as though they knew the answers. For example, when events such as the Chernobyl disaster or Tiananmen Square or the Sony purchase of Rockefeller Center occurred, the men had opinions. Their peers in INFLUENCE, however, often had fewer opinions than the men in FOCUS. Occasionally, some of the women would be self-dismissive, prefacing their remarks with "This could be off-base, but my opinion is . . ."

The men understood, perhaps at an unconscious level, that they were expected to know what was going on. These men were good, bright men, never pushy or inappropriate. They simply knew the expectations Society had for them and of them. They "knew that Communism was godless" and thus was evil. They "knew that the US was better than Japan" so the purchase by a Japanese company of Rockefeller Center was not seen as a good thing.

In our very first FOCUS group, we had men like Lieutenant Colonel Tom, one of the first B1 bomber pilots in the US Air Force; Dennis, who worked for Enron and left to start his own business; Rick, a young attorney who became managing partner of his very successful law firm; Perry, a young architect who would end up as a founding partner of a very successful architectural firm; or Gary, a hard-charging insurance salesman who rose a long way in his company. The three of us were inspired by, and learned from all of them.

Our first year of FOCUS was unfolding with interesting conversations, learning and new friendships created. In March, with just two sessions left for the first FOCUS group, Carol noticed how suddenly the guys were kind of hitting her on the arm or shoulder and/or seeming to make fun of her or tease her. She began to feel somewhat concerned. Immediately after the men left the March meeting, Carol said to Tim, "Sometimes I feel like maybe the men don't like me. They keep hitting me or kind of punching me in the arm. Sometimes they poke fun at me."

Tim answered, "What? Oh, not at all! When they start hitting you like that or teasing you, it means they like you! They consider you one of the guys."

"Well, you know I never had brothers, only my sister. It's just that women don't act that way toward each other," Carol said thoughtfully.

Both then agreed most of the INFLUENCE women developed relationships faster and deeper. Later, when recounting this to Geil, she simply said, "Try having three sons! This is what I get all of the time."

The three of us continued to observe and discuss the tendency of women to develop closeness by sharing openly and easily expressing emotion as compared to the ways men connected. The FOCUS men of the 1980s went less deep than the INFLUENCE women at the time. The guys also often signaled familiarity or closeness through the hits on the arm or making a pointed joke at a favorite friend. This was life in the 1980s.

By the final meeting in May, it was easy to see the group had grown closer. Nine months after walking into a retreat center and joking nervously about having come to the woods to sing "Kumbaya," most of these men were genuinely sad to part and became more comfortable sharing at deeper levels. Many have continued their friendships over the years.

Through this first FOCUS group, we better understood the signals and learned how the unfolding process was both somehow different and also similar for FOCUS and INFLUENCE. Both had their own rhythms and magic.

As we reflect on it today, our learnings from working with the FOCUS men were often unexpected and always rich. FOCUS provided many participants with their first real friends. We learned we could facilitate this by inviting men to reflect on their lives and share those reflections with one another. Having a safe place and a process to be real with one another made a big difference.

Most of the FOCUS men at this time presented themselves as very confident. We learned many had the same confidence issues as some of the women in INFLUENCE. We learned we could support their growth and confidence by inviting them to develop new appreciation for their natural gifts.

The vast majority of men we worked with during the last half of the 1980s were Euro-American with good educations and good jobs in large corporations in the Midwest. They were heterosexual, mostly practicing Christians, some active or former military. They typically had a wife and children. Most of their wives either raised the family or had careers secondary to their husbands.

There were exceptions, of course. Sudesh, a nuclear engineer from Egypt, exposed his group to a very different life reality. Mike, an African American stockbroker from Omaha, let the men see how difficult it is to get a business started when you are a man of Color. Dennis, a nurse educator, let the men see how a "real man" could have what in those days was such a non-typical career field.

During our many discussions of leadership and career, some themes kept reappearing. The men talked about their goals and their expectations of an upward career in a single organization. In order to make this possible, they had been taught that following the rules was very important. While it was good to take some career risks, those risks needed to be measured. Too much risk could interfere with the career plans.

Coming from the Midwest, most of them seldom talked about anything beyond the US borders. It wasn't that they were against a bigger picture, but most simply hadn't been introduced to a larger worldview. When we did our best to get the men to think about the globe or to imagine expanding power bases to women and people of color, they didn't reject the ideas. They simply seemed puzzled or wondered why we talked about all this.

These men sometimes considered change a threat as did their peers in INFLUENCE. The first year we had an openly Gay man in FOCUS was 1989. Michael was such a positive member of FOCUS he was fully accepted by the group. At the time, however, homosexuality made most of the men uncomfortable and sometimes negative in other settings. It was who Michael was as a human that opened these men to him. Additionally, many of the men worshiped at churches which were judgmental about those who were Gay. Homosexuality remained a generally difficult subject for the FOCUS men all the way to the turn of the Century.

These men were bright, good learners and great participants. They loved to talk about personal profile data, recent developments in strategic planning and marketing. Of course, before meetings, they would often discuss sports. It was a good and easy time together. Many men were more comfortable showing happiness, anger and serious thoughtfulness, conflict was usually avoided. Most of the men had 2-3 good buddies; few indicated they had any real, deep friendships.

We reflected on our experience after the first FOCUS group. The program had been a great success according to the participants. We learned everything we used with INFLUENCE worked perfectly with FOCUS. While the needs of men were in some ways different, the content and process of FOCUS worked very well.

We learned we could just as easily create communities of learners with men as we could with women. Also, looking back on it now, it is clear to us the men of FOCUS in the '80s took the opportunity provided by the program to prepare for the changes coming in the '90s and '00s. They were developing a real awareness of the changing role for men in the world and the increasing roles of women and People of Color in both the US and the world.

All groups, of course, have a unique personality. This is what keeps us on our toes and makes each group a wonderful learning experience for us as well as for the men. To this day, we remember vividly one of the early FOCUS groups. The participants seemed to go through the entire experience disinterested and not fully getting it. The groups' program evaluations were neither bad nor good. This had never happened to us, so we were eager to figure out why there was no response. We tried everything, so we were left to wonder what this meant and whether we needed to change the program.

Surprisingly, five months later, one member of this FOCUS group called to ask the two of us to have lunch with the group.

We were puzzled about the invitation.

Of course, we went! On a crisp November day, to the surprise of both of us, we met almost the entire FOCUS group at a famous South Omaha steakhouse. Everyone seemed quiet and polite as we began our lunch. As we neared the end of the meal, they began, one at a time, to tell us what FOCUS had meant to their lives. They described how they were clearer and more focused at work. They shared how they were much more available and loving, much more concerned about family, more aware of the bigger world. And they had made deep friendships with men.

So, we hadn't failed! This was not about us. This group's preferences for thinking and behaving required them to reflect longer and internalize their learnings. We understood who they really were and gave thanks for such a group. Many of them remain friends of ours to this day.

Another experience included holding a FOCUS meeting in the Enron headquarters building in Omaha the month before the last occupants left as the headquarters were moving to Houston. Our host, Dennis, received permission for us to meet in the Board of Directors conference room. This was right down the hall from the former office of the CEO, Mr. Ken Lay.

At the time we were in the Enron building, only one Executive Vice President was left in Omaha. He decided not to move to Houston but rather to retire. He graciously spent time with us talking about the end of a proud Omaha Corporation, which began as Northern Natural Gas and then became Internorth before the merger with Houston Natural Gas Company produced Enron.

During the lunch hour, we went to the cafeteria to see the list being posted for that "Black Tuesday." Tuesday was the day each week when the list of those being terminated was posted. People were crying or totally silent – all at the same time.

This was a shocking experience for most of the FOCUS men. At that time, few managers and leaders in Omaha had personally experienced such a transition. On that day, it made little sense. As the FOCUS year unfolded, the men would come face-to-face with many equally valuable learning moments. But because Northern Natural Gas/Internorth had been such a part of the fabric of the City, this one stuck in our memories like no other.

As the tragic downfall of this company unfolded some fifteen years later, we reflected on how grand Enron once had been.

As the 1980s drew to a close, we three reflected on our FOCUS experience.

FOCUS was just as successful as INFLUENCE, but quite different. Although we had some small hesitation initially about a men's program, we thoroughly enjoyed each experience. FOCUS felt different because men did not always show their true feelings in the ways women often did. However, the men used their own ways to share with us and with each other how they felt and what they thought.

Carol said simply, "For the sake of being able to know for sure, we are providing the same program in different ways to different genders. However, the three of us can perhaps lead the men to go a little deeper." She was so right. The coming decade would see the FOCUS men go deeper and deeper, forming life-long friendships, expressing deep emotions and beginning to grapple with a rapidly changing world.

Thirty years later both programs continue to thrive. Our work with men has been and is a profound experience, eye-opening and genuinely touching. But, more about that later.

## CHAPTER SIX

# Two Consultants from Nebraska

We found ourselves at a lovely "farm" just outside City Center Philadelphia. The Center for Creative Leadership (CCL) once again managed to introduce us to a new group of interesting people while we were working for them in North Carolina. It was not unusual for us to meet executives who wanted to engage us outside of CCL. In this case, it was Bob S. who was with us in an earlier CCL program. He asked us if we would be willing to work for his Bank. It was our obligation to advise CCL, who gave us their okay and wished us well. We found open dates on our calendar and off we went to meet a prospective internal client to whom Bob S. would introduce us.

As the Senior Human Resources leader of a prestigious Bank, Bob S. invited us to Philadelphia for a meeting with his internal client, Phil, Executive VP of Retail Banking. This was an opportunity to have our first client east of Chicago other than CCL. We were eager to make this trip and looked forward to how things would unfold. Once again, we were naïve. This great "engagement" would provide us with marvelous, challenging work plus lifetime friends. Life was bountiful and amazing.

That night at his farm, Bob S. briefed us saying Phil was a demanding leader who was incredibly bright and expected others would keep up with him. Few did, causing frustration in his organization. We agreed to be interviewed for an assignment working with Phil. Other consultants were also being considered. We were sure we wouldn't be hired anyway, so we went determined to be ourselves and see what happened.

We entered Phil's office on a cold day in January. Phil was and is one of the most interesting persons we have met. He was a lawyer who had been Executive Director of the Philadelphia Bar Association, a Pulitzer Prize finalist reporter for *The Philadelphia Daily News* and at the time, the Retail Banking Executive Vice President for this successful Philadelphia Bank. After Phil made a few jokes about what two consultants from Nebraska could possibly do to help him, we started the interview.

There was an instant "click" among the three of us. We felt we understood one another and valued many of the same ideas as well as ways of being. That rapid synchronicity turned into a wonderful initial assignment followed by a four-year relationship with all parts of the Bank. Phil quickly became a friend as well as a client. He and his wife, Essie, remain cherished friends today.

Because our initial assignment involved working directly for and with Phil, we decided to interview all of his peers, direct reports and supervisor. This began with his immediate supervisor, Bob, the CEO and President of the Bank. He was a soft-spoken, brilliant, intuitive leader who knew almost perfectly where the banking industry was headed and what this Bank's role needed to be. He was someone who truly appreciated Phil and the ways in which he was stretching and leading Retail Banking.

We also worked directly with Bob for those same four years and marveled how his predictions for the Bank were correct. As an interesting note about Bob: we once told him we admired the gigantic photograph posters of Degas' *Little Dancer*, which graced bus shelters all over downtown Philadelphia. These posters had been sponsored by the Bank to celebrate the Philadelphia Art Museum. The next afternoon, as we were leaving for the airport, Bob's Assistant presented us with a six foot mailing tube containing a copy of the large poster. It is mounted, framed and hangs on our office wall today.

Our work with the Bank became one week a month for four years. During that time we worked with all key executives as well as many high potential managers and leaders. During our limited free time, we were able to sample the cultural life of this very special city. Concerts, Broadway plays and other events were complemented by wonderful meals at the many superb restaurants in Center City Philadelphia.

Up the street from the Bank was the venerable Union League Club of Philadelphia. Created during the Civil War, the Union League was a prestigious organization for the leading men of the City. Like many Men's Clubs, it had beautiful high ceilings, dark wood paneling, excellent food, men smoking cigars, drinking brandy and networking. There were also several dozen hotel rooms for Union League members from other cities. The Bank owned two of the rooms. Bob asked us to stay at the Club to save expense for the Bank.

There was one small problem. The Club was for men only except in the dining room – *if* the woman was accompanied by a member. We were able to reach the hotel rooms without going through the men only rooms. However, when we entered the front door, the doorman always said, "Hello Mr. Rouse, welcome back." Carol, who would also be entering, apparently had to be considered invisible. It was a good opportunity for both of us that served as an opportunity to reflect again on social issues in our society.

There were many contrasts and a variety of social issues in such a large City. Poverty was very public in Philadelphia as in most large cities. Although the US economy was doing well, the poverty created by the 1970s was still felt by many. As we walked daily to and from the Bank, we left the lovely Chestnut Street, turned onto cross streets and generally encountered street people still sleeping on the grates over the underground subway system. This provided them with warmth in the winter and some airflow in the summer.

For the two of us, working in a large East Coast city was a very different experience than a Midwest or Western city. Age, history, pride in ancestry, generations of both privilege and poverty all contribute to a different culture. We learned how to effectively consult in this more complex environment.

Toward the end of our first year working at the Bank, a newly hired Senior Vice President arrived. This remarkable human, Kevin Tucker, would become a lifelong friend. Kevin came to the Bank from being Police Commissioner of the City of Philadelphia. Prior to this, he was a Director of the United States Secret Service. He spent many years serving on details that protected Presidents, Vice Presidents and their families.

Kevin was a genial, Irish Catholic, Republican who was also a no-nonsense, greatly appreciated leader at the Bank. As a counter-balance to Kevin's political leanings, Phil was a fairly liberal voice. The four of us shared many dinners, debating the state of American politics and history late into the evenings. It would have been a pleasure to just sit and listen to the two of them debate politics. But of course, both of us loved to be in the thick of every discussion with them.

Kevin helped Bob understand the Executive Team was not functioning as a team. They asked if we would work with them to develop this group of Executives into a true Executive Team. This was a great opportunity for us. We delighted in our work over the next two years as we met with the Team quarterly for three-day meetings. This focused work seemed to build them as a team as well as develop a shared strategic direction for the Bank. It also allowed them to assess and develop the Bank's key talent and manage the eventual merging of the Bank into the larger PNC Financial Services Group, Inc.

In order to provide this leadership for the Executive Team's development, we prepared agendas and led those quarterly meetings in amazing off-site locations near Philadelphia. During some seasons of the year, we would go to the Jersey Shore and hold meetings in a variety of vacation hotels in cities such as Stone Harbor, Margate and Cape May.

Our work with the Executive Team included a number of favorite restaurants and countless stories of life on "the Shore." Later at night, Phil and the two of us sat and delighted in the many colorful stories Kevin shared of his days in the Secret Service. At one time, those stories were confidential. However, many years later, they were educational and full of history. For example, it was "Mr. Tucker" who was personally assigned to Former First Lady, Mrs. Jacqueline Kennedy and her children after the Assassination of our President John F. Kennedy. Even during those stories, Kevin never referred to the former First Lady except as Mrs. Kennedy. His respect for his work and those whom he protected was immeasurable. One can only imagine the stories . . .

In other seasons, with the entire Executive Team, we would head to famous old resorts such as the Hershey Hotel or Skytop Lodge in the Poconos. Because these sessions pre-dated cell phones, pagers and internet, we were able to take the Executives away from their day-to-day work so they could really focus on the agenda and goals of the meetings.

We learned a great deal about building Executive Teams during those years. The members were eight men and one woman plus the two of us. We shared theory, used psychometric instruments to provide information about one another and the Team, while always working only actual Bank issues. We engaged them from early morning to late evening each day. The most important part of our work was undoubtedly encouraging them to develop their Reflective Voice both as individuals and as a team. This took their shared work to deeper, more trusting levels. They also formed new levels of relationships together.

One of the most hotly debated issues for the Team was about which Division of the Bank was most important to the future. The conventional banking wisdom had been that Lending was most important for Bank profitability. Retail was seen by some as a loss leader designed to get deposits in for the Loan officers to use in loans. In this particular Bank, the Trust Division was also particularly successful and profitable. So there was some consideration of it having the premier role in the Bank's future.

What we personally believed based on our research at the time, was that the Retail area of the Bank would soon be the most important for as long as the Glass Steagall Act of 1933 was in place. Glass Steagall required banks to not add investments and insurance to their business lines. This was designed to protect depositors' money from being lost to speculation in the investment arena. In exchange, the Federal Government created the Federal Deposit Insurance Corporation. This Bank, however, like virtually all large banks in the US, wanted Glass Steagall to be repealed so they could be in the investment and insurance businesses.

Glass Steagall was finally repealed in 1998, and banking was changed forever. Today, many observers believe that the repeal of Glass Steagall was a major cause of the Recession of 2007. But in the '80s, our clients believed it would insure their continued success. None of the Executives we worked with would have ever entered into the "deals" that some on Wall Street attempted later.

However, there was always the question whether it was more important to focus on increasing revenues from fees or from loan interest. The Executive Team never fully resolved the issue but did agree Retail fees had much greater potential than they had earlier believed.

An interesting learning for us – or better confirmation of previous learning – is how actions taken sixty years ago can have such profound effect. Unless one was a true American history buff, or worked in a bank, there is little chance that she or he ever heard of the Glass Steagall Act. It was most helpful to our work in banking that we be familiar with it.

One of the more interesting experiences with the Executive Team was to begin the process of assessing future talent for the Bank. Up to that time they followed the practice of letting the best in each Division rise in that Division. Now it was clear that effective leaders needed to have broader understanding and a shared accountability for all the areas of the Bank. This would require major development and a breakdown of Division silo walls.

Kevin and his staff assembled a portfolio containing bios and work histories of the 175 officers directly below the Executive Team. One of our first discoveries was there were few women and almost no women or men of Color in the group of 175. This concerned the two of us. The importance of diversity in a workforce was always a big deal for us. We advised both Kevin and the CEO, Bob. Both found this surprising. The information resulted in some valuable conversations with the four of us. We then led the Executive Team in a detailed evaluation of each of these individuals followed by the selection of those they considered of highest potential. The Team then decided how best to prepare this high potential group.

In addition to serious work and long hours, we often had enjoyable surprises at the various hotels and resorts where we met with the Team. One of the most surprising happened at Skytop. It was late fall, so the Resort was virtually empty. We expected our small group would surely be the only business executive team there at the time.

During the first afternoon of our meeting, we heard a large helicopter arriving on the Helipad behind the Lodge. We took a break and went out to see what was going on. Imagine our surprise when we saw the CEO of Union Pacific Corporation and his Executive Team step out of the helicopter. They were coming to Skytop for a planning meeting.

Our initial reaction was nothing compared to the surprise of the Union Pacific Corporation executives who knew us. It was if we could read their minds: "What are Carol and Tim doing here? Why are those two with one of the banks that serves the Union Pacific Corporation?" It was both a slightly awkward and enjoyable experience for us. Later in the evening, Bob, the CEO of the Bank, spent some time with Drew, the CEO of Union Pacific. Bob told us later the UP Corp. people were VERY interested in what work we were doing with the Bank.

As a result of the Executive Team's assessment of the group of 175, the decision was made to create a special development program for the 84 who had been determined to be of highest potential to lead the Bank in the future. The program had as its priorities: building cross-functional teams, individual and team assessment, examination of environmental trends that were influencing the future, thoughtful consideration of alternative scenarios for the Bank. We were asked to design and deliver the program – another great opportunity for FGI.

*Managing Through Change*, the program we designed, included a first session lasting five days followed six weeks later, with a second session of three days. All sessions were held in Hershey, Pennsylvania, at the lovely and historic Hershey Hotel. This hotel, created by the founder of Hershey chocolate, was close enough to the factory that the delicious aroma of chocolate was everywhere. At each meal there were five or more chocolate desserts available. At night, a handful of Hershey's Kisses were on each pillow in every room. It was close to heaven for chocoholics.

We divided the group of 84 high potential leaders into groups of 21. Bob, the CEO, was present for two half days with each group. He shared with them how he saw the impacts of the environment on the Bank and the alternative future scenarios we developed. He also developed closer relationships with the participants. We thoroughly enjoyed our time with Bob and the groups. His insights and intuition anticipated exactly what would very soon happen to the financial services industry. The 84 bankers learned much from being with Bob.

We used the Looking Glass, Inc.® business simulation developed by the Center for Creative Leadership, as the centerpiece of the program. Through this simulation, we were able to provide an in-depth assessment of each individual and each of the three Looking Glass work teams. Participants received more detailed and personal feedback than most had received in their lifetimes. We complemented the simulation feedback with 360° feedback from the FGI Professional Development Questionnaire© plus the Spiral Dynamics® Values Questionnaire. As often happens, the most important element of the program was teaching each participant to develop her/his Reflective Voice.

One important memory from this work with Reflections is about a man we refer to as "Allen." When Allen left the first session of *Managing Through Change*, we felt we had failed. He resisted every effort we made to encourage him to reflect during the first session. We fully did not expect to see him six weeks later at the second session. However, as we were setting up for the second session, Allen arrived early to speak with Carol. Carol is generally the one of us who introduces the concept of Reflections in our various programs.

Carol immediately said, "Oh, Allen, I'm surprised to see you. I somehow thought you might not return."

Allen answered, "I understand. I was a real jerk. I came to apologize to you and Tim. I also came to tell you what happened. I just kept thinking and thinking about this idea of Reflections. My son went crazy with me. He lost his temper and shouted his truth to me. It was terrible and yet I knew he was right. And then I learned that my wife was considering divorce because I had become unbearable. I learned so much, Carol. Thank you."

Allen then turned to Tim and simply said, "Tim, I want to thank you also. You two have made an important difference in my life."

We were both amazed and delighted. "Oh, Allen, please tell me more," Carol said.

Allen began quietly, "I went home and just could not stop thinking about Reflections. I began to set aside time to reflect every day. I learned so much. I understood many things about myself. I understood it's not about other people not liking me. It's about my own behavior that pushes them away from me. I'm a real jerk!"

He continued, "I've reflected daily since our last meeting. Basically, it comes down to the fact I've just been acting like a #xz*! I want to apologize."

Carol gave Allen a big hug and simply said, "Welcome back, Allen!" Earlier it would have been difficult to say this.

Allen went to find his room. The two of us just sat there with mouths open.

As the time for the program neared, one after another of Allen's co-workers came into the room and said to the two of us, "Have you seen Allen? He's changed!"

Or, "Oh, my, you won't believe what's happened to Allen!"

Or, "You two are amazing. You have changed our lives and the Bank for the better. Wait until you see Allen!"

It was true. Allen had taken seriously the assignment to reflect daily in between the two sessions. Through his own ability to reflect and go deep, he was able to see himself as others saw him. He changed who he was with his co-workers, with his family and, most important, within his own heart and mind.

When we meet with new clients and invite them to reflect, we sometimes get "push back." This story of Allen is one of hundreds we could tell you that reinforce our conviction that Reflection is an important key to a leader's success.

At each session, the Executive Team joined the group for dinner one evening to discuss with participants their learnings and insights. This also helped to build strength between the

Executives and the groups of key leaders. It in turn also strengthened the Bank as many of the traditional functional boundaries were crossed.

Though we were using a beautiful resort hotel, participants remained committed to the program from 8:30 AM until 8:30 PM each day. They had reading or feedback preparation assignments most nights. While there was a bit of complaining about this, most found the program such a wonderful confirmation of their work to date that they fully invested in *Managing Through Change*. For over a dozen years after we completed the work with the Bank, participants in these *Managing Through Change* groups continued to write to tell us how valuable the experience had been.

The second session of the fourth and last group of *Managing Through Change* began in January 1991. The first day, as usual, included work on strategy plus an introduction to the theory of Spiral Dynamics® (SD). SD is a process for understanding why different individuals may respond very differently to challenges they experience in life. Those different responses are described as "operating systems" in us. Just as we neared the end of the afternoon session, we learned the United Nations coalition, led by the United States, had begun Desert Storm to free Kuwait from Saddam Hussein. After the evening session, we gathered for a long evening watching the bombing of Baghdad and other targets. It was these types of every day life experiences that happened during our times together that built these teams and caused a deep closeness between us and our dear friends and clients.

The next day brought many remarkable reflections and deep learnings. Participants shared personal reactions to what the war would mean. They also spent considerable time talking about how the Spiral Dynamics® theory applied to the various dynamics in this situation. It was a very special morning session. It confirmed the work was relevant in these clients' personal lives as well as work lives.

As a token of completion of the Program, we presented each participant with a Lucite cube that had the Bank's logo and a genuine Ammonite visible, but buried within the Lucite. The Ammonite was a sea creature that lived 245-260 million years ago and, like the dinosaurs who lived in the same period, was unable to adapt to environmental changes and so became extinct. On the back of the cube was written: "It failed to adapt." The entire financial industry and this Bank experienced great change in the decade after we were no longer working there. However, the message of *Managing Through Change* became more and more relevant and many of our clients wrote us to confirm this.

A few months after the end of the *Managing Through Change* program, we decided it was time for us to leave our work at the Bank. We loved every experience. We had deep respect and fondness for our clients and friends. However, we have always believed after several years, consultants can too easily become deeply enmeshed in the client system and can no longer have complete objectivity. So, we reluctantly said good-bye to a wonderful four-year experience with the special women and men in Philadelphia. We learned an immense amount about banking. We also formed deep and lasting friendships with both Phil and Kevin.

Still, there are some additional pieces to this story.

At about the same time as we decided it was time to end our work at the Bank, our dear friend Kevin was diagnosed with an inoperable brain tumor. He was told he had only a short time to live. He returned every month to the hospital to get another MRI. His doctors and specialists would tell him there was no change. But he had an incredible will to live. He refused to allow the diagnosis to hold him back, to keep him from contributing to society. He eventually retired from the Bank, but found another way to get involved.

Kevin joined the Board of Directors at the Wistar Institute, a National Cancer Institute Center for biomedical research, where he served more than 12 years, chairing the board from 1998 until 2005. The Wistar Institute held a special tribute dinner for him in 2005. Kevin died in June 2012. We returned to Philadelphia several times during the period of his illness to be with him and his wife, Judy. He was one of the most admired men in Philadelphia, partly because of the ways he greatly improved the Philadelphia Police Department, but more so because he was simply an incredible and wonderful human. Kevin remains in our hearts forever.

Phil has also remained part of the Carol and Tim story. In 1993, Phil was a part of our second business conference in Moscow, joining us for what became an incredible life experience. In 1998, he participated in our program *Finding Our Spiritual Path* in Santa Fe. Then in 1999, he joined our *Millennium Project Part 1: Bringing Spirit to Leadership*. Essie joined us on The *China Pilgrimage* in 2003.

Since then Phil and his wife, Essie, have continued to be a part of the ongoing Wisdom Community, an offshoot of the work of our not-for-profit company, FGISpirit. The Wisdom Community is described in Chapter 20. Phil has hosted this group twice in Philadelphia. Phil's own career eventually took him beyond the Bank. He served as CEO of the Philadelphia Public Schools and later became Managing Director of the City of Philadelphia under the direction of the elected Mayor. He has also been head of a consulting practice and continued to write columns for the *Philadelphia Daily News*. Having both Phil and Essie still in our lives today is a great privilege.

Phil has also come to Omaha as a presenter in FGI/FGIS programs we were offering. He has used each occasion to tell us that he has never seen any heavy traffic on Omaha streets. We have taken him to busy intersections at the height of rush hour.

Each time we have had to concede that he is right. Compared to Philadelphia there is no heavy traffic in Omaha.

We have learned a great deal from our very special friend from the East. This would make sense because, after all, we were just two consultants from Nebraska.

## CHAPTER SEVEN

# Tall Poppies

On the fifth and final day of our Looking Glass,® Inc. program on the North Island, in Masterton, New Zealand, a senior manager in a Government Department, Janet Takarangi, was speaking:

"In New Zealand, we have many fields of beautiful poppies in season. Occasionally, a few of the poppies in a field grow stronger and taller than the others. We are taught that all the poppies in the field must be the same height in order to not call attention to the shorter poppies. So we cut down the tall poppies. But here, this week, you have taught us to be tall poppies and to be proud of it. I will never forget your teaching. More important, I plan to act on it as do many others in this room."

This was and is one of the proudest moments in our professional career. To create and honor the Tall Poppies is better than anything we could ever do. The Tall Poppies will be the ones to create a world that works for all!

We now understand the "Tall Poppy Syndrome." Apparently, this is sometimes a pejorative term describing a particular social norm in many countries; though not usually in the United States. The Tall Poppies refer to people of genuine knowledge, skills and abilities who may be often resented, attacked or criticized due to their talents or achievements. These talents and achievements are said to separate them from and elevate them above their peers. This is considered to be bad for peers who feel less.

The term Tall Poppies is considered negative in countries such as the UK, Canada, Australia and New Zealand or possibly other countries influenced by or previously controlled by the British Empire. However, often in the US, people strive to be Tall Poppies.

While we were privileged to work in numerous international venues over the years, it's quite easy to remember our first consulting work outside North America. In 1989, New Zealand, under the Labour Party government, was experiencing a stagnant economy. People were concerned with the future. We were invited by the Center for Creative Leadership (CCL) to co-lead the inaugural offering of CCL's premier program, the five-day Looking Glass,® Inc. program, *Workshop in Organization Action* in New Zealand.

The trip to New Zealand was a very important one for both of us. We felt pleased to have been invited. We learned so much about cultural differences, about how those from a small country far from the US view us, and about what it must be like to live in a country that is stunningly beautiful in every direction.

Our friend, the late Anne Faber, at CCL asked if we would work with her and her colleague, Betty Williams, as part of the Team to install CCL's *Workshop in Organization Action* at the New Zealand College of Management. We would be working side-by-side with Anne while training three leaders from the College: Diana, Wayne and David– all successful management consultants in New Zealand. So, how hard could it be to do so in New Zealand? Our common heritage was English; our common language was English; they were allies in all the wars we fought in the 20th century. We were sure it would be a great adventure.

A few months later at the Center for Creative Leadership in North Carolina, we began the initial training with Wayne, Diana and David. They seemed like nice enough "chaps," but they were initially quite put-off by Americans. It was primarily about our nuclear weapons. One in particular felt the United States was endangering the entire globe because of the nuclear arms race. Despite a history of being allies, New Zealand barred the US Navy from bringing any vessels that carried nuclear weapons into New Zealand waters.

We were, quite simply, taken aback. It took many late night conversations before the seven of us determined we would be able to work together, even if we agreed to disagree about US foreign and military policy. Despite this difference, our three new colleagues were very capable and talented.

There was another thing we noticed about the three of them: they knew more about the US and US policy than most Americans we knew then or now. This learning was to be repeated in every other country where we worked in the coming years. Sadly, people outside of the US pay more attention to what is going on in the US than most Americans do. It seemed especially true for New Zealanders (Kiwis). They came from such a small country so far away; perhaps they felt that they had to know about the rest of the world. And they did.

We were eager to learn more also. In March 1989, we headed off to New Zealand with Anne and Betty. New Zealand consists of two islands that together are about the same size as California. In 1989, the population was 3.4 million people and 70 million sheep. This was close to the population of Iowa at that time except for the sheep.

New Zealand may be the most beautiful country on earth. Within a short plane ride in country, one can find glaciers, skiing, dense jungle, geysers, beautiful beaches, rolling farmland and pasture, roaring rivers and waterfalls with every kind of outdoor activity. Perhaps due to this beauty as well as the great distance from every country but Australia, the New Zealanders have learned to be quite self-sufficient, relying on one another for all that they need. Like most countries begun as colonies, New Zealand has an indigenous minority, the Maoris. The Maoris were not given the same opportunities as the majority White population. In recent decades, efforts have been made to change that. But in 1989 discrimination was still quite apparent except in Government Service.

So here we were with people who shared the heritage and language of England, but who were incredibly different in values, outlook and priorities. Could we be successful in co-leading this program? The answer was a definite "Yes," but many learnings would come along the way.

One of the things we noticed soon after arriving in New Zealand was that the Kiwis took a more laid back approach to completing tasks. Time did not seem to be critical at all. We Americans were easily stressed when details were not attended to as we believed necessary. Our colleagues from the College seemed to take everything in a much more relaxed manner. We believed the schedule was sacred. They believed it was a general guide. We wondered if they could possibly meet our "standards of excellence." Of course, they did! They simply went about it in the way that was appropriate in New Zealand. A perfect example would be that we all stayed up preparing until 3AM on the morning the program began, finishing set-up and last minute arrangements.

The twenty-one participants came to us from all over New Zealand, employees of Government, public and private enterprises, from middle management to executive levels. They worked diligently and energetically all five days of the program. They seemed to learn more than did many groups in the US. They exceeded our standards of excellence in every respect. Based on their comments at the end, we met their standards as well.

Now, nearly twenty-five years later, the comment, "You have taught us to be Tall Poppies," has been our strongest memory and our greatest challenge. Why? Today, the stakes for leaders have become much greater each passing year since 1989. Our global economy and planet are changing in such radical transformational ways that leaders who are not ready to be Tall Poppies are not up to the challenges of leadership.

In every experience since our time in New Zealand, regardless of country or group, our goal has been to encourage women and men who would be leaders to be Tall Poppies. That is, Tall Poppies with a conscience, with values and ethics, with caring for others, with knowledge, skills and abilities for leadership. Whether those individuals limit their aspirations to the business where they work or plan to make a difference on a larger stage, the role of leader requires much more. We believe the requirements to deal with radical change, to easily work across borders, to value and motivate people who are very diverse and to accept a whole new paradigm for living are all essential.

As an interesting note, the INFLUENCE group that began in the fall of 1989 adopted Tall Poppies as the name for their group. They developed letterhead and other items that used the name and appropriate art. For years after their program ended, they continued to meet as the INFLUENCE Tall Poppies.

The inspiration of New Zealand stayed with us. Fourteen years later, we invited two of our New Zealand colleagues and students, David with whom we had worked in 1989, and Toby, a leader of the Maori people, to join us in China. Toby was a keynote speaker at our conference in Shanghai. Speaking to an audience from China, the US, Russia, Italy and several other countries, this strong and gentle leader again taught us, and each person present. Toby called upon the one hundred leaders present to bring their Work into harmony with one another and with the Creator – and so to create the world we all seek.

Toby taught us about patience, love, openness and gratitude. His spirit will always be with us. Toby was clearly a Tall Poppy.

Carol and Tim in early FGI days • Carol presents to INFLUENCE women in the '80s • Another INFLUENCE group begins their journey • Carol with INFLUENCE 2 of Denver.

Carol and Tim hold an INFLUENCE VII shirt • The venerable Union League Club of Philadelphia • Tim in the hill country of New Zealand • Carol in FGI work at New Zealand College of Management.

Onion Domes of the Russian Orthodox churches • Carol and Tim at "Mother's Flat" with Alexey Morosov, Tahir Bazarov and Lena Lopouhena • Carol, Tim and translator Svetlana presenting to Graduate School faculty, Moscow State University • Americans and Russians in an intense moment, 1992 Conference.

The 1992 Moscow Conference with song and dance • Visiting Russia's Mission Control Center in Kaliningrad, a tightly guarded, closed city outside of Moscow • American and Russian participants spent evenings in storytelling and song, 1993.

Norma Mozee couldn't resist. She had to climb up on that tank, 1993 • Tim with Dennis Hopple, 1994 • St. Basil's Cathedral in Red Square, Moscow.

Well-dressed INFLUENCE group in the '90s, Martin Marietta corporate headquarters • Geil, Tim and Carol at *Seeing Through New Eyes*, 1993 • The second decade of INFLU-ENCE women busily create introductions for Day 1.

Carol often celebrated her birthday in Moscow. Carol, with Denny Aron, holds one of the many roses she received at every "Russian" birthday • Carol debriefing a group of executives of the Looking Glass "Company" in Moscow • The camaraderie of FOCUS men is key to success • FOCUS men entertain at the Denver Holiday Party.

Gene Morton, here with Tim, was a key to our success in healthcare consulting • The *Russia Pilgrimage,* 2000, had many tender and joyous moments • Most sacred Pilgrimage site was Sergie Possad, oldest monastery in continuous operation in Russia • The long walk to the Church of Intercession on the Nerl at Bogolyubovo built in 1165.

Tim and our FGI friend and colleague, Dzhannet Gililova Kashurnikova, begin *Leadership, Teamwork and Productivity* program, our Emergenetics program in Moscow, 2006 • Tim, Denny, Carol and Dennis Hopple at the Great Wall prior to our first Looking Glass program in 2000 • Carol views the hot chips at Frito Lay, Shanghai.

Denny takes notes during a Looking Glass program in Shanghai • The first China Looking Glass program ended in a banquet • This 2000 picture is our only proof of mammoth statues to the Buddha at the famous Temple of Inspired Seclusion in Hangzhou.

PepsiCo China was our largest FGI China client, with Nina Liu and Dianna Last • A usual scene in 2000 was Beijing bicycle transportation • Carol making her first purchase in HongQiao Market, Beijing • Drying clothes on Beijing high rise building.

# The Growing Years

## 1991 - 2000

# 1991 - 2000

## 1991

USSR dissolves.

Deng Xiaoping declares the Pudong district of Shanghai to be the showcase for the socialist market economy.

US – Desert Storm

Dot.com growth

US economy up 3.8% per year.

Inflation at 2%.

Consumer confidence index reaches 145, highest in history.

## 1992

Author Frances Fukuyama book, *The End of History*, states "Capitalism has won."

## 1993

Civil War in Moscow.

President Boris Yeltsin sells off State-owned businesses in Russia; economy grows rapidly.

President Bill Clinton takes office.

## 1994

Rwanda genocide

## 1995

Oklahoma City bombing

## 1998

Russia business crash

US budget surplus for first time since 1969. Surplus

continues in 1999, 2000 and 2001.

Bella Abzug, leader of the Feminist Movement, dies.

## 1999

Bosnian War

Hungary, Poland and Czech Republic join NATO.

World population reaches 6 billion.

Glass-Steagall Act of 1933 repealed. Banks free to offer investment products previously prohibited to protect the public.

Vladimir Putin succeeds Boris Yeltsin as President of Russia.

## 2000

World survives Millennium calendar change.

Soaring oil prices panic world market.

Dot.com bubble bursts.

US economy declines for 2 years due to Dot.com bubble burst.

## CHAPTER EIGHT

# Reality vs. Illusion

## What Happened?

In 1991, the two of us were invited to come to Moscow by Laura Dodson, Ph.D., President of the Institute for International Connections (IIC). As often happens, the invitation had its own story. Some one who worked with us recommended us to a friend or colleague. In this case, it was an INFLUENCE woman who had connections with Laura. Laura had worked with the world famous Virginia Satir for some years in Moscow.

Virginia Satir (1916-1988) is perhaps best known for her work in Family Therapy and is often referred to as the "Mother of Family Therapy." She is also known for her groundbreaking work in Change Process. Satir's work grew beyond the world of therapy into business and all walks of life. Prior to being involved in work begun by Satir, the two of used her work during our time at Union Pacific as well as in our FGI consulting around corporate change.

Virginia Satir taught groups in what became known as the Satir Model. Russian psychologists and teachers became very interested to learn about Western models such as those pioneered by Satir. She led her famous Family Camps in Russia and all over the world. The Russians who spent time learning from and working side-by-side with Satir were devastated to learn of her passing. They wanted the work to continue. However, they also had a new focus of interest.[6]

After Satir's death in 1988, Laura wanted to add to the outreach work of IIC. Russia was changing fast. Laura continued the Family Camps. However as Russia changed, there were new opportunities for work among these bright Ph.D. professionals who were previously involved in psychotherapy. They wanted to learn more about working in the promised new businesses. This opportunity never existed in Russia. This is what led Laura to invite us to join her in the IIC work.

She asked us to design and convene a conference for Americans and Russians to carry on the earlier work, but with a new focus on the business world. It started out as something close to the Family Camps, but as we moved forward in planning, it was clear this was not to be a Family Camp.

We were going to enter Russia at an amazing and totally new time in Soviet and Russian history. Earlier in the mid-80's, Mikhail Gorbachev coined watchwords for a new Soviet society: "Perestroika" inferring restructuring and "Glasnost" meant openness. At some level, Perestroika also suggested a kind of revolution in what had been the tight, closed Soviet society.

This soft revolution inferred society would change to invite or initially encourage truly contested elections, legalization of cooperatives and even semi-private business ventures.

As often happens in any society, especially one that has been closed for some time, the press began to exaggerate and most likely push the limits of what Gorbachev and his Deputies imagined. For the first time in their lives, many Soviet citizens felt they were given some version of "freedom," both in speech and the written word. From our point of view, things eventually grew like "Topsy" and soon Gorbachev was seen as promoting too much change. His ability to lead such a massive change was questioned.

Gorbachev, looking for a new face, found the strong Provincial leader, Boris Yeltsin. The United States watched with delight, then amazement, then disbelief, as Yeltsin won election after election. In 1990, he was elected to a seat in the Supreme Soviet of the Russian Federation. Within months, a new position, President of the Russian Republic, was created. Later, Boris Yeltsin was elected to this new role by the Supreme Soviet.

With both Gorbachev, as the General Secretary of the Communist Party and the President of the Soviet Union and Yeltsin as the new President of the Russian Republic, there was confusion about who was in charge. Yeltsin grew in popularity.

In December, 1991, various Presidents of Soviet Countries signed accords declaring the USSR dissolved. At the end of December, 1991, the Russian Federation was recognized as a successor to the USSR. By this time, Gorbachev resigned in order to encourage Democratic Reform to Russia.

Finally, The Cold War was over!

Though the two of us had spent our childhood years in very different parts of the US, the issues of the United States and the Soviet Union were key in our minds from grade school throughout high school and college. Being educated for the Cold War was a serious part of our adolescence. We saw or heard many movies, songs and TV shows about the Soviet Union. One memorable movie was "The Russians are Coming!" Suddenly, we now were imagining going to Moscow! We would be able to discover if this was reality or illusion.

What we did not anticipate is that our hearts would soon be filled with love for our Russian friends and for Russia. Our two lives would be changed forever. Changed in deep, positive and important ways for which we each give thanks!

The thrill and excitement of the trip teetered precariously due to the many doubts and fears expressed by family and friends. Laura helped us enormously by briefing us about her colleagues and work in Russia and their many shared, significant experiences.

Though we believed we were well prepared, some things were forgotten. As is usual, one never notices what's been left behind until one needs it. We completed our third leg of the trip in Frankfurt, Germany. Now it was time to head to the Moscow Gate for the last leg of the trip. As we walked toward the gate, the gate postings and messages changed. The flight to Moscow was delayed indefinitely!

It was at that moment we understood what had been left behind, not by just one of us, but both of us! Where was the precious information about who was to meet us in Moscow? We had no Moscow phone numbers to call!

We were no strangers to airlines. We were no strangers to flight issues. Each thought about what was needed. Neither understood the other also came unprepared with how to reach our contact in Moscow. Sure, we had some official names, titles and addresses. But no phone number nor specific name of who was to pick us up at the airport!

Several hasty calls back to the US ended with someone giving us the name of a person in Moscow who MIGHT know who would be meeting us. Somewhat frantically, we called that person who also did not know who would be meeting us, but did have an idea of someone else who might know. We had a new phone number in Moscow to call.

It was at this moment we realized our many weeks of taking Russian language classes may not be as useful as we hoped. Thank goodness, the Russians with whom we spoke that first night were much better speaking English than we were speaking Russian. However, each person seemed to really appreciate our efforts.

At last, after numerous calls to names on our Contact List, we reached a woman who knew for sure that Alexey Morozov, Ph.D., was scheduled to meet us at the airport. Plus, she had Alexey's phone number! We called hopefully, only to find no one answered. This was in the days prior to phone messaging. So, with hope in our hearts, we each said a silent prayer Alexey would be waiting for us at Moscow's Sheremetyevo Airport.

Many hours later, our plane landed and we dragged ourselves into the dark Sheremetyevo Airport. It was without any working light bulbs! The only light was coming from windows far away. Later we would understand light bulbs were a valuable commodity. Once burned out, there were no replacements. If one was found anywhere still glowing brightly, someone quickly removed it from its socket and took it home to light the Flat.

Even more surprising were the armed guards with automatic weapons stationed throughout the concourse. The restrooms had tiny pieces of wax paper cut up to be used as toilet paper. Suddenly, the hard truth hit us. Could it be the former glory of the former Soviet Union and Russia had been eaten away by the demands of the Cold War?

Struggling through barely lit passages, exhausted by the long trip, we dragged along behind those who appeared to know their way. Finally, down steep stairs and around a corner, we found our way through Passport Control to Baggage Claim. Our bags were there. All was not lost!

As we dragged our bags off the conveyor belt, a friendly male voice said, "Teem, Carol, is it you?"

There he was! Alexey Morozov, Ph.D., stood before us, holding up the two black and white mug shot photos we sent Laura some months before. This brilliant and kind man became our first friend in Russia. He took care of us as if we were his family.

This was the first day of what would become sixteen years and over 55 trips to work in Russia. The incredible experiences, many new friends, thrilling adventures and all we would learn were yet to unfold.

Unfortunately, at this time, we did not understand fully what was meant by the term "Ugly American." However, within the next two hours, we began to understand.

Once at the Flat, we learned we were staying in Alexey's mother's home. We were concerned about where his mother was. Without a pause, Alexey quickly told us she was staying at the unheated dacha in the country. This made it possible for IIC to host "the foreigners." We were to use her Flat during our one week stay. This knowledge filled us with pain and embarrassment. We immediately felt this was surely going to be an example of our being "Ugly Americans." It became perfectly clear at this time. Many who are referred to in this way by others, simply have no idea.

We said we felt uncomfortable, but Alexey said, "No, no, this is Russian hospitality. Plus, Mother loves to be in the Country in Spring. She cleans up the garden and prepares for planting." However, then and even today, we regret this situation.

In Moscow at the time, we soon understood there were simply very few available choices for foreigners to stay that were safe and/or in working order. How things would change within fewer than ten years!

Additionally, we found out through further conversations the two of us arrived during an important Russian Holiday. What? Why hadn't we researched these dates? We did advise of the dates and asked Laura to confirm these were good for our trip to Moscow. No one said anything. However, we later learned the Russian way was never to make any guest feel unwelcome. We learned it was up to us as guests to Russia to do better homework! In our opinion, we were already learning how easy it was to deserve the title "Ugly American." However, our learning curve was fast and we improved.

Information known about Russia immediately after the Cold War was simply not available in the West. The longer we were in Moscow, we learned the truth would never be shared. Russia and her people were proud, well-educated and doing their best to hold things together in the late 1980s and early 1990s. This was very carefully kept from the rest of the world. And yet, the two of us felt terrible. We vowed we would do better in learning, understanding, asking more questions in advance. Within the coming year, we learned just how many holidays Russians held dear.

During the evening of our arrival, we heard most of the Russians who were a part of the Institute for International Connections had long ago made plans to be away at their dachas during these holidays. However, though no one ever said this to us, it was clear someone had to take care of the two Americans during this long-awaited short vacation time. Alexey had apparently drawn the "short straw."

Over dinner, Tahir Bazarov, Ph.D., a native of Uzbekistan, now living in Moscow, dined with Alexey and us at Mother's Flat. We concluded Tahir obviously drew the other short straw.

Alexey advised he needed to be with his Mother and his wife, Lena Lapohina, for the Holiday. Thus, Tahir was selected to entertain the Americans for two days. Tahir worked for the Russian Government. However, since his high school age daughter, Guli, had time off from school for the Holiday, the two of them met us at the Metro in the late evening. We would then travel to the train station for our trip to St. Petersburg for the Holiday. It soon became clear just how large this burden was for these Russian professionals to determine what to do with us during this period. They protected our egos by not telling us this was a holiday when we sent the dates which worked best for us.

This was big news! However, we were so jet lagged and dazed we simply followed the plan. After four hours, locked in the Flat and with little sleep, Carol in Mother's room and Tim on the living room couch/bed, off we went to St Petersburg. Immediately, we were able to see the differences between the two cities. So much to learn, so little time.

Plus, there was to be no hotel. The train going to St. Petersburg and returning to Moscow, served as our only hotel. The exact length of each one-way trip was ALWAYS eight hours. In those new post-Soviet Times, all of the Soviet ways were still in place. The trains to St. Petersburg left Moscow at Midnight and arrived exactly at 8AM. The return trip left St. Petersburg at midnight and arrived in Moscow exactly at 8AM.

There was supposedly time to sleep. Four sleeping berths were in the tiny compartment. Altogether, this compartment was about six by six by seven feet high. One could reach out and touch the bunk of the person across the compartment. The small tea table folded out of the wall under the window. In order to have tea and cookies, the four of us sat side by side on the lower bunks. Tahir and Guli both spoke beautiful English, as did Alexey. This trip was such an incredible adventure for the two of us who were so ready to gulp in all we could learn about Russia.

The night flew by quickly. We were both exhausted. However, at least for each one of us, it seemed slightly awkward for the four of us to be so closely resting on the bunks. Gratefully, however, the combination of jet lag and the movement of the train made it easy to sleep. Suddenly, we were in the Imperial Capitol of Mother Russia. We were awed and amazed at the glory and beauty of St. Petersburg. The combination of world famous museums with their incredible architecture and artwork, the beautiful churches and the amazing Russian food captivated us and began our long love affair with Russia.

Seventeen hours later, over tea and cookies during our return to Moscow, Tahir shared his surprise with us.

Smiling broadly, he said, "Ah, Tim and Carol, I have great news for you! First thing in the morning, Alexey will bring you to Moscow State University. You will present more about your work to the Graduate Psychology Faculty."

Our jaws dropped as the exhaustion set in more deeply than ever. There was only one question we needed to ask, "For how many hours?"

With his beaming smile on his handsome face, Dr. Bazarov said, "Only one day!"

WHAT!!!

Tahir and Guli each took their bunks. The two of us sat exhausted at the tiny tea table, staring out on the dark Russian countryside through the train window. The darkness outside held a variety of thoughts as we sped through the night back to Moscow. We stayed up all night and designed the first presentation signaling the beginning of our many years working in Russia.

Before we knew it we were at Mother's Flat, ate a quick meal of Russian bread, fruit and tea, cleaned up, dressed up and were ready. Alexey returned as if on cue and we were off. Both of us commented on feeling the adrenalin surge into our bodies as we walked into the Moscow State University, Manege Square Campus, close to and across the street from the Kremlin. We were pumped and ready for this new adventure. Soon, the twenty brilliant, friendly and kind faculty members, both women and men, accepted us. Their open arms, huge hearts, wide smiles and open, brilliant minds confirmed this and more.

On the train speeding toward Moscow, we decided to speak about Organizational Development, our experience and learning. Luckily, we planned time for questions at the end. Tahir advised these brilliant academicians were now ready to act on the new options available to them with the opening up of society. They were ready to become "business consultants" as well as faculty members. However, they wanted to hear stories of others who did this work inside organizations. They seemed interested in our every word. They had deep, insightful questions and ideas they wanted us to consider. One or two were already out on their own, but most were still in the planning/dreaming stages. Within the coming years, they would stay our friends, but also become colleagues who shared similar work.

As we left the University, we were full of satisfaction and

excitement about what was possible. Many of these Faculty members planned to be present at our Fall Conference. Their commitments strengthened and they barely had time to ask all the questions they had. As the time came to a close, we began our goodbyes. We spoke our tiny bit of Russian as we parted and this was met with much appreciation. With many hugs and the sweet Russian "cheek kisses," we made promises to see each other again in Moscow in six months.

The Fall Conference was to be our first big program on behalf of the Institute for International Connections. It was scheduled for October 1992. We were now more excited as well as more anxious about our commitment. Prior to this time, people were more curious about who we were. Now, they held high expectations. We began immediately to dream of what was possible.

## CHAPTER NINE

# Learning to Love Russia

Alexey was delighted with the outcome. He seemed very proud of the work. In many ways, this could have been a test to see how we would do for the Fall Conference. Or, perhaps, being good a Russian, he wanted to fully utilize us as a resource during these scarce times in Moscow.

As always, Alexey was thinking and planning. Suddenly, with the two of us hoping for some rest, Alexey, in his unique way, said, "Tim, Carol, I have something very interesting to share with you. Recently, I have made the acquaintance of a very famous State Prize Winner. There was only one person in each field of accomplishment who was selected annually in Soviet Days. This man is one of the most recent and certainly one of the most brilliant and refined. Would you like to meet him?"

Alexey, after knowing the two of us for only two days, knew in advance we would accept his invitation. Good thing, because we understood later this meeting was planned in advance.

A true thrill seemed to pulse through each one of us. Perhaps it was the promise of meeting a very special person. Perhaps it was our intuitive voices suggesting something even more: a friend we would love and hold in high esteem for the rest of our lives.

Driving through the busy, hectic, crowded streets of Moscow, we were able to see even more of this beautiful and amazing City. The locations we were passing were witnesses to some of the most incredible and even unbelievable history of more than 1,000 years. Apparently, each one of us forgot our lack of sleep and exhaustion from the past four days.

Tim, once a Russian history major, suddenly became alert and began to spout a number of stories from Russian history. Carol's head was spinning! Moscow had been one of the most amazing, incredible and beautiful cities. However, by early April 1992, it had long been ignored, due to the difficult economic times. It grew more beautiful as the sixteen years of our work in Moscow unfolded along with a booming, global economy.

Finally, after what seemed a long time on many winding streets full of marvelous architecture, Alexey's little Volga drove us into the parking area of a heavy, imposing, no-frills Soviet office building.

Alexey quickly jumped out of the little car, locked us inside and left us, shouting back over his shoulder, "You stay here. I'll be right back."

Oh my, this was a strange moment! Yet, it would be the precursor to one of the most comforting, loving, educational family friendships any human could have the privilege of enjoying. We were being blessed in this moment, without even realizing it.

Within five minutes, Alexey was running back to gather us and hurry us into the building. The old Soviet elevators were slow, but sturdy, locking us in behind metal gates. We rode up to an office and were met by a lovely Russian woman, Svetlana. She promptly took our coats and made us comfortable. As we were taught, we offered our English/Russian business card and she gave us her Russian one. We three were then seated at a conference table to enjoy our Russian Chai and cookies. This same welcome ritual was to be repeated with many different Russian hosts hundreds of times over the coming sixteen years. However, by the following year, 1993, Carol was able to respond in Russian to our many colleagues and hosts, shopkeepers and friends. Tim was also able to respond, but used a much smaller vocabulary.

Within minutes, a strikingly handsome, strong gentleman appeared to greet us. Gennady Smirnov carried himself with both grace and discipline. He was cordial and polite with broad and scholarly interests. We were caught in his aura and miss being with him even now.

The three of us exchanged business cards and sat down to a discussion. Later, both of us shared having had nearly the same, exact thoughts: "Oh my, what an incredible man! How can we ever keep up with the genius of his mind? I hope we'll be able to see this man more than just this once."

Gennady won the famous Soviet State Award, Gosudarstvennaya Premiya, for his engineering and design work on the world's largest transport helicopter, Mi-26, called "Halo" by NATO. Gennady himself rode in that very helicopter to France for the first showing of this Mi-26 helicopter at the Paris Air Show, 1981.[7]

Though Gennady was renowned in his field of design, he was just learning how to build a company, how to manage the people in it and how to market his products. His intellect and commitment were apparent. His questions were insightful. At the end of the ninety minutes, he finished his investigation. He exhibited his findings of trust in us as people and in our experience when he looked us in the eye and said, "Put me in your hands. I want to be your student."[8]

It was not a time to get the giggles or to cry. It was not a time to be speechless. This man was most likely the most brilliant person we would ever meet. His questions impressed us beyond measure. We were giddy and a bit frightened at the same time. With hearts pounding, each one of us expressed our appreciation and acceptance. Little did we understand we would also become a true part of the Smirnov family, along with our friend, Denny Aron.

When the meeting was over, we believed Gennady would join us for the upcoming Fall meeting. Now, we had met a good number of those who would join us for this meeting. Suddenly, we understood. These brilliant and kind professionals from a variety of backgrounds had big expectations for whatever it was we would do when we returned!

As we stood up to leave, Gennady said a few words in Russian to Alexey. Alexey's face broke into a lovely smile. He said, "Tim, Carol, we have a lovely honor offered to us. Gennady has just advised us his wife Tatiana has prepared dinner for us all. It would be their pleasure to have the three of us join them for dinner in their home."

Thoughts once again swirled through our heads. "Oh my, are we dressed okay? We do not have one of our many hostess gifts we brought for such an occasion. How will this go if Alexey has to translate every word we all say? How exciting! WOW!"

We arrived at the large, fifteen-story, multi-dwelling, Soviet-style building.

We just could not believe this was happening! We were with a famous person, going to his home for dinner. Life was amazing. We forgot neither of us had had much sleep. Adrenalin was pumping again. Carol began to wonder, "How long can I go on adrenalin and very little sleep?" The answer for those many years in Russia was, "As long as there is another adventure waiting, Carol."

Waiting at the doorway was a lovely and gracious, bright woman who spoke beautiful English. She was a true gift in our lives in so many ways, but for this immediate moment, the most important aspect was Tatiana's English excellence. We later learned also, though he understood English, Gennady had not yet been ready to speak English with native-born English speakers. It would be another 10-12 years before Gennady began to speak English with us. The two of us along with Denny, had by that time become considered "family." This has never ceased to be an honor and privilege, not because of Gennady's Prize, but because of the character, intelligence and deep humanity of this special man and his amazing wife.

Soon, we would consider Tanya our dearest and best friend in Russia. She also became our teacher, our confidante, our adventure and trip planner, our shopping expert, our art and culture expert, our Heart's Delight!

This friendship has never waned to this day, though the years have now become too many since we were side by side with our dear Tanya and Gennady.

That first dinner was delicious. The conversation moved quickly and covered more invigorating and mind-stretching topics than one could imagine. Gennady had a variety of word games and trivia questions with which he peppered the dinner conversation. Our three Russian friends were delighted when one or both of us could answer. They were actually testing us and later told us they were impressed. As the years passed, Gennady increased the challenge of his mealtime questions and eventually, he outsmarted us as often or more often than we could answer. Still, he always told us the answers so we would continue learning.

The stories of Tanya and Gennady's youth and courtship were delightful. The stories of college days in St. Petersburg were lovely. Over the years, Tanya's introductions and explanations of famous Russian Operas, of Pushkin, Tolstoy, Pasternak and other famous Russian authors, plus architectural achievements educated us culturally in ways no one else could ever have done. Her knowledge and understanding seemed endless. We took the information into our brains, but also into our hearts. We became true Russophiles.

The stories of the recent years of shortage in Russia were new information for us. The West had never known about the levels of scarcity in every aspect of life during those Cold War years. From Tanya, we heard about her keeping a goat on the balcony, just in case there was no food. She told us about buying bricks because this was the only item for sale on one shopping day.

These bricks were used as barter when money was short. Whatever was in the stores or being sold on the streets, they would buy. Not because they had so much money, but because the markets and stores had little inventory. Whatever someone was able to buy could be used later to trade for whatever a neighbor might be willing to exchange for the bricks or whatever commodity one might have when in need.

Later, while walking on the street with Tanya, we saw a woman with her arms spread out wide. On each of her arms were hanging about 15 bras. When Carol asked about this, Tanya said, "Oh do not worry, if you wish to buy these, they are new brassieres. The factories have run out of money, so many people are paid in whatever it is their factory is making. She obviously works in a brassiere factory."

Carol replied, "Thank you, but no, I was just interested to understand."

"Ah, Carol, you are such a good student!" Tanya lovingly said. What a marvelous compliment from this incredible teacher and friend.

What Tanya did not understand was that she was perhaps the very best teacher in multiple subjects the three of us could ever experience. We learned endless facts, stories, history and life! We learned what a precious, loving and giving friendship could really be.

Our gratitude today is as huge and present as it was over those sixteen years. Life has many blessings, but not many Americans who grew up during the Cold War were given as complete and loving an education as were we three. This was not propaganda. This was the truth about what's possible in deep and trusting friendship.

That first meeting Alexey arranged for us with the Smirnovs surely did change and enrich our lives forever.

As the last days of our first trip to Moscow unfolded, supplemented with our first, early teachings from the Smirnovs, Alexey began to feel the two of us were no longer such strangers to Moscow. We were able to be out on our own. We were able to help Alexey and Lena, his wife, with small bits of shopping. He gave us some parameters where he felt his part of the neighborhood was safe for us. We gladly took outings to the outdoor markets. It became normal for the two of us to stand in the lines for bread, to boil our water carefully before drinking it or making tea. We even began to shop on our own, using our new Russian words and our Russian Rubles.

There was never a day of boredom or without a new experience.

We shopped and walked, continued to practice our Russian, and learned more than seemed possible. Russians on the street smiled and spoke to us. We did our best to respond. Many encouraged our rudimentary Russian and wanted to practice their English.

However, one day stands out forever in our minds. This was a day in early Spring, 1992. Deep snowy slush was still on the streets. Babushkas in their heavy coats, Russian Scarves and rubber galoshes seemed to add to their numbers before our eyes. "Babushka" is the name for "grandmother" or "old woman." They had come to the market, many of them carrying buckets.

As we stood in line to purchase bread at the nearly empty, little bakery, the crowd of women gathered on the corner outside. Slowly, a large military truck with a dark green canvas canopy stretched over a metal frame covering the truck bed began to back up toward the curb. The babushkas, with only a few men in the crowd, began to slowly push toward the truck. As if they were drawn to the back of the truck by a large net, the women walked closer and closer together to the curb, gathering around the back end of the truck.

Suddenly, soldiers pulled back the canvas, shouting directions to the crowd. Slowly, the crowd was quiet and began to approach where the soldiers stood under the green canopy above them on the truck bed. Each person held her bucket in the air. The soldiers shoveled ragged pieces of raw chicken into the buckets. The Russian women and men held onto their buckets tightly. Many began to weep silently.

We read about recent starvation and heard from our Russian friends about the food shortage and hunger. Having eaten a lovely meal with the Smirnovs and enjoyed Alexey's wife, Lena's cooking at Mother's Flat, the food shortage was only a story to us. But it had **no face** until this day, this moment. We watched quietly as nearly one hundred people made their way to the back of the truck to receive their shovels-full of raw poultry.

The longer we spent time in Russia the more deeply we understood, at that moment, those babushkas were able to smell and even taste the lovely meals they would simmer on the stove for some time to renew their family's energy, health and hope for a better world. This day stopped their many previous weeks of hunger . . . at least for a short time.

Little did we understand at the time, this first trip was only the beginning of what Russia would teach us. What deep emotions Russia would bring forth. What glorious joy and life-learning Russia would provide for the two of us plus many of our friends and clients.

Leaving Moscow for home caused sadness and at the same time, excitement and ideas about our return trip in the Fall. On the way to the airport for our flight home, Alexey told us he was pleased Gennady and Tanya seemed to adopt us immediately. Then, he gave us the good news: Gennady had committed to attend the Fall Conference. This seemed to us an incredible thing! We began to imagine our American friends meeting this exceptional new friend.

With Alexey and Tahir, we began to plan the agenda for the upcoming Fall retreat. Our appetites for Russian food, Russian friends, Russian culture and now for real Russian work grew!

The return trip to the US was easy. However, once we were back in Omaha, absolutely every thing looked different. Our homes looked huge. Our food seemed bland. Each one of us was craving cabbage. The air seemed especially clear and clean. We read an endless number of books: histories of Russia, Russian novels translated into English, Russian language books and watched several Russian movies.

As a part of our planning for the upcoming Fall Conference, we began to invite, recruit and talk with friends and clients hoping they would decide to be with us in Moscow. Most of these Americans experienced the same Soviet/American conflict, with the stereotypes and fear felt as children and young adults during those years. Some of those with whom we spoke were younger than we were, some older. However, each one was called for her/his own reasons to be with us for this first Moscow Conference.

The group took shape surprisingly fast. We constantly encouraged those American friends and business clients who made the commitment to begin immediately learning and reading more about Russia: more Russian novels, Russian history and watching Russian movies.

Many from Omaha joined us in our Russian classes taught through the University of Nebraska at Omaha. We met together to practice our Russian. Those from Denver and other cities around the US, also used the FGI list of resources to prepare. Most of all, we asked people to come prepared for a life-changing experience.

The interest and excitement grew among this group of sixteen committed American friends and clients. They did their homework. They pledged themselves to represent the United States of America in positive ways with new Russian friends. They would soon meet 32 Russians, have their every word translated into Russian and work together, side-by side, living in the Profilaktika Sanitoria[9] together with the Russians for six days. Immediately after the Conference, these American friends would stay in the homes of one of these new Russian friends from the Conference. They would live their lives with these new friends, day by day for a week.

No one could imagine at the time just how this would unfold, but each one of us in this group pledged to do our best.

Soon, it would be September!

## CHAPTER TEN

# The Americans are Coming

There was something about Autumn in Moscow. It made the last treasured days of warmth very special. Late September was beautiful, warm and full of leaves in many colors. Though previously we did not experience how very special this time was for Russians, it was apparent during our first Fall, 1992. Arriving again after our recent April trip, we could clearly see how the entire City looked and felt different. An incredible golden glow seemed to be everywhere. For each of the next sixteen autumn seasons we were in Moscow, we relived the memory of this first visit. Autumn in Moscow was always our favorite season.

Fresh vegetable and fruit stands were on the corners. Food was more readily available due to Nature's Bounty, though still not enough to feed everyone. The number of Russians out walking their dogs seemed amazing to us. Where were all of these dogs just a few months ago? The sounds of children outside playing in the warm glow of fall energized us and gave us new views of Moscow.

Our dear Alexey was there at the airport to meet us when we arrived. His skin was tan and he seemed stronger and even more full of energy. His wife, Lena Lapohina, also a Ph.D. psychologist, was able to spend more time with us. Their own flat was walking distance to where we stayed again at Mother's Flat. It felt a bit like a homecoming. This was a more normal time for her to still be at the country dacha; therefore, our guilt was less. No doubt, as most Russians this time of year, she was harvesting vegetables from her garden to store in the root cellar to use during the coming winter and into spring.

Alexey was very excited to share the details of the Conference he and Tahir had in mind. We were equally excited to share ideas for the Conference the two of us had in mind. This was of course a surprise for all four of us. It was easy for us to assume since they asked us to provide the Conference, we would design it. Since it was their organization's event, they made other assumptions. However, more important was the first meal we would again share with our dear friends in Moscow.

Lena cooked up a true feast. She also spent a great deal of time searching for a special delicacy for us as their guests. Her cooking was delicious; however, Carol found herself uneasy as she stared down at the huge cow tongue placed nearby on the table. Lena was a keen psychologist. She apparently felt and read Carol's feelings. With a simple act, she quickly moved the tongue next to Tim just as he was actually saying, "Ah, tongue, I haven't had that for years." Lena's eyes lit up as she cut off a nice, thick slice for Tim. The evening was underway with ease. Tim saved the day.

How easily we all flowed together. The conversations were exciting and mind expanding. There were no issues or conflict. Both of us hoped this could continue forever, but especially during the coming three weeks. So much was planned. So much was at stake, both for our Russian friends and for the two of us. We were thinking about the sixteen Americans who soon would join us for the "Big Event." Would they find Russia as exhilarating as we did? Would they experience some of the same magic Russia provided us? Would they connect with the new Russian friends?

This big event was the continuation of the work Virginia Satir began many years before with the Institute for International Connections in Russia. It meant so much to these Russians who carried on her work and that of Laura Dodson we described earlier. The pressure began to build, we realized, "We are making history for these Russians, for our American friends and clients who will soon join us, and certainly for ourselves and FGI!" At some level, it was exhilarating; at another, it was terrifying.

Alexey wanted us to see the location where we would hold the Conference. We were very eager to do so. We understood from him this was a lovely Sanitorium, owned by the Russian State, created to serve pilots who were ill or recovering or just needed time away in healthy surroundings. He told us about the lovely, park-like grounds, about the many therapeutic services available to our guests and about the healthy, delicious food. It all sounded great. We were eager to make our first visit.

Due to our earlier Spring trip to Moscow, we were well aware of the hard times Russia had been experiencing for some time. It was impossible to guess how long. This reality was unknown to us in the US. The US press still seemed to hold onto the story of Russia's being a strong, mighty enemy of the US. However, following our earlier Spring visit to Moscow, we began to believe these hard times may have been since the time of Reagan's Presidency, some years earlier! In any case, things did not appear to be getting better any time soon.

We three squeezed in Alexey's little Volga and off we went. The Sanitoria was not far from Alexey's Sokol Metro neighborhood. We never tired of driving through new areas of Moscow and were somewhat disappointed the drive turned out to be so short. Before we were expecting it, Alexey said, "Ah, here we are!"

A very old looking brick building with a rather handsome stone facing was before us. The entire park-like area was enclosed with a wrought-iron fence about 8-10 feet high. Oh, if only we had understood our American guests would soon be climbing over this fence in order to see Moscow's nightlife! Still, at this point in time, it was best we did not know.

The Sanitoria Profilaktika was one of many such sanitariums devoted to a certain profession or even a certain trade union.

These so-called "homes-of-rest" were set up by the Soviet government in the 1930's. This particular facility and its many employees were dedicated to pilots and high-ranking airline officials. This was both a reward as well as insurance of excellent health for all levels of workers.

Sanitariums in general were necessary in an earlier time when Tuberculosis was more rampant. As the times progressed, these sanitariums became a perk for members, based on the fields into which they were placed. Their levels of luxury or service were based on the importance of their trade or workgroup to the greater society. In most cases, these sanitariums were available to both the workers and their families. The groups of workers did not mix with other trades or professions in their sanitariums. We were told this had been one of the finest.

Alexey toured us through the facility and grounds. It was both comforting and unsettling. First of all, it was a quiet place to stay, away from the busyness of Central Moscow. This would help the group focus on the Conference agenda and the interactions between Americans and Russians. As Alexey said, meals were served and many other features were available.

He took us first into the large dining area directly adjacent to the kitchen. Things were plain and basic, but certainly adequate. The aromas were inviting. Things were stark, simple. The woman in charge offered the three of us tea and juice. We began with the juice. It was a taste neither of us had ever experienced before. Certainly it was something we could never have imagined. It was definitely foreign, a taste we would never forget. The juice was considered VERY healthy. We took small sips and looked at each other. Alexey encouraged us to "drink it all! It is very healthy!" And so we did.

Later, this juice was served at every meal to the American group and our Russian friends who stayed together at the Sanitoria. Over the years, along with those of our US friends from this first Russian-American gathering, there has been agreement this juice tasted something like burned prunes, stewed with old tree bark. Thus, we came to call it, "bark juice."

Alexey toured us through the facilities along with the Director who took over after we finished our juice and tea. As with the Cook, the Director was also dressed in a white uniform. She wanted us to see everything. We went from the kitchen into the main "living room." We decided it would serve nicely as our meeting room. There were very old chairs in the room, some were easy chairs, some were regular old-fashioned straight-backed wooden chairs plus a couple of couches. Additionally, in the back part of the room was an actual row of airlines seats straight from some very old, Aeroflot airplane! However, it made for difficult seating since they were not bolted to the floor as they had been in some plane, long ago.

The room was light and airy. We asked about something like a movie screen on which we could show the overheads we used for the program agenda at the time. This was long before digital projection. No, there was nothing like a screen in the place. Tim, always excellent at coming up with solutions, suggested we might use a sheet. This seemed a very odd use of a good sheet to the both Alexey and the Director. Like everything else at that time, it was possible sheets were also in short supply in Russia. However, after much conversation in both Russian and English, it was agreed we would be able to use one sheet. No more! Ah, we had a screen.

Now, what to do about this very strange and unpleasant odor? The Director said emphatically there was no smell. She smelled nothing. Alexey agreed. He smelled nothing. We did our best to convince the two there was a very unpleasant smell in the room. But the conversation was going nowhere. And then, at just the right moment, a huge cat walked comfortably into the room, jumped up on one of the large planters, turned around a couple of times, scratched at the dirt and took his own "personal needs break." The Director seemed to assure Alexey in Russian this would be handled. He conveyed the message. We wanted to believe this. However, throughout our Conference, this cat was a regular visitor to the conference room. No one but the Americans seemed to notice. It soon became just a regular occurrence. It was Russia, 1992, and we were guests of generous, loving people who only wanted to provide the best they had.

It was time to see the sleeping rooms. We walked into the very long, very dark corridors of doors. Things were clean, but the place had clearly had a long life. Some of the doors hung by only one hinge. However, the Director carefully showed us each door still closed. Not to worry. The Conference tuition was set for the Americans in order to be able to pay for the Russians who would also stay in the Sanitoria. It was simply not possible for those Russians who were faculty, students or early entrepreneurs at this time to cover their own costs.

However, some of the actual Russian businessmen, such as Gennady Smirnov, Gennady Kureptin, Evgenny Kroshnev and others, would simply take the Metro back and forth to their own homes each night, returning in the morning. The two of us felt somewhat concerned over the age and well-used state of things. However, the place did have its charms. Certainly it was like nothing we had ever seen.

The therapeutic facilities were the reason people came to stay at the Sanitoria. The Director was eager to show us these. First we stopped at the gigantic indoor pool. It was easy to see how inviting this must have been in the long, snowy, freezing winters! The pool was longer and wider than any other pool, indoors or outdoors either one of us had seen before or after. The large room was somewhat dark, but had comfortable looking chairs and lounges for rest and relaxation. We were pleased we reminded our friends to bring their swimming suits. As with most every swimming pool in Russia, there was also a banya. This is one of the most traditional aspects of Russian life and something we would all learn to love. One really cannot claim to understand Russia without having been in a banya.

The banya is similar to, but different from the western Sauna. One difference is the banya uses heavy, moist, hot steam. The wooden banya room was built with three levels high of long, wooden benches on three sides. This allowed many people to enjoy the banya at one time. In the corner of the banya was a tall stove covered with hand-sized stones. As the stones became very hot, someone would pour water over the hot stones. This caused the very hot steam to pour into the room. Sweating is considered very healthy in Russia. Following the extreme heat, and healthy sweat, it is necessary to "switch" people with birch branches as they immediately run outside and jump into the cooler pool. In the Russian winter, people run outside and jump directly into the snow! For the best interests of our program, we decided we would have people use the banya one gender at a time.

Throughout the therapeutic areas, personnel were also wearing the white nurses uniforms. We were beginning to understand the focus on health and the work of the Sanitoria. It felt positive and useful for the Conference. We did not tour the "treatment rooms." Those would come later through personal experiences. Most likely, seeing them would not have explained the experiences.

Finally, Alexey was most excited to show us the gardens. He was certain we would love the SWANS! Perhaps, due to Tchaikovsky and his famous Russian ballet, swans held more appeal? The swans were lovely and added to the beauty of the garden, plus they brought a certain grace. We did not yet know swans can be very temperamental. This was something we would also learn later.

The gardens were lush, a welcome spot of greenery in a huge, downtown setting. The pond was peaceful and lovely as the swans swam gracefully. Large trees gave good shade and provided beautiful backgrounds plus a noise buffer to keep out the hustle and bustle of the thriving, active, noisy city outside. The trees and shrubs also helped to deal with the air pollution usual in any metropolitan city of this size. Or perhaps more so, due to the absence of any pollution control laws or devices. We became used to this. However, most of us Americans did develop small, nagging coughs during our time in Moscow. The coughs lingered as a reminder of the trip for some time. It was Russia! We all felt the trade-off had been worth it.

Before we knew it, it was time to go to the bank to exchange our US Dollars for Russian Rubles. As with everything, long lines were the only way to get things done. During each plane trip to Russia, the two of us wore money belts under our clothes with thousands of US dollars to exchange. Every trip to the banks during those early trips to Russia seemed quite a daunting task, not only with regard to the US$, but also for the vitamins, medicines and other things for just in case emergencies. In 1992-93, many of the systems were still Soviet in nature. The open economy had not yet arrived. It was not until a few years later, we easily exchanged our US dollars right in the hotel lobbies wherever we stayed.

During the spring 1992 trip, due to the money exchange rate, it was very difficult to carry the stacks of Russian Rubles away from the bank. By this second trip, we came prepared with appropriate light-weight cloth bags that zipped. The money we needed for the Sanitoria room and board plus meeting rooms and all therapeutic treatments was a huge amount in Rubles. However, in reality it was reasonable for all we were receiving. Plus, we didn't have to figure it all out! Alexey had done the groundwork and early planning. We recruited a great group and were becoming more and more eager for our friends to arrive. We imagined they would be as excited as we were and would love the Russian experience as much as we had.

Everything became more real once we began to look at the schedule of arrivals for the sixteen Americans joining us soon in Moscow. It hit us in the head this was more than just a Conference! There was more than simply staying at the Sanitoria Profilaktika. We still had the home stays and the visits to Russian businesses.

We also felt we needed to spend at least one day with Alexey and Tahir discussing all aspects of the program. In addition to the Conference design, we had several other equally important parts of the design/logistics for the weeks ahead. The Conference was to be five days at the Sanitoria Profilaktika. This would be self-contained in one location. All other aspects of the trip required major logistics and demanding details. This caused us some trepidation due to the oft repeated phrase in response to our questions, "Maybe yes, maybe no. It's Russia. One never knows."

Our pledge of flexibility became more and more important. The two of us needed to enjoy this special experience also. Sometimes, though, we faltered.

With Tahir and Alexey, we clarified the major demands of the coming week: travel arrangements, airport pick-ups, Conference agenda and coordination, Russian family host pairings and transportation, the additional Moscow outings including a performance at the Bolshoi and the train trip to St. Petersburg.

Just discussing these significant aspects of the trip caused the two of us to wonder how this would all unfold. Alexey and Tahir were also somewhat overwhelmed, but the four of us pledged our intentions to do our best to support each other and work as a team. All of this was so exciting and impressive when we planned it the previous Spring. It was now nothing short of overwhelming once we were to make it happen. But happen, it did!

During 1992, Russia was barely, if at all, recovering from the Soviet days. People were starving and food was scarce; buildings were without renovation or "remont" for more than 40 years; transportation was uncertain; assurances of following timetables and general commitments were difficult to rely upon, given the tentative nature of life. The whole notion of time, as it was known and accepted in the West, was simply not realistic. It was always the "maybe yes, maybe no" response.

This was not meant to be funny or cute or rude or non-caring. It was the basic reality of life. Would there be electricity? Maybe.

Would there be money for food? Maybe.

Would there be gasoline for the vehicles needed to transport people? Maybe.

Would there be Russians at the Conference as promised? Yes, but how many?

And on and on.

However, the two of us had seen in our minds' eyes the dream of such an endeavor unfolding with great promise and new understandings of former enemies. We believed this was all possible. It would happen!

## CHAPTER ELEVEN

# We Thought Americans Had No Heart

Soon it was time to make the trips to the airport for the various flights bringing our American friends. We felt great excitement. We simply could not wait to have them experience Russia. It may seem odd, but in just a few months, we had forgotten our first arrival, our first shock at the dark airport, the lack of any amenities in the airport, the gray color of the sky, the drab buildings, even the faces of some we saw on the streets. And yet, with the now early October glow in the air, things seemed better. Our love of Russia and our feelings of being at home in Moscow colored our views.

We were honest with these friends who were coming. Some, we knew for only one INFLUENCE or FOCUS class of nine months. Others for many years.

After several trips to and from Sheremetyevo, all of the Americans were safely at the Sanitoria Profilaktika. They arrived totally jet-lagged and exhausted. However, similar to us on our first arrival, they became excited at the new views in front of them on the long ride from the airport through Moscow to the Sanitoria. It was totally foreign!

They saw the beautiful, though still gray and dingy domes of the Russian Churches. They saw the people, waiting in long lines attempting to buy or barter some of what they needed. They saw totally unfamiliar sights and realized they were in for a life-changing experience of learning and growing. Most were ready for such a life adventure and met us with great joy and excitement.

Once they were all accounted for, we realized this was a large group for whom to feel responsible. Sure, they were adults committed to accepting whatever came their way, but we felt due to our invitation and our many stories of our own love affair with Russia, we may have swayed them some. Many wanted to quickly get a shower and go directly to bed. We coached them and then begged them to follow the healthy rule of immediately accepting the local time and fitting oneself into the daily life in order to keep jet lag with them for a shorter time. While this did not make sense to many at the time, those who had not traveled this far before, were willing to follow our advice.

Immediately, both the Sanitoria's Director and Cook insisted on tea and juice. Oh goodness! Soon our friends were sipping the strange, new drink, yet-to-be-named "bark juice." They had the same reactions as we did for our first taste, but eventually, we all learned to drink this daily because it was "very healthy."

We set to work orienting our group of American friends for that first day. They had many questions combined with some blank stares. We kept in mind our own first trip and the times of adjustment and need for understanding.

Before we knew it, it was time for dinner, for wine, for friendly conversations and a few reminders from "TeemanCarol." It began to feel as if the two of us had only the one name. The Russians especially came to calling each one of us "TeemanCarol."

The meal offered a good boost of energy for the tired Americans. They seemed to enjoy the food and had a new buzz about them. We suggested they go to their rooms to unpack. We agreed to meet back in the main room for a brief orientation and promised an early bedtime. We also prepared them for the fact many Russians stayed up most of the night. Tahir and Alexey were both there with us as the Russian hosts. Their talks and warm welcomes gave the newly arrived Americans a great first taste of just how endearing our two friends and other Russians could be.

The refreshed Americans were back before we had imagined they would be. It seems Tahir had promised to sing and play his guitar for them. Many stayed up into the night, intoxicated with the Russian spirit, music and warm way of welcoming us all.

The next morning, the Americans told us they were eager to get out on the streets and see Moscow. We were taken somewhat by surprise, having given them the entire schedule in advance. The schedule clearly indicated our first week would be the Conference, held right there within the Sanitoria Profilaktika. Oh yes, we should have known!

As we expected, the Americans were considerate and spent many late evenings with their new Russian friends. However, before the week was over, some of the Americans were indeed climbing that very tall wrought iron fence and making their way out into the Moscow night. They were very proud when the news was finally clear to us all. The two of us gave thanks for their safe returns to the Sanitoria and knew it must have been an exhilarating escape experience.

However, the time for the Russian participants to arrive was the day after the Americans' arrival. These Russian business and professional people set aside the days from their jobs with hopes of learning. As individuals, their learning goals were different. They wanted to understand information about business useful to them for the newly open economy. They wanted to learn more about life experiences in the US and make new friends from the US. They were curious about who Americans really were. Many Russians seemed to love nothing more than being with new friends in social environments. Perhaps this was due to the many long years of stark Soviet times.

A handful of those Russians present were older gentlemen who arrived with Soviet medals covering an entire half of their suit coats or jackets. Their lives were full of rich, but difficult history. They had survived. Among the group was a nice mix of somewhat formal clothing plus some more casual sports coats, sweaters, dresses and so on. Many of the American women were in slacks and jackets. Some were in skirts and tops. The American men were in casual slacks and nice sports shirts. The group looked very professional and was a great mix of age, gender and occupation. The stories behind the people were even more varied and amazingly interesting. We were delighted our new friend, Gennady Smirnov, had accepted Alexey's invitation to be a part of the Conference.

We began the meeting by asking people to introduce themselves. Tahir and Alexey told us the Russians would not say much. This was 180° from what happened. There was no understanding of a time limit. The three minutes suggested for each person's personal/professional introduction in some cases stretched to over 30 minutes! We had planned two hours for introductions. It took over four!

We heard incredible creativity in some introductions and true order and safety in others. There were stories of real hardship, of fear, of military experience, of family and growing up years during the Cold War. As Americans, we learned so much. There were quiet tears as we heard stories of pain, loss, fear, heroism and deep character. Few of us had experienced such lives.

After lunch, we were ready to jump into the rest of the agenda. Our prepared charts were ready and on the walls; our transparencies were ready to project. Our focus was on business. This would serve those Russians ready to begin or who had already begun new businesses once the State-owned organizations or a military career were no longer the only options.

We started with something we believed to be simple and obvious: "networking." We talked about how a good manager uses her/his network to accomplish goals and make the work successful. We attempted to draw diagrams of people, surrounded by little circles which indicated the friends they called on to help them succeed. One Russian after another wanted a more specific definition. We gave one explanation after another. Were they not understanding or not believing or genuinely not clear? Were we really so inadequate this early in the agenda?

Carol attempted one more time to provide an explanation, something such as: "Your network is the collection of people you use to help you get your work done and to have success."

More questions, more confusion, some growing frustration early in the program! Not a good feeling . . .

Pavel, already a practicing business consultant said, "This question of networks needs more time. The Russians and Americans do not perceive the same thing with this word, 'networks'."

Different Americans took turns in explaining "networks" from their perspective. After much grumbling from the Russians and a series of side conversations with Americans doing their best to explain, there was a breakthrough. Dan #1, one of the Americans, said something such as, "Try this. Networks are the people who help you get what you need or want. For example, here in the group, Sasha is now in my network because he is the one who bought the beer I drank last night. Nina, the kitchen cook, is in my network because she has been giving me apples."

Long silence, and then a loud sigh came from the Russians, followed by these two statements.

Vladimir said, "We have a word 'mafia' which gets much coverage from the Press. It sounds like networks."

Alexey K., another consultant said, "It sounds to me your network includes those who get your bribes."

The Russians breathed a sigh of relief. They felt they understood.

Well, not exactly, but . . .

Somehow, this strange struggle seemed to break the ice. Things began to work more easily. The small mixed groups of Russians and Americans seemed to have excellent discussions. Even disagreements were met with joy and learning.

We were delighted to have Alosha, a brilliant psychotherapist, serve as our translator from English to Russian and Russian to English. His ability to move from one language to another on a variety of subjects amazed us all. He soon became a member of the planning team along with Alexey, Tahir and the two of us. His humor and insights added value and meaning to every interaction. Alosha had a way of making what could have been a difficult or even culturally inappropriate incident float away with his quick humor or deep wisdom. His presence kept a certain feeling of trust and safety alive for all.

The agenda plus the spontaneous questions moved us from one topic to another. All sense of time was forgotten. Luckily, this was good due to the larger Energy present which just carried us where we needed to be in forming and developing a learning community.

Prior to the meeting, different women and men signed up for the offering of therapeutic sessions. This meant people were coming and going throughout the Conference, but all were eager to have their therapy. The individual therapy sessions were all gender specific; however, we did not understand this until later. Nor did we have any idea what these "treatments" would be. The Americans were encouraged to take their turns first. Russians said they had such therapy before and preferred to have us make sure we had the healthy experiences.

The men were scheduled to come and go first to their individual treatments. As one man after another came back into the room, they appeared to either be limping or walking with caution or in a rather fragile way. Finally during a break, we began to ask about the treatments. One thing led to another and the entire group somehow gathered to listen.

Dan #2, was one of the first men to have had his treatment. Carol simply asked in a friendly way, "Well, how was it?" Dan, still looking in pain, simply said, "Did you know what they were going to do to us?"

Carol said she had no idea. Dan then described quite a process. Basically, it began with leaving one's clothes in the dressing room and walking into a large concrete room with a drain in the floor and with only a metal bar at about waist level on which to hold. While Dan was standing at the bar, holding on, a male attendant came in across the room facing the bar. He held what we would call a fire hose. The Russian man said something in English that sounded vaguely like "Ready?"

As the American man said, "Ready" or "Yes," the attendant opened the water pressure and began to spray the man with a piercing force of water. Every part of the body was shot with a tremendous force.

Thus, each American man came limping back into the room. The American women now began to wonder what their "treatment" would be. It would not be our turn until a day or two later. Carol for one was beginning to dread this.

We continued to share business concepts and definitions which were discussed in small groups. Those small groups led to the deepest and most significant learning experiences. We used the agenda to provide lighter moments with the theory. One of the most enjoyable parts of the Conference for the two us came when we discussed favorite maxims or proverbs in both Russian and English.

We found this gave us our best understanding of the two cultures. Plus, the entire group seemed to have a great time, laughing and explaining their various maxims, sayings or proverbs. We found only a few to be the same or similar in both Russia and the United States. We learned the most from those maxims which were very different. This helped us better understand the two different cultures.

When the two of us put this into the design, we did not understand just how deep and meaningful the learning would be for the two different groups. It was fun, touching and educational; one of the best times of shared learning we experienced.

The Americans arrived from a country where things were plentiful and life was good for those of us present. The Russians were living in and coming from a time of scarcity and sacrifice. The history of those who came before them held many sad and difficult stories.

The proverbs and maxims helped us inform each other and taught us so much. What did we learn?

One of the first American maxims to surface was the old favorite: "If at first you don't succeed, try, try again!"

Russians found this amazing and inspiring. They said it explained so much about America. They told us in the times of their parents, if one did not succeed, it could be he was not allowed to live. Or else, the person lost all contact with others, simply to be ignored and sent off on his own.

They said many people often just gave up and accepted what they had.

One of the Russian proverbs we heard we would also experience in the home of our Russian hosts: "The stores are empty, but the table is full." Even if Russians had nothing, they would entertain their friends. They offered whatever they had, sacrificed for themselves, in order to share with and feed their friends. The generosity of spirit we experienced touched us all deeply.

Other Russian proverbs and maxims were things such as:

- "You die today, I die tomorrow."

- "Every rooster has to sing."

    ❧  "Be brave and take a piece of the pie."

    ❧  "If you wish to receive the Magic, share the food."

Most touching was perhaps this: "Go nobody knows where, bring nobody knows what." Those Russians present referred to this as "The anthem of purposelessness." However, they were not depressed or without energy over this. It was just how Soviet life had been the past seventy-plus years.

This kind of sharing continued to open up the group and add to the understanding, shared laughter, depth of emotion and true learning, not from books, but from life.

The learning continued. Panels of Americans and Russians were chosen to sit before us and respond to the same questions about life, work and goals. There were both amazing similarities and new, interesting differences.

The time was flying by. Soon it was time for the American women to have their health treatments. Similar to the men's, but somehow different, the women's treatments also included water, as well as massage. When it was her turn, each woman entered a room alone with woman attendant: very tall, large and strong. She wore the usual nurse uniform and cap.

After a short, rather strong and even somewhat rough massage, the deep bathtub in the middle of the room was filled with hot water. For most of the women, this was a first experience to enter a bathtub with a total stranger present.

The attendant then used some kind of scratchy mitts to scrub each body with a source of power and energy never experienced before! When this was over, she said in English, "Okay." Most of us took this as a sign we were to get out of the tub. No, this meant the hefty loofah mitts were done.

Carol could really only describe her own experience: "We were not done. Without time for relief, her large hands were now pushing me under water. I took a few quick breaths and sensed I was going to have to hold my breath a while. When I could stand it no longer, I reached my hand out of the tub and grabbed her hands on my head, attempting to push them off. I was able to pop up and say, 'Enough.' She did not know the exact word, but understood."

"Just when I thought we were done, I saw I was going to get a version of what Dan Kline and some of the other men had endured. However, this was not a fire hose, but a tiny, but very powerful water pik. But, oh my, it put out a powerful jet of water, all focused under the water with my head now above."

These treatments did not really last that long. However, for most of the American women, they were a true test. As one by one the American women returned, the Russians wanted to know if it had been "wonderful?" Each one of the American women did her best to smile and answer, "Yes."

At some level, it was wonderful experience. Certainly nothing like this would have been possible in an American Spa.

The days of the Conference passed all too quickly. For those who stayed at the Sanitoria, the nights were spent talking, laughing, singing, together in large groups of Russians and Americans. We were dancing to Elvis and other Golden Oldies from the US. As some Americans drifted off to their rooms, full of exhaustion; others stayed up most of the nights, talking with new Russian friends, singing together as Tahir played his guitar and just sharing stories of life. The group became very close.

One night, very late, or perhaps very early in the morning, Carol looked out her window, having heard some kind of noise.

The grounds were dimly lighted, but it was not easy to see. Still, suddenly, Carol saw one of the very quiet American men go running by, with three large swans chasing him. He did not look frightened, but he did look as if he had had too much vodka. Suddenly, it was clear the swans were actually chasing him and nipping at his heels. However, he was laughing and would occasionally run and do a series of somersaults to confuse the swans. "Oh my!" she thought. However, it appeared he was having fun and was not in danger inside the tall fence! Exhausted, she said to herself, "I'll check on him in the morning. He's an adult and they are only swans."

The two of us told the Americans they were soon to be going on "home visits" for five nights and partial days with Russians who were present at the Conference. This caused some concern and stress. Each American felt she/he wanted to choose which Russian it would be. This was simply impossible. The days went by and neither the two of us nor the Americans knew yet where they were going.

Tahir and Alexey said they would handle it. We knew they would. However, we all learned things were often not acted on quickly, but always in the knick of time. Apparently, the night prior to the last day of the Conference, the Russians had decided. We would share this information prior to our leaving the Sanitoria Profilaktika.

However, there was still much to be accomplished during our final time together. The primary reason for the Conference from the Russians' point of view was to introduce more concepts and deeper understanding of business and what would hopefully develop into "the open economy," though no one yet used the phrase "market economy." The Russians from the Conference were eager to learn whatever we had to share.

This also included having the Americans visit some of the newly formed businesses of those who joined us the prior week. After much discussion with Alexey and Tahir, we decided to choose only three of the various young businesses represented within the group. We felt we could send larger teams into each business in order to not put such a large responsibility on one or two Americans.

In some cases, the Russians felt they were actually going to receive true business consultations. We did our best to clarify this. However, in the end, each one of the American business/professional persons we brought to Russia had many years more experience and true understanding of a life in a business or large organization than most of those Russians with whom we shared the Conference. The Russians with us had just come from 20-30 years within State-owned organizations. They wanted to understand about "real business."

The three businessmen from the Conference who were welcoming us into their businesses included: Gennady Smirnov, President and Chief Designer of a new venture spun off from the Mil Helicopter Plant; Gennady Kureptin, President of a new Industrial Construction Company and Evgeniy Kroshnev, Manager of PROFIS Advertising Agency.

These business visits were much easier to organize because we asked the Americans to make a choice regarding which of the three businesses they wished to visit. Their decisions were fast and easy. Prior to leaving the Sanitoria, we assembled each of the Americans into the three groups with their sponsoring Russian "business leader" and others present for the Conference.

Each group had an assignment to agree upon the primary goal of their visit plus other suggestions that would serve learning as well as give value to the three businesses being visited. Everyone worked together with excellent focus and process. As the week drew to a close at the Sanitoria, we were all able to see this group who seemed so different from one another, become a true working team of colleagues who respected and deeply cared for each other. The business visits would take place the following week, after the Conference adjourned.

Closing the Conference was a loving and emotional experience. The last Reflections and final words took nearly an entire day. Clearly the most moving comment from a Russian participant who began his final reflection by saying, "We thought Americans had no heart. How much you have proven us wrong."

It seemed each person, including the two of us, was deeply

touched and leaving with minds spinning and hearts full of love. It was difficult to leave after this period of "cocooning" with people of all ages, from different countries, different walks of life and the stigma of once having been "enemies" hanging over our heads. Now, only friendship, trust and love flowed.

At long last, Alexey and Tahir shared the assignments for the home visits. Americans were quickly paired up with their new Russian hosts. There was a bit of nervousness in the air, but this lasted only a minute or two.

On Friday afternoon, the Americans left the Sanitoria Profilaktika. The personal experiences since their arrival six days earlier virtually changed their worldviews. Nothing would ever be seen in quite the same way again.

Only a few of the Russians had their own vehicles. In those days in Moscow, if you were without a vehicle, you simply stood outside on the edge of the street with your hand in the air. Or you walked a good distance to the nearest Metro. Imagine the surprise of those Americans who were going home with a Russian without a vehicle! This meant the American dragged her or his very heavy, large American suitcase out onto the street and actually hitchhiked to the apartment or flat with the new Russian friend. At first it was frightening for the Americans. Within only a day or two, however, most became quite accustomed to this approach to transportation.

Due to the lack of telephones in most of the Russian friends' homes, we knew it may not be easy to connect with our friends for whom we felt a certain sense of responsibility. Alexey assured us he would check on people during the evening. He also reminded us we would all meet again at the Moscow Leningradsky Train Station the next evening. We seemed to find it somewhat difficult to part from this group of American friends with whom we had become so close. No one but these people could ever understand what we had experienced together.

We later learned the Americans had many different experiences of their home visits, depending on the family with whom they stayed. Dan#1 who went home with Gennady Smirnov and his charming wife, Tanya, stayed in a Moscow high-rise. This high-rise was just a part of the State Prize Gennady was given for his breakthrough design work in creating the Gear Box of the world's heaviest Helicopter, the M-16. It was a lovely neighborhood close by the Moscow Metro's Red Line stop, Krasnoselskaya. This made every thing convenient within the entire City.

Others Americans went home to communal apartments with shared kitchens and bathrooms or to very small flats with two rooms, a small kitchen and a bathroom. Judy was one who experienced how a family of three generations lived together in a tiny space, full of love. The two main rooms were converted into bedrooms during the night. Drawers and wardrobes held the "bedclothes" and five people sat close together as they ate in the tiny kitchen. It was clear to Judy that her hostess Lena and her family were delighted to have an American stay with them. They shared stories into the night about their lives and life experiences. Others also found these home visits very educational and very loving.

Within hours, the American group was reunited at the Moscow Leningradsky Train Station. Packed with one tiny carry-on bag, they would sleep through the night (though not many did) and wake up the next morning as the train pulled in to St. Petersburg. In those days so recently Soviet, many Russians still referred to St. Petersburg as Leningrad.

Two of the Russian group accompanied the Americans exploring a new and very different City. The Americans returned with the same kind of exhilaration and amazement we experienced earlier that year when we took our first trip to St. Petersburg. It was as if one could understand history in a totally different way. Now, it was alive and more relevant!

In fact, all of us felt we were more alive in Russia. It was as if we were drinking from a fire hose of history and culture. Plus, we began to understand we were visiting a country in the midst of great change. The Americans had now traveled within Russia, spent at least one night in the homes of their Russian hosts and were ready for the next outing.

The next learning opportunity was to be the business visits. Even though the three companies being visited were in totally different business lines, each one was hoping for the same outcomes: input on confirming strategy, clarity in moving from strategy into operation, understanding how beginning operations move to customers. The notion of marketing was a major topic of the Conference, but turning it into reality was another thing. Many of the Americans who joined us for this work, were actually excellent in and understood how to offer concrete ideas and coaching specifically in marketing.

The next day the Americans headed off into actual consulting roles. The three business leaders were delighted and could not thank us enough. The Americans themselves were satisfied, energized and hungry for more. Over the coming years, some of those who joined us returned to Russia to continue their work with these friends in the three businesses. Certainly, we did this and more.

Alexey, never one to want to end an adventure, decided there was more to be included in the agenda of this incredible experience. While we had believed it would be a quiet day of rest, reflection and long walks in Moscow parks, Alexey came up with a new idea.

"Carol, Tim, I have made a contact you and our group of Americans will find very interesting. You will be the first group of foreigners in Russian history to visit the Russian Space Center in the 'Closed City' of Kaliningrad. We can go tomorrow!"

Aghast again, we were interested and asked to hear more. What we heard made us jump at the chance. Thus, we enjoyed an incredible trip with an outing to the "Cape Canaveral" of the

Soviet Union.

Our Russian hosts, who worked in this secret, closed city, were eager to greet us and show us sites never before seen by Westerners. Unfortunately, they were also hoping that we might be ones who could invest in the future of businesses in Kaliningrad. This was not something we were able to do. However, they seemed to appreciate our interest and our knowledge of the early Russian space history.

We knew the name of Yuri Gagarin, the first human in space. This delighted our kind and generous hosts. That Carol remembered the name of the first living being to orbit the earth simply delighted them. This was not some kind of information Carol consciously kept in her mind. However, as she rounded a corner in the museum and saw the actual stuffed body of the little Russian dog, Laika, Carol exclaimed with delight and called the dog by name. While it was rather odd to see the little Laika, it was still a one of a kind experience. The afternoon trip was a wonderful capstone to our 1992 trip to Russia.

## CHAPTER TWELVE

# The White House is Burning

Our energy was high as we prepared for our fourth trip to
Moscow and our second Conference with Americans and
Russians. Our 1992 experience with the Russians and Americans
working together in such creative and positive ways whet our
appetites for the next step. We began to imagine the new things
possible to continue building bridges between Americans and
Russians. We could see even deeper conversations, new program
designs, more dancing and singing, more times spent inside
Russian businesses, more sharing customs, history and life.
While 1992 was still in our hearts as an incredible life happening
for both of us and for all our American friends who had joined
us, we were also living ahead in our minds dreaming of what
could unfold now.

This was a new year in the life of Russia. It was September 23,
1993. We arrived in Moscow believing we were ready for
whatever unfolded. We were thrilled to be convening an even
larger group of both Americans and Russians than had gathered
in Fall 1992. Life was somehow different in Moscow, which
meant the beloved Sanitori Profilaktika was no longer available.
However, dear Alexey Morozov found a new and more
interesting site for convening the group. We did pause to wonder
if this was code for something rather different or was it really
more interesting? We could honestly say each new experience in
Moscow was more interesting and only added to our learning
and awe of this country climbing out of those bleak, dark days of
Soviet Rule.

These were new times for Russia as well. Mr. Yeltsin, now settled in as President of Russia, began to experience additional challenges to his leadership. He had been in a power struggle with the Russian Parliament for most of the past year. During the months since January 1993, both sides did their best to strip each other of power, with no success. We read the news and watched the little coverage US television could provide. Therefore, perhaps we were naive to imagine this trip would unfold as easily as our trip with the 1992 group.

As we thought about the group we would welcome to Moscow, we found some things reassuring, some not. We realized we knew and worked more closely with many of the American friends from the 1992 Moscow group than with those who would be arriving soon. Some we had not yet met, but they were friends of friends coming. Others were new to our FGI programs, but expressed a keen interest in the Moscow work. Stories of our 1992 work in Moscow spread and many more Americans now wanted to share in the learning and life experiences possible from such an experience. However, the reassuring aspect was at least one third of those who were with us in Moscow in 1992 were returning to join us for the 1993 trip. This gave us even more reason to have confidence that things would unfold as we planned with Alexey, Tahir and other leaders of our Russian friends in the Institute of International Connections. They also recruited more Russians, many of whom asked to be involved. Positive stories and good news travel fast in any country.

As always, the two of us traveled ahead of the group in order to ensure all was in place as planned for their arrival and the unfolding of the new Conference program. For the first time, we wired money ahead to Alexey in order for him to make down payments at the hotel and Conference center. We were pleased and excited to meet Alexey when he met us at Sheremetyevo Airport. We felt quite at home arriving in Moscow. The promise of the golden fall weather invigorated us. We longed to see the young Russian women with the traditional Autumn woven crowns of huge yellow leaves around their heads. The women were so beautiful and free as they played and danced outside in parks and with their friends at various historical sites in the City and in the countryside. We were eager to return to Moscow. Our spirits were high!

Prior to the flight, the Fall Conference topic of Marketing had been very invigorating for us. Our friend, Dan Kline, then a marketing professional at University Hospital at the University of Nebraska Medical Center, agreed to work with us on the design. This was exciting for all three of us since Dan also was with us for the 1992 Moscow experience and would now take a more up-front role. Our Russian friend, Evegeny Kroshev, owner of the Moscow based marketing firm, Profis, was present for our 1992 Conference and would also attend the October 1993 gathering. He was also a part of the planning committee and became a dear friend of Dan. We felt confident in our research, materials and program design. We were eager to arrive and get down to business.

Our arrival in Moscow was much like the earlier arrivals. This time, however, there were lights in the airport and even some rather rough toilet paper in the restrooms. What a huge improvement over the dark airport and the wax paper in the restrooms on our first arrival long ago. It had been only eighteen months earlier in April 1992; however, we had changed and the world was changing before our eyes.

Alexey's smiling face was visible through the small crowd gathered to greet guests and family members. Oh my, at that moment, we realized Alexey had become a dear friend and valued professional colleague to us. In fact, Alexey and Lena, along with our dear friends, Tanya and Gennady Smirnov, had become our "home away from home" family. We felt secure, comfortable and safe with each one of them. We enjoyed our deep conversations. We found we already developed memories and stories of times past that when recounted made us all laugh with joy at shared experiences.

Once we were in the little Russian Volga with Alexey, we knew the next Conference would be here as if it were tomorrow. There was still so much to accomplish!

Alexey's mother was once again staying at the dacha in order for the two of us to have our usual rooms in her Flat prior to the Conference. It was definitely less expensive for all of us and Mother did not plan to return from the countryside until later in October. This worked out perfectly for our schedule.

When we entered the Flat, it was sweetly familiar. Carol ran to the windows to enjoy the well-remembered scenes. We counted the days in our minds until the American friends would arrive and were eager to see Alexey's list for the Russians who made commitments for the Conference.

As soon as we entered the Flat, Alexey went directly to the TV and turned it on. It was clear he was eager to see what was going on. This seemed odd to us. We were vaguely aware of news prior to leaving the US. President Yeltsin dissolved the Russian Parliament and decreed new parliamentary elections were to be held on December 12. We thought little about this and apparently imagined it was, as often happens in some countries, another parliament being dissolved; some new coalition would rebuild soon. As much as we imagined we knew what was going on in Moscow, the truth is we were clueless. Alexey listened a bit longer, then, muttered some words in Russian. Then he smiled and asked about how we were doing plus other matters about the Conference.

The three of us began to talk immediately and became excited about our work ahead and the arrival of the American group. Alexey looked forward to being with the returning Americans and was very eager to meet those who were making their first trip to Russia. Our attention quickly turned away from the Moscow TV scenes and current events to planning and remembering the success of the 1992 Conference.

Alexey went to the kitchen and returned carrying bowls of food to the table for dinner. Suddenly, he gave a moan and grimaced. We looked up, feeling worried.

"Tim, excuse me. Would you help me please?"

It was clear something was bothering Alexey physically. We looked at each other in alarm. Tim rushed to take the bowls of food from Alexey's extended arms. He wanted to make everything perfect for the Americans arrival, but we saw he was now in pain. We wanted to hear more and asked directly about his pain.

Alexey said, "Carol, Tim, please do not be alarmed. Now and then if I do too much, I feel some pains. I might as well tell you now. After you wired the extra three thousand dollars to me, I went to the money exchange to pick it up. There, I got US $3,000 cash in Rubles. Apparently, I was watched as I went into the bank. I was mugged, my ribs were hit, I crumpled and the money was stolen. I don't know what to do. The money is gone. Can you forgive me?"

He was in tears. We reassured him we would find a way to have more money wired to us and the three of us would make things work. He breathed a sigh of relief, however he was in pain both physically and emotionally.

We did our best to soothe him and reassure him things would be okay. All we had to give him was some aspirin. He seemed to feel a bit better and the three of us carefully embraced. We were careful not to put too much pressure on Alexey's ribs.

We sat down to our dinner, discussed politics, life and our plans for the Conference. Alexey seemed to feel better. The first night in Moscow came to a close. There would be much more to accomplish the following day.

The two of us were eager to see Tahir and Alosha again. They were good friends and great resources for us and for our shared work. Alexey began to explain about the new site for the

Conference. He was excited about it and believed both the food and the sleeping rooms were better than at the Sanitori Profilaktica. Additionally, Alexey said it was much easier for the Russians to come to the Janj Joeu/East Hotel. It was nearer to a metro and this would make life more convenient for the local participants and friends taking part in the Conference. Alexey seemed to be very excited about the "airy meeting room, spacious enough to hold the larger group" who would attend the Conference.

We trusted Alexey as always, but did ask about the name of the Hotel. We were curious about a Chinese hotel doing business in Moscow. He reminded us of the previously close ties between Moscow and Beijing during the Cold War. It wasn't until we were working in China a few years later that we began to more fully understand the extent of the SinoSoviet relationship, on and off again during the Cold War. The exchange of Russians to China and Chinese to Russia was a big part of history. The more we worked in both Russia and China, the more we often met clients who had either a Chinese father and a Russian mother or a Russian father and a Chinese mother. When we traveled to China for the first time, we were stunned to see an exact replica of the famous Moscow "Stalin's Wedding Cake" building in China.

Not yet having been to China in 1993, we did our best to imagine being in a Chinese hotel in South Moscow. "Well, this sounds interesting," Tim said to Carol after Alexey's sharing. However, the thought of great food and ease in metro travel did sound like a good addition to the work. Still, we felt so far away from Center City.

Alexey began to describe again how pleased he was at the large, airy conference room only a short walking distance from the hotel. Oh, this was a surprise for us, but we knew we were in Moscow and took it in stride. Alexey told us this conference room was actually a part of a large Institute, capable of meeting our needs. This seemed like good news.

We still chuckle today when we think about our first trip taking a group of Americans to Moscow when we wanted to share Russian culture with our American friends and ended up at Moscow's grand Bolshoi Theater without understanding earlier we were taking them to a Bolshoi showing of the famous Tokyo Kabuki theater. Then we think about taking our American friends to Russia in 1993 and ending up in a Chinese hotel in Moscow. It's just too perfect for our many world adventures. Luckily, we usually were able to find our way through the surprises the Russian culture offered us. We grew as did our American friends and clients who trusted us and shared these adventures with us.

Alexey wanted us to move into the Janj Joeu/East Hotel the next day, prior to the Americans' arrival that afternoon. Though he did not say this directly, it seemed clear he wanted us to see the conference room and appreciate all of his hard work and planning. This was easy to do because Alexey carried the load of managing all of the logistics in a logistics-starved environment. It was still Moscow post Cold War. Things were not readily available.

On our trip to the south side of Moscow, the ride seemed a hundred miles away from where we had been in Moscow prior to this time. It all seemed quite different. The look and feel of this part of the city was very different from the beautiful City Center and from the older Soviet neighborhoods with which we were familiar during the past trips. However, we loved seeing new things and trying new adventures. We were ready to go.

The Janj Joeu/East Hotel seemed a bit tired in our eyes, but this was Moscow. The area was considered a "newer" neighborhood. Most of the buildings were from the Krushchev era. Tim believed this hotel was somewhere close to where the Nazi Advance on Moscow stopped during World War II. He always knew these things intuitively. Maps and history books later confirmed he was right. This was a relatively new area as compared to where both Alexey and Lena lived and where Tanya and Gennady

Smirnov lived.

We entered the hotel, eagerly imagining ourselves within these surroundings for the coming 8-9 days. While the hotel was a bit of a surprise to us at first; we developed the ability to adjust in a short time. The people who ran the hotel were obviously delighted with our business. We believed they had not seen many Western visitors and hoped our group would not be too demanding. The rooms were simple and adequate. Later we would discover we shared the rooms with a large village of very active mice.

We remembered Alexey told us the hotel was a short walking distance from the Conference space. We were eager to walk over and see it. Alexey was happy to take us. What a surprise when we discovered the circuitous route through the hotel, outside the hotel onto a narrow slightly elevated walkway, through a large metal door.

The floor on which we entered was humming with busyness and noise.

This was a very active vocational school. The industrial education rooms were full of young men who hammered on cars, spray painted cars and practiced auto mechanics in several different large labs. Large car and truck engines in various stages of assembly and disassembly were in additional open labs as we walked by. The smell of caustic auto body paint and chemicals assaulted our nostrils. The teachers' looks indicated we were a nuisance to them and their work with the young men.

"Ah, Carol, Tim, this is the Institute I spoke of to you. They are very busy creating jobs for young Russians who do not go to the Universities." Alexey was very proud of this additional approach to education, though he spent his time as student and as professor at University levels. The two of us had imagined something quite different. However, as with every new Russian experience, there was much for us to learn.

Eventually, we found our way to the Conference Center. It was situated at the end of the complex, away from the noise and the smell of strong paint fumes. The Conference Center, while nothing like what we might have seen in the US, was quite fine by the current standards of this country just climbing out of a long, hungry Soviet reality.

The room was long and narrow, with an open feeling due to the three walls of windows. There was sturdy, strong Soviet furniture around the walls. We knew our Conference friends would be comfortable. We could move some of the chairs into groups for small conversations and had plenty of room for a variety of activities. Oh yes, the furniture had been there a long time and the room was in need of paint, but this was Russia 1993. We had a Conference room and we were pleased. Once we saw this, we became more excited and began to imagine the room full of new friends and old.

Later that afternoon, several of our Russian friends from the Institute for International Connections stopped by to welcome us and see how we were. It was another sweet homecoming for us. Their joy in seeing us plus their gratitude for our returning again was deep and real. We felt trusted and grateful. We were also delighted to be back in the marvelous Russian culture.

One of the friends said something in Russian to Alexey. We noticed Alexey became concerned in some way, but we had no idea what was going on. As they spoke we did hear the familiar names "Yeltsin" again and again. We recognized the second name, "Rutskoi," the Vice President of Russia. We had missed the world news of the past two days. As it happened, throughout our flight to Moscow, history was unfolding in Moscow. However, at this time, we did not know the details and would not find them out soon.

The tensions between President Yeltsin and Vice President Rutskoi had heightened. Once Yeltsin dissolved Parliament, Rutskoi called an emergency session of the Russian Parliament in the Russian White House. Rutskoi announced he was assuming the office of President. Parliament and all of their supporters refused to obey Yeltsin's orders. Things were heating up at the same time we were preparing to welcome Americans to Moscow.

Today, we look back and wonder in amazement that our American friends all boarded planes and flew to Moscow to join us, just as the Russian government began to fall apart. Surely US television shared this information, but we weren't there to see it. Life above the clouds in a large Delta jet in 1993 was without world news. Once in Moscow, we did not understand Russian well enough to listen to news and understand events were escalating.

Thus, with ignorance being bliss, we moved forward in our preparations to welcome our American friends to Moscow. We were full of anticipation and excitement at what would unfold.

The Americans arrived. They were happy and excited to be in Moscow. Those who were with us the year before were eager and happy to be back. Those travelers who were new to Moscow were a bit nervous, but clearly ready to learn. It was an exciting time for us all.

We made the long drive from Sheremetyevo airport to the Jang Joeu Hotel. Our American friends were taking photos from the bus windows and getting acquainted with each other. Others were already asleep against the headrests of their bus seats, oblivious to all of the new sights and new friends. It was a long and hard trip from the US to Moscow in those days.

As we came from the airport to the hotel, we both knew we were taking a much different route than we had ever seen. We wondered about this, but thought it was simply "Bus driver's choice."

Arrival at the Hotel was somewhat frenzied. The hotel desk staff appeared never to have had so many guests arrive at one time.

This was especially true since none of the guests spoke Russian and poor Alexey was running back and forth helping everyone. We noticed he appeared to be in pain. When we asked him about this, he said, "Ah, dear friends, do not worry about me, I am simply a bit sore. Let's take care of our guests." He gave a big smile and we all carried on.

Checking into the hotel had been a quite a challenge for everyone. It seemed the hotel staff may have had a more difficult time than the tired Americans. Soon all Americans were in their rooms, unpacking and preparing for dinner. With all of the guests in place, making noise, running back and forth to each other's rooms, the village of mice were awakened. Soon, one after another, Americans were coming to us saying there were mice in their rooms. We assured them the hotel was putting out mousetraps and we hoped this would help. We then took the group and went off to the hotel restaurant for a dinner of Russian foods. Our American friends were won over immediately with the delicious Russian food.

After experiencing their first taste of Russia, the Americans were eager to experience more. They all wanted to run outside immediately to snap photos of Moscow. We encouraged them to wait as the early evening gave way to darkness.

We knew our scheduled outings the next day would take them to the glorious spots so famous in Moscow. We loved to imagine the joy of taking people for their first time to stand in Red Square. They could gaze in every direction at the still functioning, beautiful and historic buildings surrounding the Square. We were eager to show them the Kremlin, the Kremlin museums with amazingly preserved coaches and furniture from the time of Peter the Great. Our own excitement gave us great energy for the days ahead.

The next morning, it was difficult for the jet-lagged Americans to get going, however, they were in Russia. The group seemed quite eager to get out and about experiencing Moscow. They could not wait to walk around Red Square and experience the famous landmarks face-to-face. They were as eager to see the Kremlin history museums, as we were to show them. This was always a marvelous way to learn quickly and enjoy amazing and incredible art.

We were delighted to be taking our American friends to Red Square in the daylight. Because most of the group had never been to Russia, it was even more thrilling. This is because if one takes a certain route, it is not possible to see Red Square until one is actually stepping onto the "red" bricks. We had been told the bricks were once red; however, in the early 1990s, the bricks were black without any maintenance having been done for most of the last years of Soviet Russia.

As we walked from the North toward Red Square, we purposely stood with the group behind the ancient State Historical Museum built by Czar Alexander III in 1873. We felt it was important to provide our few minutes of history and background. However, our ulterior motive was also to keep the view of Red Square unseen from behind the museum. Our hearts were beating with excitement knowing the view our friends would soon see. Even with the dirty grime from the Soviet era still shading the amazing structures, Red Square was marvelous.

We slowly led the group around the Museum and allowed them to take in the view. The large brick watch towers built into the Kremlin walls were taller and more awesome than one could imagine. There on the right was Lenin's Tomb which until earlier in 1993 had been flanked and protected by two Russian Honor Guards. Long, stretching lines of Russians paid respect. Many in the 1992 group stood in the line a long time to enter the Mausoleum. For most they regretted having done so. Viewing a body after over 60 years of being "mummified," was not easy. We were not sad the tomb had been closed.

During the early months of President Yeltsin's term, he decided to take the Honor Guard Unit away Lenin's Tomb and close it to visitors as a sign of changing times and beliefs in Russia. However, bouquets were still left outside by faithful Soviets in 1993.

On this 1993 trip, the two Honor Guards were now protecting the Tomb of the Unknown Solider in the Alexander Gardens. The changing of the guard, the rigid, strict requirements of the two young men, most likely only 18 years old, were still followed. This remains so today.

Visible behind Lenin's Tomb and along the entire right side of the Square were the red brick walls of the Kremlin with those multiple, tall, imposing towers placed at corners and other strategic spots. At the far end and to the left was the famous and colorful St. Basil's church, built in the 1500s. Immediately to the left was the famous GUM department store. All buildings were amazing and beautiful, each in their own ways. The tops of official buildings in the Kremlin were a dirty yellow and showed above the wall. Beyond the amazing St. Basil's to the South was the Moscow River. One could stand on the Square all day and feel history shout out.

It has never failed to touch us to stand there in the middle of Red Square and take it all in. History, before our eyes . . .

Our American friends knew they were truly in Russia now, spending hours in Red Square, listening and learning from the Russian guides with us, photographing each other in front of the various historical landmarks and letting Russian history and culture flow into their beings. It always delighted and surprised those we took to Russia how friendly and eager the Russians were to meet and please Americans, have their photos taken with us and just have a minute or two to use their English with native speakers. Many exchanged addresses on the spot and ended up in "pen pal" relationships. This was before computers were used in most of the world.

We couldn't help but notice throughout the morning when Alexey began to look worried. We believed this was due to the pain from his mugging incident. It came time for us to enter the Kremlin. This required a short walk around Kremlin walls to the main tourist entrance. There were also guards at the entrance to the Kremlin, but they were different from those we had seen in early visits. Holding automatic weapons, these guards looked serious and did not make eye contact.

A large group of people was standing outside the Kremlin gates, through which we walked during our past two trips to Moscow. Most of them looked angry or uncomfortable. Alexey went up to the ticket window to present the tickets for our group. He waited quite a long time. We were all excited and became quite a find for the vendors selling Russian army hats, Russian flags and a variety of Russian souvenirs. Perhaps we lost track of time. As we saw Alexey walking toward us, we saw he looked even more uncomfortable. He motioned the two of us to come to him and took us aside, slightly away from the group.

"Oh my!" Both of us began to worry about Alexey's physical pain. We were both right, but also had incomplete information. Alexey was in physical pain. However, he was more concerned about the news he had to convey. The much-awaited trip for the Americans' visit to the Kremlin would have to be aborted. The Kremlin was now off-limits and sealed due to the threats brought about by the conflict between President Yeltsin and Parliament. President Yeltsin had an office in the Kremlin.

The two of us now had to walk over to our group of friends and give them the news. They were very unhappy of course, but also concerned in a new way due to understanding there was now a civil conflict. Things were beginning to sound ominous.

While the two of us somehow kept our faith in Alexey and in the group's safety, it was clear others were worried. We did our best to divert their feelings as well as decide to take them somewhere exciting to forget the "war" and to give them another important Russian experience.

It was Sunday. This meant the Vernisage (a large outdoor art exhibit) would be open with hundreds of booths selling Russian goods. There would be beautiful art work, incredible jewelry in brilliant designs of silver and Russian amber in several colors, matryoschka "stacking dolls" painted by gifted artists, handknit sweaters, amazing crafts beyond one's imagination to believe. Ah! The Americans immediately came to life, ready to drive the hour to Ismailova park where the fun would begin.

All worries faded from our minds and we set about introducing our American friends to one of our favorite pastimes, exploring the Vernisage!

The Americans had cashed their travelers checks for Rubles the day before upon their arrival at the hotel. However, before they knew it, some had gone through their entire stash of trip money. The Vernisage was just too enticing and exciting for them. They had never seen such beauty as one finds in Russian crafts. These were not crafts as we know them in the US. Many Russians were amazingly gifted artists. This was not their job; it was their love.

The artwork staggered our minds and delighted us. Sharing this with our friends was such a joy. Much of what was in the Vernisage was also a huge collection of amazing and valuable antiques from over the past 50 years. The Russian economy had gone through many difficult times. People needed money on which to live. The only way was literally to sell the "family jewels" and treasures.

It had turned into a marvelous day of meeting Russians. Americans had a chance to use their halting Russian as well as engage in exciting conversations with Russians for whom Americans were something special. Everyone had a marvelous time. The sun began to set and it was time to head back to the Janj Joeu Hotel. Oh, those Americans had not had enough shopping time, but we dragged them away anyway.

On the bus back to the hotel, our American friends began to complain they had spent all of their Russian Rubles. We promised them tomorrow the two of us and Alexey would go for more Rubles plus also visit the Moscow American Express office to bring them more American dollars. They were happy.

Little did we know by the next morning, the City would be overtaken with the war! We were able to find 2-3 Russian friends who would join the Americans on the bus for a nice tour of Moscow sights not close to the Russian White House or to the Kremlin. Everyone seemed fine with this plan. The three of us set out in Alexey's car. Apparently, even Americans living in Moscow felt the need to increase their US dollars in hand. We waited in a long line outside the building in which the AMEX Moscow office was located. Finally, after what seemed to be hours, we came away with over two thousand dollars in US $50 bills.

The two of us believed we would be joining the group again to settle them down by giving them their US dollars. However, Alexey surprised us by saying, "Carol, Tim, I have something I would like to show before we return to the group. It's only a short drive."

Alexey looked very sober, but we also felt an urgency in his voice, though it was not emotional, just very clear. He had something he wanted us to see. Apparently, it was not something positive.

The drive was indeed short! Within only minutes, Alexey wound us around several small streets in the City. We went from the Red Square Kremlin areas to the well-known Barrikadnaya Metro Station, one of the closest stops to the Russian White House. As we came close to the Barrikadnaya Metro station, the streets were crowded and full of people on foot. Hundreds of people!

Alexey asked us to walk together tightly and stay close to him. "This is something you must see in order for us to plan," Alexey said quite soberly. This did not sound good. Soon, we heard the noise of a crowd, shouting and even messages shouted out in Russian over powered megaphones. The two of us looked at each other with discomfort. Alexey was quick to say, "Carol, Tim, do not be alarmed. There is a small disagreement between President Yeltsin and Parliament. I want you to see what's going on."

It was not one of the highpoints in our Russian experience. It was, however, memorable. We walked cautiously toward the Metro station. As we approached, the large crowd seemed to be jostling with some kind of barricade! Within seconds, we realized it was, in fact, a human barricade! Russian soldiers were side by side, each one holding a large protective shield and wielding some kind of large club. Tim has since called those clubs "truncheons."

Carol's heart began to beat very fast, falling into her stomach. All she could think was some kind of terrible outcome. Alexey, in his best comforting way, said, "Do not worry. This is simply protection for the White House, just down the street on Arbatskaya." Thoughts ran through both our American brains, "What, don't worry? Are you kidding?!"

The crowd was made up of hundreds of people, pushing and shoving against the Soldiers who protected themselves and held back the angry citizens with the human circle of shields. Most amazing was the number of little old ladies, the traditional babushkas, wanting to do whatever they came to accomplish and not be stopped by the Army or anyone else.

Alexey said, "Most likely, this will be over in a day or two. We are staying far away to the South, so our group is safe. Please do not worry." At last, the real reason for our staying so far away from City Center was revealed. The Chinese Hotel was nice. The Vocational School Conference area was light and airy. But the real reason for our being in both places, was about civil unrest. Things were becoming very clear.

Our short trip was over. Alexey found it easier to show us an example of the civic unrest rather than to tell us. Now, we understood, but was this better?

Each one of us later shared we had the same thoughts and fears without knowing it. In this kind of scene, things could have gone out of hand quickly and without warning. At any minute, the crowd could begin to fight back and violence would erupt. It was not a good situation!

Alexey indicated it was time to leave the scene and drive back to meet the Americans. Their largest worry was no doubt finding more US dollars. This one was easy for us to fix. We had the newly exchanged money in our hidden money-belts. We were ready to return to our friends, determine how we would advise them of the situation in Moscow and get things back to some sense of normal.

It was clear our only option was to tell them what we had seen and assure them for the coming few days we would all be far away from the City Center and Russian White House, in the South part of Moscow. The truth was, we were in no danger. However, the two of us began to imagine what friends and relatives of ours and of the other Americans might be watching on TV.

Alexey and the two of us drove back from Barrikadnaya to the agreed upon meeting place to reconvene with our American friends and the 2-3 Russian friends on the bus who were with them on this last outing.

We knew providing them with US dollars would set the American's minds at ease. They now had money to spend! Prior to this little outing with Alexey, this seemed like a big deal. Now, things were different. We clearly agreed we did not want to frighten anyone but we had to share what we knew.

We stepped aboard the bus and joined our friends to visit different "safe" landmarks and other interesting areas. We calmly and quietly used the loudspeaker system to share with them what was happening at Barrikadsnaya and in the City. These old friends and new friends seemed not at all concerned. There were few if any questions and people were mostly interested in where we would go for our next stop. The news from Barrikadsnaya was simply a small blip on the screen of life in Moscow for the Americans.

The two of us decided to move forward as planned. People were light-hearted and ready to see more of Moscow. As with every site where Americans might visit, there were Russian vendors selling souvenirs, Coca-Cola and Fanta. The Americans began to spend their new US currency. It was not long before our first complaint tinged with fear was heard. Linda came to Carol and said, "Something is terribly wrong! The vendor assures me my US money is counterfeit."

Oh my, our stomachs dropped again. It was becoming too familiar and too common for one day!

Before an hour passed, more and more of the American's came to us with the same news. All of the money was simply useless. Most of the Americans were now close to being out of US dollars. In those moments, this seemed more important than the war going on across town. Luckily, the two of us were each wearing several thousands of dollars in our money belts for all expenses, including surprises. We advanced our US friends money and they paid us back in the US.

Still, the war was becoming worrisome. The current edition of *The Moscow Times* was delivered. On the front page was a huge photo of the Russian White House burning! How would this unfold? At the moment, we had no answer. However, we understood something clearly: at this time in Moscow, with so much going awry, the entire group of Americans simply had to adjust and accept. It was easier for some than others. This makes sense of course. Each person is different. No matter what we had written them in advance of the trip about things being a bit unpredictable in Moscow, this was too much for many.

Our dear, ever present friend, Denny Aron was there for us. He was always ready to support us, advise us and remind us of a favorite approach the three of us came to use for the next 14 years as we worked together in Moscow, "This is Russia. We are working and learning in ways many other Americans will never experience. We give thanks." And so we did!

## CHAPTER THIRTEEN

# Stay Off the Tanks

Moscow 1993 was about to come out of a long, difficult economic and political past. The people were challenged in many ways for generations. Our earlier trips in 1992 showed us a Moscow beyond our ability to believe. There were struggles and deep learning.

Now here we were in the second week of our 1993 work. The first week with our group of Americans included a few grueling days in Moscow due to the news of the Russian White House being under attack. Receiving thousands of dollars in counterfeit US dollars, concerns about the injury of our partner and dear friend, Alexey, plus the normal demands of bringing American friends to Russia added new challenges. We were ready to get on with the actual program. Our group of Americans made it back to the Janj Joeu Hotel. All of us felt quite at home in the Russian Chinese hotel by now. We were ready to be in the vocational school for the Conference or in our sleeping rooms for at least the next three days! For all practical purposes, we were safe. The mice continued to be a bother, but as Alexey said, the food was good and the conference room was close.

We already experienced what seemed to be challenges. Yet, the main event, the Conference, had not begun. It was quite a relief to realize we would soon be away from the violence and unrest in Moscow City Center. We looked forward to the Conference and the group who would assemble.

Our one new concern was how or if our Russian friends who

were joining us for the Conference would be able to leave their homes and arrive safely at the Hotel? Alexey reminded us the Metro was a safe, fast, inexpensive way to travel. He told us he was not worried. He would call each one of the Russian Conference attendees after dinner to confirm the Conference would go on.

Both of us were busy going over the agenda and design for the coming three days. This 1993 agenda was far more business-oriented than the 1992 agenda which focused more on understanding how Russians and Americans saw the world and approached business. In 1992, the idea of "business" was still new to Russians. By 1993, more businesses were established and many had been quite successful in their first year or two.

Throughout our evening's planning, Carol began to think about the unrest close to the Russian White House and City Center. With her usual curiosity, she jumped up, intent on going down to the lobby to see if by chance there would be some additional news available. By this time, it was 11PM, still quite early by Russian standards. As Carol stepped into the lobby, a scene beyond even her imagination stopped her in her tracks. Knowing she obviously stuck out as an American, she stayed close to the wall and stared in disbelief. To this day there is no one else, except those involved, who know what was going on.

Quietly, she crept around a corner for a better view. Her inner voice shouted out, "Yes! Those are definitely sturdy metal posts from which are hanging butchered sides of beef!" Additionally, there were smaller slabs of meat and roasts, sitting there on tables in all their raw, red glory. Being careful to stay out of sight, Carol was soon aware this was some kind of midnight meat auction!  Both Caucasian and Chinese men were gathered around, with some standing and some sitting. The voices were loud and it was clear a certain style of bidding was taking place.

"What! This can't be true. No one will ever believe me," Carol thought. However, she was too caught up in this moment to move or return upstairs. Had she gone upstairs earlier, perhaps there would have still been American friends awake who would have come down to see this spectacle. But, alas, she stayed and stayed and stayed, saying to herself, "I have to see more. This is unbelievable!"

Finally, exhaustion set in. Carol turned around and took the elevator up to the American's floor. Moving quickly to Tim's room, she pounded on the door. Maybe he was here and not in some evening conversation. Tim was there, but had apparently been in a deep sleep. He came to the door, exhausted and still half asleep. The second his door cracked open, Carol began to talk at a rapid pace, describing all she had seen. Tim listened graciously, but was apparently ready to get back to his bed. The best either can remember is Tim saying, "Oh my! Let's talk more in the morning. Goodnight." Tim closed his door.

By morning, the Conference was on everyone's mind. Carol did her best to share the meat auction story with Alexey who simply shook his head and then commented, "Ah, yes, you must have stumbled into the Russian Mafia's business. Don't be surprised if you see more of this during the evenings." Apparently, it was just another evening in Moscow. What did we Americans know?

During this short conversation, Carol noticed Alexey was not his usual self. He was moving more slowly and seemed to look as if he was in real pain. In asking Alexey how he was feeling, he appeared ready to admit he was in severe pain. The mugging was more than we had originally understood. He admitted he needed some help. Carol immediately called Dennis Joslin, a close American friend and medical professional who had come for the Conference. Dennis told Carol to have Alexey come to her room. Dennis also said she was to bring aspirin, panty hose and duct tape.

All four assembled in Carol's small hotel room. Within minutes, Alexey was face up on the bed. Dennis somehow gently set Alexey's broken ribs, bound his torso in Carol's panty hose and covered all in duct tape. Two aspirin were supposed to seal the deal, but Tim decided to offer Alexey some remaining pain pills from his minor surgery the week before we came to Russia. All four of us breathed easier, but especially our dear Alexey.

While we may have wished to sit around, rest and comfort Alexey, we remembered our big event. It was time to welcome the new guests to the Conference and to embrace old Russian friends from last year. By this time, Carol realized the meat auction story was really no big deal, except to a naive American. Apparently, one had to have been there. We moved on and were off to the next event.

Tim and Carol followed a rather slow-moving Alexey on the long walk from the hotel to the conference room in the Vocational School. The vocational instructor looked even angrier than during our earlier walk to the conference room as the group of Americans and Russians walked through the school. This was the way we had been told to come. We guessed he had not been advised this would happen.

The conference meeting room was as bright and welcoming as it had been when we first saw it. Tim had the FGI music playing and positive energy was palpable. The morning bustling had begun in earnest. People were coming in, conversations were starting, welcome hugs were being offered among old friends and new friends, tea and coffee were being poured. Things were underway.

It was very easy to forget the war was just miles away. The agenda was far more complex than the year prior. We all expected more from ourselves.

The Marketing topic drew a good crowd of both longtime Russian friends and new ones. Marketing was only a "Western term" at this time. The Russians were eager to understand business and what it took to sell things. They were especially eager to work with Westerners to learn about this exciting part of business. During all the years of their lives "marketing" had never been a part of the reality.

Prior to this trip, the two of us spent long hours determining how to find a simple way to bring marketing alive and to explain the "value" of a product in marketing. Most Russians up until now, had never had choices in what they could buy. Whatever was available, they bought if they were able to afford it.

Now, the goal was to develop a "market economy." However, it was still a new concept even for these bright Russians to understand. We wanted a very simple example. As often happens, the Universe provided an idea. One day in Omaha during work on the agenda and actual content, Carol remembered the delightful, delicious smell of chocolate drifting through the air in Hershey, Pennsylvania. The town of Hershey smelled like chocolate!

Suddenly, Tim heard Carol shout out, "AH HA! That's it! We can use Hershey's Bars. We will have them work on marketing a regular Hershey's Bar as compared to the Hershey's Bar with Almonds." The plan to carry along to Moscow a suitcase full of Hershey's Bars, with and without almonds took shape immediately.

This course of action proved to be just what we needed during the Conference. Being able to differentiate by adding a new ingredient clearly was a reason to raise the price and change how to market the different candy bars. Changing how we spoke about the candy bar with almonds moved the group toward understanding how this difference was used in marketing. The bright minds of these Russians ate up the idea. Within minutes of digesting the theory, our Russian friends also digested the Hershey's Bars, both those with and without the almonds. Most of all, everyone present seemed to enjoy and understand the approach.

This opened the door for other Americans to give examples in their own work. Additionally, some of our Russian friends who were the first to begin marketing firms, added additional value to the discussion with concrete examples of their own. Their explanations to other Russians, in Russian, provided new comfort and increased comprehension and readiness to learn even more. As the days progressed, this Conference began to thrive in a new way as more of the Russians were willing to provide their own stories of marketing, of the business successes they had had during the past year and to take more leadership in sharing their actual business stories. In 1993, as opposed to 1992, we were more one group of business people sharing with each other than one group teaching another. The colleagueship was as sweet as the Hershey's Bars.

On the last day of the Conference, we walked the long route to the conference room. The route we had been shown to the conference room now ended with a heavy padlock on the door and the door had been welded shut! This had all of us, Russians and Americans alike, following our steps back to the front desk of the hotel. Carol had to use her Russian to explain we needed a new entrance to the conference room. With about 20 Russians all chiming in to "help" Carol, the front desk woman did understand and said in lovely English, "Follow me." All this time, there had been other options for our walk to the conference room. It was Russia and we should have known there is always more than one way. However, this was only our second year in Russia. We were learning.

The final day of the Conference was a great success. Plans were made for continuing the shared learning. Five Russian business leaders had offered their businesses for visits for those interested in spending a day with them. The group of Americans and some of the remaining Russians divided themselves up easily and evenly into manageable groups. The scenes of the "war" in City Center had left our minds. We were feeling grateful and relieved this Conference was another success.

Saturday evening, the Americans went off with their new friends to become a part of a Russian family for a couple of days. This was very exciting for everyone. One group of Americans ended up having to hitchhike for a ride since this was how their hosts came from home and returned. A second group of Americans were driven with their hosts to the homes where they would stay. The third group took the metro as their hosts did every day for their transportation needs. As a result of sending our American friends home with different Russians, whatever the hosts suggested as an activity became the next event. In most cases, the generous and caring Russians asked their American guest what she/he would like to do. Having heard about the War, most Americans wanted to see it first hand.

The Americans were, of course, eager to get where the action was. They were also eager to have their "home stays" with Russian friends from the Conference. We were somewhat concerned about sending our people out into the City, given the serious conflicts happening. At least 3-4 of our Russian Hosts lived within walking distance of the Russian White House. As it turned out, October 2-3, the days of the "home stays," were the most violent clashes with the police and army. A mob constructed barricades and blocked traffic on Moscow's main streets. On October 3, a mob of parliament supporters overcame the police cordon around the White House territory and also seized the Moscow City Mayor offices. President Yeltsin was in a struggle for power with Vice President Rutskoi who later in the day encouraged the mob to seize the national television center at Ostankino. Some Americans were also staying near Ostankino.

Our American friends were out of our reach and the City was at war! That same evening, October 3, a small division of Russian Airborne troops were able to stop the assault of Ostankino. News from a Russian TV shown around the world showed significant damage to the Ostankino tower had already taken place.

Now and then, one of the Americans would call us at Alexey's Mother's Flat to exclaim over the war from their point of view and wanting to talk with the two of us. But that was it.

Dr. Katya, a Conference participant and homestay host, lived within walking distance of the White House. Her home was apparently within range of the explosions. One corner of the home was damaged due to firing from the tanks. This was our most concerning phone call! Still, our American and Russian friends all remained calm. The two of us and Alexey, being the ones "responsible" for bringing the group to "a war," remained the most concerned.

Alexey, after a long phone call, walked into the living room of his Flat where the two of us were gathered with 1-2 other Americans having tea. He sat down and began as usual, "Carol, Tim we must talk." Alexey advised us the committee of Russian organizers were also concerned and suggested we postpone the business visits and plan instead to have a trip out of the City. It was easy for Alexey and the two of us to accept this idea.

We ended up making two trips out of Moscow. The first was a day trip to Sergie Posad, about 2 hours away via bus. As a part of the famous "Golden Triangle" of Moscow, the trip to Sergiye Posad was a beautiful drive. Once there, all thoughts of the "war" disappeared. We were surrounded by the most beautiful architecture and taken back into history. Named after Saint Sergie of Radonezh, a 14th century monk, Sergie Posad is the Russian Orthodox equivalent of the Vatican, with an amazing complex of medieval buildings rivaling those of the Kremlin!

Every American was intent on bringing home to the US the famous Russian wooden nesting dolls, known as Matryoshkas. Our group delighted in learning St. Sergei himself carved wooden dolls, horses and other toys to give to the children he met. The Americans brought home great collections for themselves, family and friends.

The City was filled with history and beauty. In fact, it is said Sergie Posad is the only city in Russia whose churches were allowed to continue in operation throughout the Soviet period. This trip gave the group energy as well as insights into the true Russian character, history and beauty. What a contrast to the tense climate in Moscow.

We had had a lovely day together. Three of our Russian friends went with us to Sergie Posad and added information and great caring. The drive back was peaceful, with most of the group napping from exhaustion. Suddenly, as we reached the outskirts of Moscow, the bus driver pulled over to the side of the road and began speaking loudly. Though we could speak some Russian, it was impossible for us to understand his emotional words. Alexey and Tatiana (Smirnova), called the two of us to the front of the bus.

In whispered tones, they told us the bus driver understood there was a war going on in Moscow and found this a perfect time to demand we pay a bribe to return to the hotel in safety. At first, the two of us were outraged. We spoke loudly to Alexey and Tanya saying we did not pay bribes. Alexey used his oft repeated phrase, "Carol, Tim, this is Russia." The driver had shouted in Russian he would simply not drive any further. Tanya told us she was concerned about the situation and whether it was right or wrong of the driver, we had no choice. She felt uneasy with the responsibility of finding transportation for this size group during these uncertain times in Moscow.

Not wishing to put further burdens on our two dear friends, we each went to the back of the bus. One of us went behind one seat, one behind another. Finding one's hidden money pouch discreetly with a wide-eyed group of American friends looking on with keen interest, while crouching to recover a money pouch is not easy!

We were able to find some $100 bills we knew were not counterfeit and hand them over to the driver. As if this were simply a normal transaction, he smiled and said "Spasibo," "Thank you," in Russian.

We all took our seats and drove back to the Chinese hotel. Whew! Just another day in Moscow, Autumn 1993.

The following day, we talked to Alexey about all of us going to the Russian White House to give everyone the chance to see the sights they saw on TV. Alexey was not thrilled with this request, but agreed to take us. Two or three of the other Russian friends joined our group as we took the trip via Metro to Barrikadnaya station.

Once off the Metro, Carol gathered the group and said a few words. Our concerns were not to look like "crazy Americans" going to see a war. Both of us asked our American friends to act concerned and appropriate. As a last remark, Carol seriously said, "Please stay off the tanks. Do not make a scene. Use your own good judgment. We are Americans and will attract unwanted attention."

The group split up into smaller groups and wandered about the area of the Russian White House. The window where the fires had been were blackened and still smoking. There was obvious damage to the building. Several tanks manned by Russian military surrounded the building and were also out into the streets where we walked.

The Soldiers were far more interested in a group of Americans than in watching or protecting the aftermath of a skirmish. Many of the soldiers were practicing their English on us and seemed to be almost light-hearted.

We set aside a certain amount of time for seeing the scene and reconvened as a group to walk to the Metro.

It was only later that we saw the photos from this little outing. Really, we should not have been surprised. The various photo collections showed some of our American women sitting on Russian tanks, surrounded by Russian soldiers. Our American friends, women and men, were posing with the soldiers, holding their automatic weapons and having a good old time! These were of course, bright, independent, successful Americans. Like the Russians, we made friends easily and loved to meet people and connect.

Alexey, bless his heart, worked in so many ways to care for us, to bring all of the best Russian business leaders and to provide a variety of learning experiences and trips to share his Russia with us all. Tatiana Smirnova knew we would listen to her advice and guided us through more than one challenging experience after another with grace, wisdom and love.

Our trip continued for another four days. Our participants had their "day" in Russian business and we also continued to see important landmarks. There would be many more trips to Russia for the two of us, both taking Americans or just the two of us plus Denny Aron, our partner in the Russian work. Still, this trip remains a special one. We can now read about the events as history on Google. We look at the photos of the Russian White House on fire and see photos of our friends with the Russian soldiers on their tanks. Only our small group has the photos of some of our American perched on those tanks!

Had this been 2013, imagine all of the Social networks on which those photos would have been shared . . .

## CHAPTER FOURTEEN

# Influence Comes of Age

The three of us, Carol, Tim and Geil, met in spring, 1991, to select participants for the new INFLUENCE groups. We were encouraged with the quality of the women who were joining our new Denver offering. We felt positive about the great support from our sponsors. Additionally, women from six states had applied for INFLUENCE in Omaha.

The value of a single gender program was now more clear. We received feedback the INFLUENCE approach was making a significant difference for both participants and sponsors. Research has repeatedly found women learn more deeply, more rapidly and with longer retention in a single gender group than in a group with both women and men.

Linda drove 100 miles each way to the Denver INFLUENCE meetings. She described herself in September and then in May. A single parent with a big job, she arrived strong and tough. She could handle anything that came along and do it better than any man. Of course she also did it the way the men in her organization would have. But in INFLUENCE, Linda became totally herself, had greater confidence, explored areas of concern more openly, developed learning partners more fully than would be true in a mixed group. The stereotypes and social norms didn't interfere, as they might have with women and men together.

The two-day format also helped as learnings from the first day "cooked" overnight and increased both understanding and retention. With the one-day format, Linda would not have had the reflection time needed to internalize the things she learned about herself. Expanding the focus on the broader world also allowed Linda to understand herself in a global context.

This was particularly valuable for a single parent who might have otherwise been consumed by the obligations of both parenting and career. Increasing our focus on understanding one's self in this way allowed Linda to develop herself from the inside out. Linda came to us a leader – a strong one – and left not just as a leader, but as a much more complete person.

At its essence, INFLUENCE invited participants to give birth to themselves as leaders over the nine months. The program used many development tools and experiences. However, the most important source of learning came from the community of women who learned while experiencing life together. In 1998, we intensified the process with the introduction of the 2% initiative and the creation of 2% teams.

Our first intro to the concept of the 2% projects caused some confusion for Kim. We calmly said, "What is something in your life that if enhanced would add value?" We invited her to select a personal development initiative and during INFLUENCE focus on it with a small team of peers. Thus, her the 2% team was used to develop progress and achieve her goal. The title is "2%" because we do not believe that any INFLUENCE women need to "be fixed." So the 2% is a result of identifying some aspect of life where a change or improvement can produce significant positive impact.

For Kim it was about determining what she wished to do with her life. As a single woman with a good job, she was faced both with deciding her personal life choices and also deciding to remain in the corporate world, or leave it to join the family business.

After a great deal of thought and feeling, Kim took our suggestion to take some time to travel to a place far removed from her present circumstances and let her life choices choose her. In fact, she expanded on our advice. She took a leave of absence from her job at the time and moved to Asia alone. Kim took a job teaching English in a village in Thailand for six months. When she returned, she had life answers. She joined the family business, married and had children and is very active in her community. There are no boundaries on what is or is not an appropriate 2% for any individual.

It is not necessary, of course, to find your answers by traveling to Asia – though Kim is not the only one who used travel as a 2% muse. Usually the answers can be found very close to home. It is amazing to see how participants have used these initiatives to make adjustments that add great value to their lives.

One woman reported during the last session of INFLUENCE she had been completely "stuck" on her initiative. She decided to fly to Europe to gain perspective via a new venue. During the week she spent there she created a self-portrait in pastels showing the beautiful things about herself she re-discovered and appreciated. This same portrait is prominently displayed in our office today; a touching, meaningful gift which daily confirms our shared work.

The three of us were privileged in ways greater than we could have expected to witness twenty-three groups of INFLUENCE women in the '90s as they developed their individual leadership "from the inside out." For instance, we saw women who were professionally trained as musicians, dancers, artists who then gave up their chosen fields to move into business. Their INFLUENCE experience allowed and encouraged them to return to the field of their love, if only on a part-time or hobby basis.

Although it happened in 1998, we fondly remember the day Jo Ellen interpreted her INFLUENCE experience with a classic ballet presentation. She completed the program believing she had re-discovered herself. The group sat silently, with tears of gratitude and joy for witnessing such depth of beauty and meaning.

In the '80s, we heard many stories of challenges in participants' lives. But with the '90s, came many INFLUENCE women ready to act on the real barriers keeping them from being all they could be as women, as professionals and family members. A floodgate of deeper and often more painful stories opened. The stories were ones some women had kept bottled up for most of their lives. The seemingly strongest, most put-together professional women were often the ones who were victims of incest, rape, physical and mental abuse. Without the support their INFLUENCE groups provided, the stories would never have been safe to tell. Typical stories of participants would begin like this:

- "I was seven when my grandfather came to my room and raped me for the first time. He returned at least weekly until I was 12. I have had trouble trusting anyone since then . . . "

- "I was regularly burned and beaten by my mother and told by my father that I was worthless. It is hard for me to believe that I am an effective leader now . . ."

Some of the women actually said their lives were saved by the INFLUENCE experience and/or a member of their 2% group.

And yet for some there was no saved life or happy ending. Lisa was one of the most talented women we met. She was a part of our first INFLUENCE of Phoenix program. To meet her she seemed a bright, sociable, upbeat single parent of a delightful young son.

Her life story, though, was one of abuse, alcoholism, drugs, early sex, a dysfunctional family, the need to care for her mother from a young age.

Lisa was always successful at work, received promotions and job offers from other employers. But the "demons" of her life chased her despite her success. Tim worked with her regularly after

INFLUENCE ended. She also received professional help in the city where she lived. Finally she decided she was spiraling out of control in the corporate world AND her son was not receiving the parenting she wished. Lisa decided to leave the corporate scene, moved to a different city and obtained a job as a math teacher in the local public schools.

She was assigned by choice to one of the toughest schools in the District where poverty was extreme and violence was always present. Tim talked with her off and on through her first year of teaching. She seemed to have really found peace and satisfaction. For two years she had successes with young teen boys that no one in the District had ever achieved. Then the depression Lisa had felt for so long caught up with her and during the Christmas holiday break she took her life. We remember her regularly even though it has been over a decade since she died.

The conversations and development of the INFLUENCE women in the 1990s were influenced by an amazing period in US and world history: the fall of the Berlin Wall, Desert Storm, rapid growth of the economy and all the other events of the period. Participants who, in the '80s, were too consumed by their lives in a small geographic area were slowly replaced in the '90s with women who began to realize the larger world was increasingly influencing their lives.

In the '90s, the participants in INFLUENCE gradually, but significantly changed. They had more confidence, held demanding positions, felt more confident in their rights and seemed less afraid. Organization change was becoming routine for most participants, though some fear persisted. There were more and more women of Color being sponsored by their companies.

We remember Lorinda, a manager in the Finance Department of her company in Phoenix who was also an elder of her Navajo tribe. It is important to the story to mention that the Navajo are a matriarchal tribe. The role of women is very important. Lorinda was quiet and calm. But when she spoke, she filled the room with wisdom. All of us listened with great interest and learned from her. Though she was a successful business woman, she desired to return to the reservation.

Yi Fong taught us about the actual realities of China at the time. She came from China to the US to earn her Ph.D. in Engineering and stayed to work for a Denver manufacturer. She quickened our growing desire to work in China. During the INFLUENCE year, Yi Fong went back to her home city for the first time in many years. At that time, a trip home to a city of millions of inhabitants required two plane rides, a train ride and a bus to finish the journey. It took nearly four days each way.

When she returned she brought us our first large-scale map of China. We later used that map for many years in our work in China. After her return, we began for the first time to set our clear intention to be working in China within five years. We purposely stated this intention to each new group we met. Our intention would manifest in only three years.

There were other INFLUENCE women whose life experiences are even more challenging. We remember the US Army Captain, veteran of Desert Storm, a talented African American woman, who was sponsored for INFLUENCE by her civilian company. We all shared the hope we could aid in her transition back to civilian life.

Most of the women in her INFLUENCE group had not known the trauma that was a part of women in the military returning from war. A few of the women had husbands or other loved ones who had been at war. But for most of America, this was the beginning of wars where many Americans did not have personal involvement. Much difficult but important learning occurred for all of us.

The Captain's injuries in Kuwait and Iraq challenged her ability to be as successful as she desired within her civilian company.

Carol continued to work with her for nearly ten years after INFLUENCE. Another INFLUENCE alum who was her friend, also kept in touch with her. Now almost twenty years later, this woman has finally found some level of peace, started her own company and has an income to sustain her. We give thanks.

During the '90s we saw a coming out of Lesbian participants in INFLUENCE. Most were in the Denver or Phoenix programs because it was still not safe to "be out" in Omaha. The stories they told of abuse while growing up, rejection by parents, discrimination in their workplaces and rejection by neighbors in upper middle-class neighborhoods were shocking.

We heard of crosses being burned in their yards, homes being egged. It was not unusual for an INFLUENCE woman to report having been summarily fired when her employer discovered she was a Lesbian.

Many of these women only grew stronger as a result of the challenges they faced. Additionally, heterosexual women in INFLUENCE learned more about themselves as they dealt with their own prejudices, the many stereotypes they believed, plus their own questions about homosexuality. As the '90s ended, fear was dissipating. Lesbian women in INFLUENCE had fewer difficult life stories to tell. However, acceptance of both Lesbian women and Gay men is far from reality in our society, despite the legal and social progress that has been made.

Throughout the '90s, the number of women from cities beyond Denver, Omaha and Phoenix continued to grow. We had participants from California to Massachusetts, Georgia to Washington State plus Arizona, Denver and Nebraska.[10] Many INFLUENCE women have traveled to different countries for their work. During this same time we began to see women born in other countries joining us in INFLUENCE. Their homelands included Brazil, Canada, China, Egypt, Iran, Poland and Russia.

Of course, all of this diversity greatly enhanced the richness of learning.

Lorees, from Egypt, was an engineer, educated when women didn't yet go to Engineering school. She had a significant role in an electric utility. Soraya, who sometimes referred to herself as the little Persian girl, fled Iran before the fall of the Shah. She became an executive in a successful communications company.

One of the women raised in another country was very helpful to the learning of us Native-born Americans. Fan came from China. In fact she had been one of those young Chinese who marched in support of Mao during the Cultural Revolution. When she came to the US, she lived on the West Coast where she went to college and subsequently began a career that brought her to the Midwest.

One day we were discussing terrible pay and working conditions being experienced by immigrants. Fan joined in the conversation to tell us she had put herself through college working at one of those "terrible" jobs. She wanted us to know that without such jobs available to immigrants she could never have received a college education and would not have the career that allowed her to be with us in INFLUENCE.

≈    ≈    ≈

Interest in the world beyond the US borders was growing, especially after the fall of the Soviet Union and the apparent ascendancy of the United States as head of a "Unipolar" world. In 1992, the author, Francis Fukuyama, had declared "the end of history" as liberal democracy had been proven to be the unquestionably "best way" for countries to operate.[11] Some INFLUENCE participants found this exhilarating, others found it scary. The bottom line, however, is more of the women were ready to be involved.

The '90s were a time when women began to feel more accepted and confident in professional and managerial positions. And, while the glass ceiling was very real, women in INFLUENCE were beginning to pass through it.

Jacquie was promoted to Superintendent of the Westside School System. Joan was promoted multiple times until she became Chief Operating Officer of Alegent Health. Shirley went from an engineering job at the Rocky Flats nuclear site in Colorado to Site Manager of the entire operation to clean up the Hanford Nuclear Waste site in Washington.

The list of successes is very long. Executives began to understand women increasingly brought gifts and talents to the workplace organizations had not experienced prior to this time.

We were working with some of the brightest, most capable women from the sponsoring organizations. It was easy to see they brought attributes critical to success in the emerging world, especially the world beyond the borders of the United States. Research studies have now confirmed women in general are more effective in building and maintaining relationships; they are also more flexible and resilient.

Early examples of INFLUENCE women making a difference in the international arena included:

Marti, Denver INFLUENCE; was responsible for the white paper USWest used to develop a major international training center in Moscow.

Patti, Omaha INFLUENCE; was making software deals in a number of countries for Applied Communications.

Brenda, Denver INFLUENCE; was working with start up cellular ventures in Czechoslovakia for USWest.

Major Fran, USAF, Omaha INFLUENCE; was participating in the SALT talks in Geneva as an advisor to Secretary of State George Schultz. She later retired as a USAF General. And, of course, there are many others.

We were interested in understanding whether women or men were better prepared to build the relationships and have the sensitivity required by the global business arena. To explore the question, we decided to do some research on the women and men we worked with in the INFLUENCE and FOCUS programs. We were curious to understand how women and men were viewed in some areas of leadership and management.

We had rich information on the respective INFLUENCE and FOCUS group members through the feedback data in the FGI 360° Professional Development Questionnaire© we use every year. Insuring total confidentiality, we wanted to see if the characteristics believed necessary for success in the global economy were more attributed to women or to men.

We looked at the comparative results of the FGI 360° evaluations of over 13,000 co-workers who rated more than 1,100 women and 875 men who had been a part of FGI programs. The largest number of individuals were from INFLUENCE or FOCUS. We compared results for 45 behavioral items. In 28 out of the 45 items, women were rated stronger than men. In three items, men were rated stronger and in fourteen cases there was no significant difference between women and men.[12]

Our 1997 research was in no way intended to show up men or elevate women. Rather it was intended to identify areas of both strength and developmental need for women and men. To be effective in the global arena, women needed confidence and experience. They typically were stronger in key success factors. To be effective in the global arena, men needed to recognize the United States was no longer always dominant in its international relationships. Success required more sensitivity, flexibility and relationship building than may have felt natural or familiar to men.

The findings from this research helped us understand what would become major challenges after the turn of the Century. Both women and men in the United States would need to expand their repertoires in order to have business success in the global economy.[13]

The two of us had many conversations about this topic, especially as our international work expanded to China and then to India. The things we learned about women in our work all over the world seem very important. And these learnings are applicable to men as well as women. US companies still have a long way to go in understanding the global requirements for success.

It is important for leaders to assist our country in understanding what the global economy requires. It is exciting to see how INFLUENCE women are beginning to see the importance of developing their natural strengths, and FOCUS men are increasingly valuing relationships, flexibility and resilience.

INFLUENCE and FOCUS continue to be one of our greatest teachers as well as significantly meaningful work.

As the '90s drew to a close, we felt INFLUENCE was a gift we received each year. The women were special; the learnings were incredible. The opportunities for women seemed to be opening up everywhere. Plus, the economy was doing well; the national deficit had turned into a surplus; the nation was not at war; outsourcing was growing rapidly; consumer confidence was high.

Internationally, the crises in Central Europe had been stabilized; reform of the Indian Government opened up rapid growth for that country; China was about to take on a new leader, Hu Jin Tao. The BRIC[14] countries were leading the way to a new century. The stock market was soaring. Now, if only we could all survive what was threatened as a crisis with the coming of the Millennium.

We did. And it wasn't a crisis!

## CHAPTER FIFTEEN

# One Ringy Dingy

We saw the wonderful Lily Tomlin live for the first time in 1988. We were in Philadelphia working with our bank client. Our friend, Kevin, was able to get tickets to her new show, "The Search for Signs of Intelligent Life in the Universe." He and our friend Phil went with us. Thus, we met "Ernestine" on the stage and in person. Her telephone operator characterization is one that has lived in American comedy folklore since 1969.

However, when we saw Ernestine in 1988, her character took on new meaning. The telephone companies were in a state of confusion and some disarray. The "children" of AT&T, or as they were known, the "Baby Bells," were doing their best to create new identities and live with the realities of deregulation and divestiture. Some of them were not doing very well. Customer Service was suffering. "Ernestine" helped Americans both laugh and cry at the same time.

We just finished working with one of the Baby Bells and happened to be in the second year of a long-term consulting assignment with another.

No client of FGI, regardless of success or failure, has ever had higher quality, better-trained managers and leaders than the two different RBOCs (Regional Bell Operating Companies) with whom we worked. They also had more leaders who were women and men of Color than any other company with whom we worked.

Additionally, women managers and leaders in those RBOCs were in a category by themselves. As a group, they seemed much more capable and confident than their peers in other industries. This was largely the result of an AT&T settlement with the Federal Government to remediate discrimination against their women employees. The Baby Bells continued to develop and fast track the careers of their talented women. With such talent in place and businesses with such an important role in the lives of all Americans, what happened to the telephone companies?

Shortly after divestiture and deregulation, we were invited to work with the strategic planners at Pacific Telesis. This Baby Bell was considered "most likely to succeed." It had the smallest geographic territory (California and Nevada), a large population and a huge need for telecommunications services.

We thoroughly enjoyed working with the strategic planners. They were smart, engaging and enjoyable. When we asked them to imagine the issues necessary to change the Company culture to being competitive, they understood the issues fully. However, when the deliberations turned to implementing the new vision, the "how" became more challenging. Changing the regulated culture of a nineteenth century company seemed beyond imagination.

These strategic planners had been told by executives the Company would now be somehow free to raise rates, introduce new services at a premium and make more money by doing largely what they had been doing. This concerned us. Our growing experience in other industries made us believe deregulation would require a whole new paradigm for doing business. Pacific Telesis ultimately was acquired by SBC Communications, which later changed its name to AT&T.

Our next experience in telecommunications deregulation and divestiture came in early fall, 1987. Carol was approached by Lois, one of the communications team members at the new USWEST. People told Lois that Carol had experience working with large organization change. Our knowledge of the industry was limited, but our experience in organization change was solid and real. After interviewing Carol, the article Lois wrote about the change process was widely distributed across the fourteen states of the Company. Suddenly we were "experts" and the FGI phone began to ring.

One call came from the Engineering department in one of those states. Victoria, a senior leader, asked us to present to her management team how these changes might impact their work. These engineers were proud leaders of a strong engineering-based organization. The change scenario we presented was that deregulated reality would require maintaining quality with lower capital as well as lower general and administrative costs. This seemed difficult for the group to digest at the time.

We designed our workshop and headed off to the Double Tree Hotel in east Denver. Transparencies and notes in hand, we entered a large theatre style room to meet nearly 150 Engineering leaders and managers at the new USWest. They must have felt like captives in a hotel conference center in east Denver, wondering if these two strangers really knew what they were talking about. These USWest women and men were expert engineers. We were former railroad employees. After a very flattering introduction by Victoria, we began. The time flew by as we shared change theory using examples from other industries.

We then invited them to evaluate their present business environment using an FGI approach. We also asked what they believed would be the necessary business environment under deregulation. They were interested, engaged and – in our opinion – excellent in their analysis of the situation. They acknowledged the need for change, and seemed to appreciate their new understanding of what was unfolding. We felt confirmed in our work. How they would translate their new insights into action at USWEST was left for them to decide. We had opened minds. We soon realized this was an important way for us to serve.

Later, we started new work with another area of USWEST. We were able to integrate some of what we learned earlier in California and Denver. This USWEST territory included Idaho, Iowa, Minnesota, Montana, Nebraska, North Dakota, Oregon, South Dakota, Utah, Washington and Wyoming as well as Arizona and New Mexico. Headquarters were in Colorado. Experts believed USWEST received the most difficult Region. It was the largest geographically with the smallest population and industrial base. However, their top two leaders, Jack MacAllister and Dick McCormick, were experienced and respected.

Our major work with USWest for ten years was with the Home and Personal Services (HPS) sales organization and its many capable leaders. In the very first meeting with them, we "caught" their optimism, enthusiasm and commitment to success. Looking back on it now, we still remember the many enjoyable times we had with those women and men. We laughed together, cried together, "plotted and schemed" together and thoroughly enjoyed each others' company.

It may be difficult to imagine today, but in 1987 sales were an afterthought to customer service in the telephone companies. Why? Because earlier, when business was regulated, prices on all services were set, options were few and all customers were thought of as equal. A unionized sales force was incented for courteous, respectful service and prompt, correct answering of customer inquiries. They had no control over the actual provision of service and little control over what actually happened to customer requests.

Suddenly there was deregulation! All the rules were changed. The long-dedicated customer service reps suddenly had dozens of "products" and were now incented to sell premium products to everyone who fit certain profiles. This was a totally new business approach for them. Their goal was to serve the customer. They felt they were being encouraged to "push things down customers' throats." The immediate results were frustrating for many. As we met with more and more service reps, it became clear the new job requirements were a huge psychological as well as behavioral shift for these women and men. They prided themselves in serving each customer in a certain way.

Our friend and INFLUENCE graduate, Jeffrie, was the first to ask us to partner with her on this issue. Director over a large call center in Omaha, Jeffrie brought us in to observe her customer service representatives plus work with her to develop a program to transform them into actual sales representatives. For days the two of us sat with headsets listening in to customer service/sales calls. The customer service representatives (CSR) were union workers, some of whom had been with the Company for over twenty years. They were very nice, professional women and men who took their work seriously. However, it was a foreign notion to accept being Sales Reps. Though devoted, they had little training in basic sales skills.

Jeffrie was pleased with the insights and outcomes we offered. She asked us to meet Linda, her Vice President of HPS. Linda was headquartered in Phoenix. Thus, we began nine years of very satisfying work with Linda and her talented team of directors.

We listened in on sales calls all over the USWEST system – Belleview, WA; St. Paul, MN; Des Moines, IA; Denver, CO; Phoenix, AZ; and other call centers. It quickly became apparent there were significant differences among the customer sales reps we heard. It seemed to reflect differences in geographical regions as well as how their brains processed what they thought and heard, plus what motivated them. Some were naturally eager to sell and succeed in sales. Others had little interest in sales and just wanted to make customers happy. The work for the Director became: how to incent the first group and retrain and/or motivate the second group? All of this was to occur while honoring the fact that all the CSRs were Union members.

During the many weeks we spent in the call centers, we often found opportunities to chat with the CSRs in informal settings, such as break rooms, areas outside of the buildings, even restrooms. We were able to naturally learn more and even offer coaching through these casual conversations. The women and men were sincere and eager to learn more and be successful with customers. Myths that existed about union workers in those days did not apply to those we met. They were dedicated to customers, worked hard and cared deeply. Many, however, did not grasp the idea that the "Spirit of Service" effort the Company was making at the time included the notion of selling additional features and services.

Because we were introduced as the consultants, many reps saw us as an opportunity to both share and receive important information. Some of what we shared with them about the impacts of deregulation was possibly concerning. However, they always remained dedicated to both the company and their customers. The conversations with the CSRs seemed to make a positive difference.

Our work with the CSRs also allowed us to develop more meaningful and animated coaching sessions with Linda's direct reports. We worked with this leadership group to develop processes that enabled the new requirement to "sell" and give excellent service as a part of the new approach. Working with the Senior Team, we developed a list of desired behaviors for the new culture. Together, we assisted the directors in implementing this new culture in each local area. Directors such as Leslie, Denise, Bob, Ken, Char, Eunice and Jeffrie jumped at the opportunity and rather quickly enabled significant changes to happen. We had the honor to serve beside them fine-tuning the processes and helping to measure the progress.

One favorite area of work for us was to use our newly designed FGI 360° Culture Development Questionnaire© to measure annual progress in changing the sales culture after three years of work. The results were gratifying. Each year the management teams debriefed the results of the 360° reports to review their progress and then decide how they would move the culture forward in the coming year. At the meeting in Seattle, we barely covered the reports before Leslie, the Director of HPS for Oregon and Washington, had a strong response. She understood immediately what it meant and was ready with a step-by-step team plan for the coming year. Within less than an hour, her team was ready to go! We left Portland that day feeling tired but very happy. We felt well utilized.

Over the years, we were fortunate to spend literally hundreds of hours with Linda, diagnosing, strategizing, evaluating and reflecting on successes and failures. Linda was a strong, compassionate, goal-oriented leader, a true role model for her team. The team all seemed to understand this, learned from her and became incredible leaders themselves. We still use one of the analogies Linda used for change management. It was simple baseball truism: It is a lot more doable to hit bunts and singles than to hit home runs. Implementing change is mostly achieved through bunts and singles.

However, there were dark clouds on the horizon. Cell phones arrived and became a difficult product line for USWest to integrate effectively into its business model. Cable Television and the Internet arrived, bringing new competitors. These newcomers to the market were a tough bunch who really knew how to compete and how to "skim" the best customers from the RBOCs.

Regulated telephone companies, USWEST and the other RBOCs, were required by law to provide Universal Service. This meant they had to serve every household, business and government organization in their territory. The cable companies had no such requirement. They could go where the profit potential was the greatest and skim off the most important customers, leaving the RBOCs serving customers who, in many cases, were unprofitable. Similarly, USWEST lost a share of its large business and industrial customers to the new fiber-optic competitors such as Global Crossing, Telemedia, Level 3 and others.

Many historians believe USWEST was the most progressive of the RBOCs in adopting new products and technology. However, they were not able to match up effectively against competition on either the retail or wholesale sides of their business. The drag on the bottom line became too great. In the year 2000, QWEST Communications acquired USWEST in a hostile takeover.

We felt privileged to work with a part of this proud and successful company. We worked with women and men who were exceptional managers. Many were exceptional leaders. Despite their best efforts, events beyond their control kept them from success. Due to what was happening with technology, a deregulated market, new players, fierce competition and finally, the billions of dollars available during the dot.com bubble, a new history began to unfold.

We learned so much from our work with USWEST. It was the first time we had encountered discontinuous change on a massive basis. Technology was the biggest cause of the discontinuity. Almost as important was the blurring of lines among industries. Suddenly satellite, Internet, cable and cellular companies were all in the phone business. Unless the phone companies could seamlessly cross into those industries as well, there was no future for landline phones only.

In our consulting practice, we quickly saw the importance of being able to serve our clients in understanding this discontinuity phenomenon would repeat itself in many industries. In our work with power companies, health care providers, insurance companies, manufacturers and others, our message has been consistent. History will have almost nothing to do with future success. Some clients have embraced this reality; others have not. This often leaves us wondering about alternative ways to present the messages effectively.

## *Epilogue*

Any business school professor wanting to teach the maximum number of leadership and management concepts in one case, could surely select the breakup of the old Bell System and the birth of modern telecommunications in the US. This story has it all: deregulation, divestiture, mergers, technology, discrimination remediation, customer service and more. In some ways it was "the perfect storm." We had the chance to experience it all while serving these fine professionals. It was surely the most complex set of change initiatives we encountered anywhere.

Today, nearly 30% of US homes no longer have a telephone landline. For adults under thirty-five, the landline seems redundant, irrelevant and an unnecessary expense. During the '80s and '90s it was impossible for our clients to imagine that in such a short time their primary product would become obsolete to many customers. The telephone company of 1987 was vital to the American economy. It has disappeared. Today the more complex and constantly evolving telecommunications sector is one of the most critical to business success in the world.

Who knows what the next twenty-five years will bring? We believe that much of what we now know as telecommunications will change even more radically than it did in the past twenty-five years. Maybe Ernestine knows the answers, wherever she is!

## CHAPTER SIXTEEN

# The New Business in Russia

We stood at the front of our meeting room at the Russian Academy of National Economy sharing theory and teaching about organization development. Since Soviet times, this academy was known as one of the most prestigious education centers for the advanced development of national leaders. From time to time we had to raise our voices to be heard. Outside the window of our meeting room was a large cement plant, clunking away all day long. It was a good reminder of the fact that the Soviet Union had consciously placed factories next to educational institutions, museums, theatres, to remind people that nothing is more important than the worker. Our new Russian friends seemed not to notice the noise.

Through an amazing chain of coincidences, we came to share our experiences with key staff members of the Center for Business Skills Development (CBSD). CBSD was originally the brainchild of Marti, an INFLUENCE woman who worked for USWest in Denver. USWest purchased a number of cell phone licenses in Russia. This produced a need to develop Russian employees across the country. The Soviet system had not prepared these workers for a market economy which was ready to ignite and grow. Marti was asked to prepare a White Paper proposal for how the Company could develop the needed employees. Because she knew we worked in Russia, she asked us to review the proposal.

Meanwhile our friend Dennis, a business executive who had been with us on the 1992 trip to Russia, called us for a favor. He decided he wanted to return to work and live in Moscow. We arranged meetings with USWest decision-makers in the US and Russia. Because of his credentials and experience, they hired Dennis in 1994.

In 1995, USWest abandoned its Russia plans and CBSD reverted to the US Agency for International Development who originally provided partial funding. USAID, which was not in the people development business, eventually arranged a sale of CBSD to Thunderbird University in Arizona. Within months, Dennis became the President of what was a complex organization with multiple locations in Russia, but with little money and few prospects.

Dennis, however, had two very important resources. First, he had several very bright and talented, bi or tri-lingual Russian faculty members. Second, he had his own incredible Spirit and drive. It was and is still remarkable to reflect on all he and they accomplished.

Dennis and his staff determined CBSD's initial market would be Western multi-nationals who were setting up operations in Russia. CBSD would educate their new Russian employees of those Western multi-nationals. The two of us were invited to share our learning and organization development experience with key CBSD faculty. The main focus was on approaches that would meet the needs of these Western companies. We developed a series of classes to serve the CBSD staff in fine-tuning their skills and knowledge for CBSD to be successful. We spent five wonderful days with Dennis and his key CBSD staff members. During the evenings that week, the three of us talked, planned and created the future vision. But there was always the cement factory.

Our memory holds on clearly to that first afternoon in the classroom. It was a particularly hot Moscow summer day. We opened the windows for air. The grinding-clanking noise from the cement factory was so great people could not hear one another speak. Tim began to apologize for the unfortunate noise and heat problem. The Russians hastily told us not to apologize. One of them quickly but firmly said, "Tim, Carol, we are grateful to be here, working with you. We are grateful to have our jobs. We are also grateful that the cement factory has work. Think nothing of the noise and heat."

Of course, depending on one's perspective, different lessons emerge. To us the surroundings were a barrier to learning. To the Russians, there was only gratitude that they were free and able to create a business without the direction of the State. It was exhilarating for them! It became exhilarating for us as well. We felt privileged to be there during incredible change, to work with bright, caring, intelligent women and men. We learned lessons in humility and appreciation that day which would remain with us forever. Those of us born and raised in the US are used to basic freedoms and conveniences. We often have no concept of what would be normal in other settings. Russia in the mid '90s was just beginning to stabilize from the Soviet period. They were slowly adding amenities of life that were "givens" in the US. In our future work in Russia plus China and India, this lesson was reinforced over and over.

We heard many stories from Russians about how they viewed Americans. The Russians had met Americans in Russia who complained about the shortages of food, about any and all inconveniences they experienced, about the pollution and the general decay in the cities, about the absence of good customer service. And much more. We began to understand the meaning of the term "Ugly Americans." Then we remembered our own reactions to the cement plant.

As we look back, we now realize we shared every bit of theory we could about how to develop leaders for Western style business. We exposed them to organization development theory, small group and team development, organization life cycles, planning, marketing and adult learning theory. It was a glorious experience for us!

Our Ph.D. "students" in most cases had better formal educations than we. They were great learners, actively involved in every exercise, freely asking questions and able to disagree. Boris and Tanya, for instance, were quick to challenge statements we made about how organizations make decisions based on finance. Mikhail had great theoretical knowledge of group process and would occasionally challenge our approaches to group work. However, he was also a wonderful student who was ready to learn new approaches as we shared our practical experiences with the group. Tanya and Lena were like sponges who absorbed everything we shared about process facilitation. They would soon be using that theory as they adapted it to the specific needs of their clients. Kevin, who was the head of Marketing, saw the week as a great springboard for creating and then marketing a variety of new courses. Dennis was like a proud father, excited by the possibilities yet worried about how to make them come alive.

The time flew by and we were sad to see it end. The Academy of National Economy and the section of the City in which it was located, was an area of Cold War Soviet architecture and zoning. Grey was the predominant color. Buildings were generally non-descript. Shopping was limited. High-rise blocks of flats and office buildings were close together. It was becoming clear to us that during the final days of the Cold War, 1988-1989, the threat was not as real as the US believed. However, the missiles in the Russian silos were likely still armed.

Prior to our leaving Moscow, Dennis asked if we would like to see what would soon be the new location for CBSD. We were eager to do so! The trip took two hours to the opposite end of Moscow. We approached a small bridge crossing a small lake onto an island in a forested part of the City. Suddenly we were in the 17th Century! The lake surrounded Izmailovo Island. This island was the site of a beautiful late 17th century summer palace built by Alexi I, Czar of Russia and father of Peter the Great. Peter spent much of his adolescent years at this palace. It was in the lake surrounding the palace that Peter was said to have first sailed the small boat that would later encourage him to build the Russian Navy.

It's difficult now to fully explain how exciting it was for us to be in this magical place. As we drove over the bridge, through the large steel arch, we found ourselves in the midst of very old buildings allowed to decay for many years. Only recently were various business enterprises recognizing the significance of the place and the beauty of the surroundings. Both Russians and International businesses were remodeling and rescuing these marvelous, old structures.

Sergei, our driver and friend, approached a long, narrow, two story building facing a beautiful birch forest. The road to the building was rutted and muddy. "Where are we?" Carol asked. Dennis responded, "We are approaching the Officers' Quarters of the palace. This is where our offices and training rooms will be located."

We entered what appeared to be a long abandoned building in the early stages of renovation. It was hard to imagine that this could become a modern training center. The only feature truly noteworthy was the badly marred maple floor in what had been the officers' ballroom. Everywhere around us was debris, spaces that had been bathrooms, large hallways and rooms that could be turned into classrooms and offices. The opportunity was there! We used our imagination to picture smartly dressed young officers going up and down the halls, holding meetings and training sessions, planning field exercises and serving the Czar. It was exhilarating!

After our week with Dennis and his key staff members, we were off once again to spend a week with the dear friends Tanya and Gennady Smirnov and their family. It's impossible to adequately describe the warmth of their welcome every time we returned! It was like coming home to a dear family to rest and enjoy life. Our times with the Smirnov family always offered hospitality of love, great food wonderfully prepared and active enlightening conversations about culture and world events. As a family, they enjoyed and deeply appreciated cultural events and arts.

Every visit with Tanya and Gennady included excursions to see historic sites both in Moscow and out in the countryside, usually a live opera, ballet or concert, conversations into the night about politics, world affairs and history. Over the years we visited at least fifty monasteries, one hundred churches, dozens of homes of famous writers or poets, a dozen palaces and every conceivable historic site in Moscow, St. Petersburg and other Russian cities. We saw Tanya and Gennady on every one of our over fifty trips to Moscow. Their home became our Russian home and they included the three of us, Carol, Tim and Denny, as their family.

After our week with the Smirnov family, it was time to return to the US. We left Russia eager to set the date for our next trip!

When we returned to Moscow in 1996, the Izmailovo Island Officers' Quarters was transformed. The maple floor in the ballroom had been sanded and polished, hallways were carpeted, classrooms and offices were beautifully furnished with the help of USAID. And, the bathrooms were modern! A food service caterer brought in beautiful and delicious food each day.

Two bright young men, Victor and Velodia, were in charge of logistics. Both men went out of their way to make us feel special whenever we came. They quickly became good friends who worked with us the entire time we worked at CBSD. Dennis had worked magic! For the next seven years, this was the site of our work in Russia. We loved this beautiful, historic and very functional space.

Because of the number of people who came to the CBSD/FGI programs, we always had the pleasure of working in the ballroom. We were never in that room without being able to envision the officers in their colorful dress uniforms dancing the night away with beautiful young ladies from the best families in Moscow. It was magical.

In 1996 and 1997, we traveled to CBSD 2-3 times a year. We felt honored to serve as main presenters for CBSD and/or the Russian Chamber of Commerce sponsored conferences offered for Human Resources professionals from multi-nationals doing business in Moscow. The participants were hungry to learn best US practices in the HR arena. The impressive professionals took great notes, asked insightful questions and often stayed after for individual coaching. We continued to work with the CBSD staff. At this time both the staff and overall business were growing rapidly. It was a "heady" time for all.

On one trip, Dennis invited us to accompany him in marketing calls with prospective new clients. Dennis managed to land a significant contract with an international company who bottled and distributed the world-famous cola.

Our mistake, perhaps the largest of our careers, was we took our information only from Dennis and the key-leader of the organization. We failed to follow our own rule and listened only to "the Boss" of the organization and to our colleague. We did not gather face-to-face information from those with whom we would work. We did not hear the issues most important to them. We trusted the information we received from the General Manager of the Russian operation. We went against our most important FGI belief: gather information from all parties; do not assume we know the issues.

At the time we had uneasy feelings about it. But we convinced ourselves that the "Boss" must know what his people needed. And Dennis had gathered information as well. How wrong we were. It was a painful lesson to learn, but essential. This serious mistake was compounded by a terrible trip from the US. Northwest Airlines mismanaged the flights out of Minneapolis and required us to arrive in Moscow a day later than planned. The result was that we went into the first session with this client group with no time for reducing jet lag.

While we had worked with ex-pats for some time, these men and one woman had moved all over the world to open up markets in emerging countries. They were tough, motivated by money, competitive, non-collegial, very self-confident and hard to reach – true mercenaries. In their eyes, we were "soft," irrelevant Americans.

We agreed with the boss that a 360° questionnaire would be a useful intervention with this group. They would complete it and have their colleagues complete it on them between our first and second sessions together. So in early evening of the first day, we distributed the packets of questionnaires and explained the process. Almost every person threw the handouts back at us. Using very colorful language, they told us in no uncertain terms that they were not going to have colleagues give them feedback. After the day ended, we were ready to return to the US.

That evening, we decided to become more like them – to become tough. They needed us to show we could become strong, assertive, demanding. They immediately respected and positively responded to our new, stronger approach. They cooperated. We managed to get through the rest of the first session and imagine the second and last session with these leaders.

The CBSD trainers sat in that first session with us, because they would be working with other levels of the organization after we finished with the top leaders. Our contract with Dennis called for us to continue helping to develop his staff. They were, of course, taken aback by our experience and wondered what it would be like for them when they took over what we started. Because most of the trainers were Ph.Ds who thought they were smarter than we were. Some of them may have had a feeling of satisfaction in watching us do so poorly. The two of us were mortified. Others were observing this "disaster." What would they think of the client organization? More important, how would they feel about us? Would we lose all of their respect?

Our second session with this same group from the client

organization was much different. We passed their test. They arrived reflective, seemingly aware of how dreadful their behavior had been. We worked together well as we covered the planned material. Their final comments were very positive and confirming. Their final words were reminders to us about not treating the rest of the world with the so-called "soft" approach Americans use. This was very useful. We left respectful of one another.

Following our initial programs with the senior leaders of the organization, CBSD carried on the work with other levels of management and supervision called for in the contract, using our program design. The contract proved very profitable for CBSD, and their trainers learned from working with the groups. The two of us learned never to take on work without first a deep assessment and an understanding of the entire client system. Looking back on it later, having an experience with true mercenaries taught us a lot about the world.

CBSD continued to grow and thrive. Students came from all parts of Moscow via the Metro. The nearest Metro station, Izmailovskaya, was a mile away. By American standards it was not easy to get to the CBSD offices. A person needed to take the Metro almost to the end of the "Blue" Line. Then, walk for about a half hour onto the island. Six months of the year, the path was either muddy or covered with a deep snow pack. Russians were used to walking because during Soviet times there were no civilian automobiles and walking from the Metro or a bus line was the only option.

CBSD decided to provide busses for students and staff from the Metro station. Two very large, blue Ford vans became signature vehicles at CBSD. However, these were rapidly changing times in Moscow! Within two years, the situation had changed radically. The majority of program participants and staff began to drive their own automobiles. This created a different problem on the small island, which had almost no parking.

One could almost chronicle the transformation of Moscow by the autos that came to CBSD. In the first years there were none. People walked a mile from the Metro. Then people started arriving in Ladas or Zhigulis or Moskvas. The next phase included used Volkswagens, Toyotas or Datsuns. Then came a phase of shiny new Hyundais, Toyotas and an occasional Jeep. Finally after about five years, the parking lot held BMWs, Audis, Lexus, Renaults and a few Mercedes. Moscow was beginning to thrive; CBSD was doing very well and we were invited to be a part of it all.

Throughout those years at Izmailovo, the three of us, Tim, Carol and Denny, had hotel rooms in a nearby complex of high-rise hotels. Each one of the Hotel's four towers had over 1,000 rooms! The complex was originally used as headquarters for the foreign press corps who came to cover the 1980 Moscow Olympics.

The rooms were typical for the late Soviet period, minimalist in every respect: poured concrete, heavy doors, few electric outlets, limited furniture, plus a loudspeaker in every room so that the government could make announcements. We imagined there were also microphones so conversations could be monitored. The bathroom fixtures worked some of the time. When faucets or showers leaked, we used duct tape. The three of us loved the adventure and came to consider the hotel complex as a home away from home.

Moscow heat came from central facilities and was piped to every building. There was never a thermometer to control the heat. It was turned on in October and turned off in May. If a room became too warm, the windows were opened. If too cold, one used extra blankets. Occasionally, Carol piled her coats and clothing on top of the bed and then crawled in. In the bathrooms, there was a warm shower in the winter and a cold shower in the summer. This was all part of the earlier Soviet system, which kept citizens dependent on the Government. Private citizens were not allowed to have their own heating units.

As Americans, the three of us were used to temperature control all year long plus always a hot shower. We discovered living could be just as enjoyable without those familiar conveniences in the US. Why? We were experiencing a new culture, new people and situations all day every day; this produced an incredible adrenalin rush. How lucky we were! It was all new to us and we learned while doing. We witnessed history being made, while also experiencing history hundreds of years old.

Each floor had a "Concierge" who collected one's room key whenever we left the floor. We were told she also served as the government informer during Soviet times. Over the years, some of these women became our good friends. Instead of spying on us, they looked out for us. Every floor also had several housekeepers who cleaned the rooms and the common areas. These delightful ladies brought us gifts and went to special efforts to treat us with great care. We reciprocated with small gifts from home and shared family photos and warm hugs.

From the windows of our individual hotel rooms, we could see CBSD in the distance across the lake. In the winter months, we watched thousands of women and men trudging across the frozen water to reach the Metro. This made their walks much shorter. In the summer, we could watch them on the street below walking to our favorite weekend spot in Moscow, the Vernisage. It was a year-round open-air swap market that also sells fine art, antiques, jewelry, rugs as well as handicrafts and souvenirs.

During the tough times in the post Soviet period, people brought what they had to trade for things that they needed or might need.

As we described earlier, over the years we bought everything from beautiful lacquer boxes and matryoshkas to clothing for children and carved, painted wooden Father Christmases. Open every weekend, the Vernisage attracted thousands from all over the City. In the early 1990s, it was simply a bunch of tables and tin sheds set up on an open field. By 2005, it was an immense reproduction of a Russian village of the 19th Century. The three of us must have been to this marvelous place over 150 times. Treasured purchases have included original oil paintings, two accordions, hundreds of pieces of amber jewelry we gave as gifts, rugs from Persia, Tatarstan, Kazakhstan and other Soviet Republics. We never could get enough of the culture, excitement and interaction with thousands of Russians and foreigners who seemed to also thrive in this environment.

Naturally, with so many shopping trips to the Vernisage, we developed a number of friendships among the vendors. Sasha became our friend. He sold amber and so looked forward to our visits. We exchanged family stories and greeted Sasha with warm hugs. Our dearest Vernisage merchant and closest friend was Galena. She sold us the most beautiful matryoshkas we prize today. We never visited Moscow without stopping to see her. We will never forget our wily young friend, Boris! Boris became our prime source for hand painted sports matryoshkas, which we gave as gifts.

Things were always exciting.  One very cold winter day, as we were walking through the snow and cold mud in the Vernisage, Carol seemed to have disappeared. Denny and Tim thought she had gone into one of the stalls to look at some special merchandise. They searched in all her favorite spots. Almost an hour later, she was still missing.

At last the two men remembered, Carol had been chatting with two Russian Babushkas in long fur coats. As Tim and Denny rounded a corner into another row of booths, the sound of Carol's laughter came through the frigid winter air. There she was, sitting on a wooden crate between the two older women. She had been invited to have a bit of vodka with her friends who simply said in Russian, "She was so very cold. We showed her how Russians stay warm on a day like this." Then, all three each raised a tiny glass of vodka. Though none of them knew English, Carol's Russian was apparently enough for them all to have a great time.

On another occasion, a wonderful old accordion "found" Carol. It was made before The Great Patriotic War (World War II). We believed that it had either come to Moscow with a German prisoner of war or as a souvenir brought back by a Russian soldier after fighting in Germany. When we brought it back to the US, a local accordion repairman confirmed for Carol it was very special with its leather bellows. It was the product of the famous German manufacturer, Hohner – a prestigious "Verdi iii" model. What a story this accordion still holds today.

It's hard to explain it now, but at the time everything we saw, smelled, tasted or touched in Moscow was thrilling. We were there and understood we were witnesses to history. We saw riots and protest marches, watched the erection of new statues and the creation of a "grave yard" for old ones. We watched beautiful ballets and operas at the Bolshoi, saw *avant garde* theatre and heard beautiful orchestras. We hitchhiked around the City when a car was not available. Most of all we met fascinating and wonderful people.

We were experiencing Moscow not in a five-star hotel in the Center City, but rather in places where average Russians would stay. However, our hotels in Moscow were better than the housing of more than half of the population of Russia. We were grateful to have access to excellent and plentiful food which was better than 99% of the population could afford at the time. We could freely come and go anywhere. Our experiences could not be considered the norm in Russia. We worked hard and long; yet we were blessed with these years in Russia!

In 1998, we were honored to take the Center for Creative Leadership's Looking Glass® Inc. (LGI) simulation to Russia for the first time in history. We were delighted to be trusted in this way. We called the new program the Looking Glass Leadership Program (LGLP). It became our signature program in Russia.

LGLP was our four-day FGI intensive assessment program

tailored for emerging markets. We embedded the LGI simulation content that stretched, challenged, confirmed and supported our Russian clients. We learned to love them deeply. Our FGI/CBSD team worked long, hard hours but also felt satisfied.

By 1999 and into the early 2000s, we were blessed to provide three to six Looking Glass Leadership Programs a year in Moscow. The profile of our average participant was a professional woman or man, mid thirties - forties, who held a significant job usually in a Western multi-national. These impressive young professionals were generally working 70-90 hours a week while supporting their nuclear family. Often they also supported many other relatives who could not earn enough to live in Russia at the time.

A brilliant young man we recall broke down in tears with Carol. "I am so tired. It's good to have you here to counsel me. I feel stretched beyond my limits. At this time I support 28 other people. Without me, they cannot eat or have a place to live. I must keep going."

Many of these exceptional, young leaders touched us deeply. Some became long-term friends. One of these is Olga. Olga, a remarkable leader, was responsible for a start-up company in Russia, owned by foreigners. Today, the company has had incredible growth and success. Olga has joined us for each of our different programs in Moscow, plus other FGI/FGISpirit programs in China and the US.

In reality, we also worked 70-90 hours a week while in Moscow. We arrived back in Omaha sick and exhausted. However, we had the luxury of coming back home with down time to rest and recuperate.

The lessons from the Looking Glass simulation always seemed to make a positive difference and significantly improve the work performance for our clients. However, a majority of participants were just as eager to learn how to balance home and work. They desired to succeed and avoid burnout. They looked for opportunities to get ahead with seemingly impossible job demands.

Consider the following example as one of a thousand we could share:

Late one Friday afternoon, about an hour before the program was to end, we were listening to participants state their intentions for change or improvement in themselves as a result of their Looking Glass learnings. Dmitry, a tall, good-looking man in his late thirties had one of the most challenging real life jobs of any one in the group. He was always traveling, working late, carrying multiple, heavy responsibilities in a huge business. He was one of the last to speak and began by saying, "I have not been a Believer (of God). But this week has enabled me to learn something incredibly important. I am not living up to the potential that God gave me. He expects far more of me than He has received to date. I must completely re-direct all of my work and actions."

Here we were at a business leadership development program and Dmitry is learning about God. Some of the group were stunned at his comment and none spoke for what seemed like minutes, though it was probably only seconds. Headshakes suggested that some others were having similar feelings. Atheism was never very effective in Russia. While closing the churches and denying the use of God's name may have pushed it underground, the spirit of the Russian people never lost their connections with God.

We have never had God as a conscious part of any of the leadership development curriculum of FGI. However, a consciousness of a loving, Higher Being is always present.

## CHAPTER SEVENTEEN

# Russia's New Young Leaders

We often discuss the participants who received the greatest gifts and learning from FGI and FGISpirit[15] Programs. In Russia, it was the three of us: Carol, Tim and Denny.

During our many years in Russia, we learned about the country, its culture, its history, its people with hearts of gold. We learned about the early transition from Communism to a form of "Crony Capitalism," where bribes, nepotism and assassinations were part of everyday business. Then there was experiencing up close and personal the development of the global economy as we worked with multi-nationals doing business in that exciting and often challenging environment.

In the mid to late '90s, managers and professionals in the US were feeling stressed about how to work effectively with members of their teams in remote locations. In the US we often heard, "If I can't be face to face, how can I effectively supervise?"

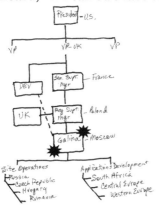

However, as we worked for a number of years in Russia almost everyone in a multi-national had a boss in another country. An excellent example of this would be Galina who came to LGLP (Looking Glass Leadership Program) from a large American company. She was an IT manager who officed in Moscow.

Here was Galina's organization chart

showing the multiple relationships. She reported to a Regional Superintendent responsible for the Commonwealth of Independent States (CIS)[16] locations. He was headquartered in Poland. This man reported to a Senior Superintendent headquartered in France who reported to a Vice President in the UK who reported to the organization's President in the US. Galina also had dotted line reporting to a technical center in England.

Reporting to Galina were development offices in South Africa, Central Europe and Western Europe. She also supervised operations sites in Hungary, the Czech Republic and Romania. Galina was about 33, on the job for eight years. She loved juggling her priorities among bosses, offices and team members.

In 2010, US clients were still telling us that it is ineffective to have team members at remote locations. With her attitude and experience, Galina made it seem easy and ordinary. As we observed her during the Looking Glass,® Inc. business simulation, her ability to communicate easily and often with every other person by phone, mail or in person, seemed to allow her to operate with ease in cross-border business relationships. This made us think about the many US managers struggling to supervise people in other cities or states.

After much consideration, we understood possible reasons it was much easier for Russians to work with a greatly disbursed team than equally bright Americans with similar responsibilities. It seemed to us that there were three reasons.

First, the young Russian professionals were introduced to this way of working from Day One. Communism was gone. They entered their professional careers in an emerging market economy where cross-border teams were the norm. They had no other experience so learned to make it work.

Also, those who had lived in poverty and with limited freedom developed a deep burning desire to be successful. They also knew they had to support large extended families. They adapted to what ever was expected.

Additionally, many in the US were used to organizations modeled after a military structure of the 1940s. In this model, the manager was geographically close to her/his people and would oversee them directly.

We were given the opportunity to provide the Looking Glass Leadership Program over 50 times in Moscow. The incredible participants always told us they had learned so much. However, we were never sure if it was they or we who were learning more.

Prior to our work in Russia, our experiences outside the US were few. Yes, Carol had lived in Turkey where she taught mathematics, but these were American Military men who were her students. This work for many years in Moscow was different.

In Russia, our teachers were our students – women and men business professionals from Russia, France, the Czech Republic, the Netherlands, the United Kingdom, Romania, Moldova, the Ukraine, Turkey, several of the Central Asian Republics and even China, Canada and the US. Each was there representing the thousands of multi-nationals enjoying the flourishing Russian economy of those days.

Our participants were mostly young women and men holding leadership positions in fast growing companies. People in Western economies holding similar positions were typically ten to fifteen years older than the young people we worked with in Russia. In Moscow, Western multi-nationals set out to hire only bright, young people. They insisted on employees who had no "Soviet baggage." This meant they wanted young professionals who had never worked in a business during the Soviet period and thus had no familiarity with how work was done (or not done) then.

In addition to our regularly scheduled open enrollment programs, we had two contracts for custom programs offered for specific client groups. The first was for Unilever, a global foods company headquartered in the Netherlands. The second was for the coal subsidiary of Severstal, a Russian company, one of the largest vertically integrated coal and steel companies in the world. Both were new clients for us, though Unilever "tested" us first in the open programs.

We passed the test! Unilever then asked us to develop a special version of LGLP for their top 90 middle managers. We were sure not to repeat our earlier mistake with the beverage company. We wanted to learn more. This meant we toured a mayonnaise factory in Moscow and interviewed the HR team, then agreed to move forward. That mayonnaise factory was built before the Great Patriotic War (World War II in the US) and therefore not exactly new, but still taught us much.

Those four FGI/CBSD Unilever programs brought us some of the brightest, most energetic young managers a company could hope to have. Though only in their thirties, with women in the majority, the participants made every program a delight.

The most exciting results were that every program produced the same attributes! Our main corporate client, Frank, was pleased with our report. However, he and we agreed these bright young Russians brought their own fast-moving, free-flowing culture. The old European company had a culture at odds with these bright young leaders. This was another primary learning for us. Older, well-established US and European companies with well-known, market leader brands had cultures in which bright young leaders felt their "wings had been clipped."

This experience highlighted the challenge for multi-nationals who promoted young managers to positions of significant responsibility and then continued to closely manage them as though they were entry-level employees. The young managers believed their positions should have considerable freedom to act, even though they did not have the seasoning of managers at similar levels in more mature markets.

Another learning experience came through our work with Severstal's Coal Division. This was our first opportunity to work within an old Russian company. This company was in a basic extraction industry. The group of participants stretched us with a mixture of senior men who had been with the organization for many years plus young women and men who were much like those from Unilever.

The culture the group created was hierarchical and certainly more traditional. The younger women and men wished for more openness in communication and more freedom to act. The more seasoned employees felt more comfortable with a top down approach. We understood we were seeing a microcosm of the country itself. The Russian country was, and had been, in a deep change since the moment we first arrived in 1992! History was being made before our eyes.

✎   ✎   ✎

Through the early years, the Center for Creative Leadership had developed international performance norms for the Looking Glass,® Inc. simulation. We were able to show participants their results compared to participants in other parts of the world.

We were initially surprised to see Russian participants performed far better than participants from the US. Although the simulation was based on a US company and American participants were used to the business processes for decades, the young Russians with whom we worked were doing better at the simulation than peers in the US. This was true, despite their limited experience and no tradition of capitalism.

Eventually it became clear to us that the significant variables were the quality and level of education that these young Russians and others from the CIS countries received under the Soviet system. In the mid 1990s – early 2000s, Russian participants typically had multiple degrees, often in scientific and engineering professions. We also had many middle managers from multi-nationals who had PhDs.

At the same time, the Russian culture was one that relied heavily on relationships to do work. Thus, our participants were capable of making good decisions once they felt a connection to the members of their teams. These professionals took the simulation very seriously. It was a pleasure to observe them and debrief their performances.

In the late '90s and early 2000s, the Russians we saw were, on average, better educated and smarter than their peers in the US. It could have been a clear competitive advantage. However, tragically, the old Soviet education system quickly collapsed for lack of resources. The young Russians from 2004-2007 were scoring comparable to Americans in the simulation. The edge was gone.

≈   ≈   ≈

The stories we could tell about experiences with LGLP would fill a book by themselves. For example, in one early program we had several Mary Kay leaders in a group. On that occasion, the simulation became primarily a marketing company as the Mary Kay women inspired all their peers.

On another occasion we had two young men from Intel. Earlier we were asked to assess the two of them for their Company, to determine their long term potential. It was clear from our assessment work plus the experience at LGLP that these young men WERE high potential. A few weeks after they were in the program, Alexei was transferred to Palo Alto to take an assignment at Corporate Headquarters. A couple years later he was the first Russian heading an Intel operation in Russia.

Another person who also became a lifelong friend was Elena. When we met her she was marketing for RJ Reynolds. Shortly after, she was hired by Clorox to take a job in California. When she came back to Russia several years later, she was to take the COO role for the company that had the contract to construct a new city south of Moscow. It would be the education and healthcare capital of the country. Elena now lives with her daughters in Walnut Creek, California. In 2003, she came with us to China and was one of the keynote speakers at our *Commons Café* in Shanghai.

Maria was one of the best-educated, most intelligent persons with whom we ever worked. With a Ph.D. in Nuclear Physics, she was in a key role in the Soviet Union. When the Soviet Union dissolved, Maria was selected to head the Russian operations of the Pioneer Fund investment advisors. She began her work knowing nothing about investments. But such a quick mind!

A year later we had Maria join a different program that used the Clare Graves Spiral Dynamics® theory. The SD theory, which we have used for thirty years in the US, is quite complex. Many Americans have trouble initially understanding the nuances of the theory. Maria and other Russians understood the theory instantly.

Galina Smirnova was a young woman from HP when she came to LGLP. Within a year she became head of Accenture Russia, probably the youngest female General Manager in Russia. While many women held management positions in the multi-nationals in Russia, almost none rose to the top ranks. Galina remained a friend of ours throughout the rest of our years in Russia. We would see each other at least once a year. So we watched as she grew in stature in the business community, gave birth to two children and blossomed in all aspects of her life.

Perhaps our most famous student was one of the so-called Oligarchs.[17] Gregory was an intense young man, holder of advanced degrees in nuclear physics and owner of multiple enterprises. He came to the program to find out if he was truly a world-class leader. Because he arrived daily in an armored car with security guards, it was a bit unnerving for some of the participants.

He was a delightful participant who was active in all parts of the program – with one exception. During the week of the program, the participants have a big reading assignment to prepare to run the company. Gregory did not do his reading himself. He had members of his real life staff do the reading. They then briefed him on the content before the program day began. He was always on top of every issue.

His peers elected him to be President of the Looking Glass Company. In that role he excelled, proving he was a world-class leader. At a point during the day, one of the other participants made up information in order to get a decision to go his way. When Gregory heard this, he called the participant to his office. Gregory looked at him with an icy stare and then said, "If this were real life, I would see to it that you would not be here." We all knew what he meant.

On the last afternoon, one of his security detail came into the classroom and took Gregory out into the hall to tell him something. A minute later he returned to the room and announced regrettably, "I must go early because President Yeltsin has summoned me on an urgent matter. Thank you for all you have done for me." Then he kissed Carol's hand and disappeared.

And for a final story, we remember Amal Chakir. Amal was born in Morocco of a Moroccan Dentist father and a Russian woman that her father had met while studying in the Soviet Union. Amal was educated largely in Russia and was trained to be a dentist as well. But she decided business offered more allure, so became affiliated with Lens Master.

Lens Master was the brainchild of an Iranian and an American. At the time, it was impossible to buy stylish eyeglasses in Russia. All that was available were what you could get from the old Soviet stores. So Lens Master began to build dispensaries. Amal was the COO, responsible for all dispensaries. During the eight years we have known her, Amal opened over 100 eyeglass dispensaries in all parts of Russia. Her energy has been amazing to behold.

During LGLP, we told her that she needed some other stimulus in her life to allow her to decompress from time to time. We suggested she do something that would be perhaps outrageous and something she had never done before. Several months later we received a photo of Amal parasailing over Rio de Janeiro. While doing so much for Lens Master, she has also married and given birth to a child. Amal traveled to China for our *Women's Leadership Program* in 2009.

~ ~ ~

Because we provided LGLP over fifty times, we could tell you interesting stories about well over a thousand women and men we met during the program in Moscow. We were able to see the re-birth of Russia through their life stories.

Through the eyes of these young leaders, we watched the City of Moscow transform. In 1992, it was a dingy city with long lines everywhere waiting to buy food and non-existent merchandise. By the early 2000s, it was a City where everything was for sale, where most of the City sparkled with remodels, where crime was exploding, where conspicuous wealth was to be seen everywhere.

One day while out exploring the Center of the City, Denny and Tim turned an unfamiliar corner and found themselves in a dead end street that featured a Bentley Dealer, a Ferrari Dealer, and a series of designer brand clothing and jewelry stores. The security guards looked them up and down. They would probably not have allowed Denny and Tim to enter, because they were not the kind of customers the owners wanted!

When we first came to Moscow, there were two colors to be seen: gray and brown. Everything was run down, collapsing. This was the world in which the young women and men we had in LGLP grew up. By the turn of the Century, it was hard to find gray and brown anywhere. The City was alive in every possible way.

By the time we would end our work in Russia in 2007, it was as glamorous as San Francisco, as alive as New York, as expensive as London and as beautiful as Paris. It is easy to understand why young leaders felt the urge to purchase an expensive car or designer jewelry. Think of how much adjusting our students in LGLP had to do!

Through all these years, while we were doing the most stressful and demanding program leadership and coaching we did anywhere, we were also soaking up as much of the culture of Russia as possible. Thanks to the love and leadership of our dear friend Tanya Smirnova, we probably had the most active arts lives of any Moscow natives.

One Sunday we traced the life of Boris Pasternak (author of *Dr. Zhivago)* from the house where he was born, to every place he lived including his dacha outside the City. We ended up at his gravestone in a country graveyard. At every stop we talked about what was happening in his life during the time he spent at that spot.

We visited the New Jerusalem Monastery where the original church had been built as a replica of the Orthodox cathedral in Jerusalem. The monastery had been the headquarters of the Nazi Armies when they laid siege to Moscow. As they withdrew, the Nazis largely destroyed this magnificent property. It has been under reconstruction for a dozen years.

A couple of miles from the Monastery we visited the site of an enormous tank battle that ended the siege. In an open field are hundreds of German and Russian tanks, guns and supporting vehicles, sitting exactly where they were destroyed during the battle nearly seventy years ago. The feelings Tim had while walking through that field were overwhelming. It was easy to imagine the carnage that happened on that day and ended the siege of Moscow.

For those living in Russia who were alive during The Great Patriotic War, their memories were as strong and clear as if the war had ended yesterday. Mercifully, the young women and men we worked with had only the stories of grandparents to remind them of this terrible period.

Perhaps the most enjoyable outing during all our trips to Moscow was the one we took to Leo Tolstoy's beloved home, Yasnaya Polyana, about 50 miles south of Moscow. We walked the beautiful grounds where he wrote so many of his books and essays; we saw the rooms where he slept, the table where he ate, soaking up so much of that amazing man's life. Several years later an American movie, "The Last Station," focused on the days of Tolstoy's life and was filmed at Yasnaya Polyana. We later reported to each other that each one of us cried while watching the movie with our families.

And there is no question about our most humorous outing. The night after an LGLP had finished, Tim managed to break a foot in his hotel room. He called Carol for aid in the middle of night. She supplied a spare pair of panty hose, which was used to wrap the foot tightly and reduce swelling. On top of the panty hose wrap were tied cold bottles of Fanta to also help with swelling and pain.

Despite this, Tanya Smirnova took Denny, Carol and Tim on an outing to Tsaritsyno the next day. This was a grandiose palace begun by Catherine the Great outside the City. The palace was never finished because of fights between the Czarina and the architects and builders. The area is now a beautiful park. Tim wanted to stay behind because he could walk only with great pain. Tanya said to not worry. She would handle it. How she handled it was by hiring a young woman who had a horse drawn cart. Tim was put into the back of the cart and transported all over the vast estate. Keep in mind the cart was intended for a couple of small children. Then put Tim in the cart and imagine how the scene looked. But otherwise it was a typical outing: beautiful setting, historic buildings each with a story, picnic in a grassy area, lots of cultural lessons from Tanya, lots of laughter with Tim, a late drive home.

The following week we provided an LGLP at CBSD, then returned to Omaha. Later, Tim's doctor said, "How could you possibly work? You have at least three broken bones in your foot." While it was a good question, there was never a question about us working. A new classroom of Russians was gathered; the adrenaline kicked in and we all made it through.

In 2001, our LGLP was given an award for being the Best Leadership Development Program in Russia. The award came from an on-line survey of human resources directors at companies in Moscow. It was an honor to receive the recognition and certainly helped CBSD market the program. But for us, the real joy came from our experiences with the Russians.

We learned more, had more fun and made more friends during our trips to Russia in the '90s and early '00s than we could ever describe. The capacity of the Russians to endure pain and oppression, to remain deeply spiritual, enjoy life, despite all that was happening to them was incredible. We each became stronger in our respective approaches to spirituality and more resilient as learners and teachers than we could have imagined. And there was much more to come.

CHAPTER EIGHTEEN

# Focus Comes of Age

*"FOCUS was as much a personal as well as professional*

*journey. It was a great feeling of validation that 'I'm OK.' There*

*are others in the business world who feel as I do. This was extremely*

*important to me. Today I understand myself so, so much better than I*

*did nine months ago. It was the single greatest period of internal change,*

*discovery, awareness in my entire life."*

- Dan, FOCUS 1991

From the beginning of the new decade, the men who came to FOCUS during the '90s were somehow different from those of the 1980s. Their responses to the program content were in many ways new to us. The changes occurring across the globe in the '90s made life seem better to most participants. We Americans had "won" the Cold War. The "American Century" was ending on a positive note. Americans were pleased the US economy was growing. Men participating in FOCUS were in the group whose income was rising and whose prospects were very positive.

Steve was a participant who joined FOCUS to improve his leadership skills and left wanting to experience the world. A real IT guru, he felt there was more. In 1992 and 1993 he accompanied us to Russia. Shortly after, the whole course of his life changed. He and his wife moved to Italy and later to

Thailand, finding work that nurtured him while he experienced the changes going on around him in the world. Later he returned to the US and joined the administrative staff of Duke University.

His passion for refugees became the driver in his life. Today he continues to help dozens and dozens of refugees from Southeast Asia find ways of living new lives in the US. His work both delights and humbles us.

The old notion of career had changed. Things were new. Apparently, one's career would require working for multiple employers and taking care of oneself. At the same time, there were more People of Color and Euro-American women competing for professional and management jobs previously held almost entirely by White men.

In their homes, more FOCUS men had partners with full time jobs. The approaches to family life now required a different role from men. Society seemed to expect them to develop their sensitive side, claim all parts of themselves. This was the decade of the "men's movement." Authors like Robert Bly[18] held seminars in the woods across the country to help men truly "discover themselves."

We remember many conversations at FOCUS (and elsewhere) about how the men's movement was not a part of the reality here in Omaha or Denver but instead for other men far away. That may have been true, but whether individuals embraced the movement, it had major impact on men as a whole. Just the encouragement by authors such as Bly caused men to think about topics that had never occurred to them.

Because the economy was growing in a healthy way for most of the '90s, evidence of the change came as FOCUS men could "focus" on themselves and their families. This resulted in many discovering new aspects of who they were, with a commitment to further develop who they really were.

The "fellowship" which Bly and others shared, became a

characteristic of FOCUS in the '90s. One group in the Denver program became so close that they stayed in each others' lives long after the formal program ended. They continue to meet on the first Saturday of every month even to this day.

Some men, however, seemed to insist there was no need to change. For this group, a few had the fear "Carol, Tim and Geil will make us hold hands and sing 'Kumbaya'." We never did!

Interestingly though, one of the men who had feared it the most, a corporate attorney for a large insurance company, eventually led the group in singing 'Kumbaya' to let everyone know he had been wrong. It was actually the one and only time in all the years of FOCUS programs we sang "Kumbaya."

These men seemed to go deeper, became more vulnerable and discovered many things about themselves that felt unthinkable in the '80s. Laughter and tears became a part of the FOCUS year.

Perhaps a short anecdote explains this. In the '80s, most participants would introduce themselves at the Retreat by telling us about their company and job. They would mention being married and having children. In the '90s, they would tell us a bit about their job and then talk about family and outside activities. We remember Bob from Salt Lake City. He had a large family, and family was far more important to him than job.

Another result of the growing '90s economy was the number of men of Color sponsored for FOCUS. It increased dramatically. We also began to have homosexual men sponsored by their companies. We remember the year Tom and Dan were in FOCUS together. The group had several very tense conversations about homosexuality. And then learning to know the two gay men in their group helped them know there was nothing "wrong" with these men. For after all, they knew Tom and Dan! We could not have had this kind of conversation in the '80s.

One of our favorite memories is of Terry, an African American whose wife had given birth to a baby boy during the FOCUS year. He asked his FOCUS 2% Team to be godfathers at the Baptism. All of these men who happened to be White, agreed joyfully.

On a bright, Spring Sunday morning, the FOCUS 2% group, plus Tim, went to a Baptist Church on Omaha's north side. It was a memorable day for both the FOCUS men and the parishioners of the church. Most of those FOCUS 2% men said they had never before been to this part of the City. There is no better way to learn to value diversity than to experience it in a positive setting with positive outcomes. It was the joyous group participation in singing hymns, in hearing the "Amens" and in the loving welcome they remembered.

This day was a happy one. We grieve, however, for the hundreds of thousands of Omahans who are unwilling to venture into the part of our City which is majority African American. They are missing a lot. We had similar experiences of Whites in Denver and Phoenix who were sure they would come to some kind of harm were they to venture into the sections of the cities where many wonderful people worshipped, shopped and lived.

We believe the deepest learning for a FOCUS group came the year Barry was in FOCUS. Barry knew on the first day of the program he was dying from an inoperable brain tumor. His company had sponsored him because of his deep desire to have the experience. As the FOCUS year progressed, Barry became weaker and weaker. However, he remained firmly committed to being with the group. His contributions were always supportive, insightful and on target. Barry made it through FOCUS, but died just weeks after the program ended.

His funeral was an amazing and moving experience. Virtually all of the men were in attendance. The tributes to Barry and his life were many, heartfelt and moving. There was another set of tributes offered that were also very memorable. These were the tributes Barry's family offered to his FOCUS group.

The family said FOCUS had allowed Barry to approach death

with confidence, love and peace. They added that he had given enormous credit to those who had loved and supported him throughout his FOCUS experience. The family shared with us that their gratitude was unbounded for FOCUS. As we filed out of the church that day, we could only talk about how Barry had made a positive impact on our lives. To this day, a mention of Barry's name brings tears to our eyes, tears of joy.

All FOCUS participants have been expected to identify an area of personal or professional improvement and act on that area during the program. In the early years, the performance on these improvement initiatives was quite uneven. But in the '90s, the three of us introduced the concept of the 2% initiative: "the 2% that really matters." To ensure success for the individual, we had the men work in small "2% Teams" to support and coach each other through both the identification phase and the action steps. The results were often magical.

Over the years, we have seen FOCUS men accomplish amazing outcomes with their 2% initiatives, which is the same as the 2% initiatives for INFLUENCE described earlier. There was the lawyer who decided to return to his music in order to bring more balance to his busy life. He composed and performed an original composition which included references to each member of his group.

There was the engineer who was working so many hours that he felt he was missing time with his young son. He asked the boy to help him remodel the basement. He created a video showing the moment his son broke through the basement wall with a sledge hammer, so he and his dad could finish their shared remodeling project. The smile on the boy's face was beaming. The entire group then heard the boy say, "Thanks for letting me help, Dad!"

Perhaps the most remarkable 2% initiative was chosen by a man with major management responsibilities in a large health care system. He came in to talk with Tim about his initiative in January. He told Tim that he had not yet been able to get his hands around the 2% initiative – so many choices with nothing standing out.

Tim told Bob that since he had been so successful with career and family up to that point, the question he might want to look at was "What will be the 'Big Project' for the rest of your life?" Bob said he couldn't imagine what it might be.

Tim's response was that Bob was so gifted he could have a significant positive impact on the world. So he suggested Bob could continue doing what he was doing, clearly an effective use of his energy. Or he could stretch himself to imagine what could be a "Big Project" that would give meaning to the rest of his life if he decided to take it on. Either decision was a good one.

Bob went away to think about the conversation. We had often told the men an excellent way to get perspective on a challenge or opportunity is to get physically removed from the current situation. You can then clear your mind and really imagine what is in your best interest.

Bob acted on Tim's suggestion. Both Bob's church and his employer were active in Tanzania. They were working to expand healthcare services in the district of Kilimanjaro. So he joined a trip to Machamo Lutheran Hospital, Moshi Tanzania.

He returned to the United States and decided his "Big Project" would be in Africa. A few months later he returned to Tanzania, where he remains to this day living in Machame, Kilimanjaro. Bob is home several times a year to be with his family. However, his life's work is in Tanzania.

He continues to receive financial support from his former employer as well as clinical volunteers who work for short periods throughout the year in Africa. Bob has built multiple clinics, has improved the care of HIV+ and AIDS patients and has greatly raised the quality of care in the surrounding area of Tanzania.

In the last two years, he has expanded his work by building small houses for families affected by HIV who live in villages near the clinics. Bob has completed over sixty homes and has raised the money to build over a dozen more. He is a White man who has become a part of daily life in Tanzania.

Perhaps a "capstone" of FOCUS experiences with the 2% initiative came in 2012, when we received a note from Mark, one of the FOCUS men of the '90s. He wrote to tell us that he had just completed his Ph.D. His dissertation examined how organizations develop and market energy efficiency services. Because he works for a utility, his research is directly applicable to his work.

What is more important to this story is that in his research he discovered his true 2%. And as he said in his note, "Thank you so much for laying the foundation (in FOCUS) that supported my search for truth and meaning. With love, Dr. Mark." For some, the concept of "the 2% that really matters" is elusive. For most it has had a significant impact on their lives as men.

The three of us, Carol, Tim and Geil, continue to marvel at all the men of FOCUS have accomplished and how deep they have gone. They have been successful in their careers. Most have consciously worked to become better husbands and fathers. Many have increased their sensitivity and ability to relate and to feel. Statistically, some of this is measured by the changes we see on the assessment questionnaires they complete as a part of FOCUS. But more is our professional judgment as we work with one group after another.

The FOCUS programs in both Omaha and Denver were very special throughout the 1990s. We learned much from these men about the potential for positive change in our country and in our world.

## CHAPTER NINETEEN

# Open Your Mouth and Say, "Ahh . . ."

It was November and the two of us had been invited to a lovely resort in Florida to speak at the annual meeting of a large healthcare system. We received a warm, professional welcome.

The CEO's goal was to ensure attendees understood how important it was for the System to undergo major change in the coming years. In our remarks, as always, we began by speaking about global/national trends and the direct impact these would have on US healthcare.

Some in the audience were skeptical US healthcare would soon experience as much change as we were suggesting. These professionals had been in healthcare all of their lives. There were many others, however, who wanted to speak with us after our remarks to determine how this System would need to change in order to be a healthcare leader for the future. Most of those who spoke with us seemed to clearly understand and sincerely wanted to move the System into a continuing positive future. One of many things we learned in working with healthcare leaders throughout the '90s was that many of them knew exactly what was coming and what needed to be done to be ready. Taking the actions necessary were sometimes resisted by physicians, other times by nurses and/or other professional groups.

Later that day, many outings were scheduled for attendees. Nearly twenty-five of us ended up on a large catamaran in the Gulf of Mexico. Along on the outing were the Chair and Vice

Chair of the Board of Directors, our client the CEO and a number of others.

While we moved across the water, we couldn't help but watch the Chair and Vice Chair. We heard much about them from our client, the CEO. We wanted to understand for ourselves more about the distance between the CEO and the Board Chair.

Carol leaned over and whispered to Tim, "Have you noticed the Board Chair? She looks quite agitated. I'm not feeling it was our presentation. She and I had a very nice conversation immediately afterword and she said our remarks were very relevant and useful. But, just watch how she looks at Bob (the CEO). I'm concerned about this and where Bob stands."

After glancing in that direction again, both noticed the Chair with a small group of Board members sitting with heads together talking and now and then glancing at Bob. Tim said, "Yes, it looks like they are giving a performance appraisal of the CEO with their eyes. He is not receiving a high rating."

We then remembered the meeting we had with the CEO only one month earlier in his office. After working directly with him for several years, it was clear that he was a true visionary and had the courage to take actions others in his position may never have attempted. During our work with this Health System, we had the occasion to meet some of the members of his Board of Directors. After only a few hours of conversation, with questions and answers going both ways, it seemed clear to us that the Board did not have the readiness or understanding Bob and the majority of his key executives had for significant change.

On that day in his office, we slowly, clearly and directly as possible told him, "Your Board is not ready to go where you want to take the System. You need to spend more time talking to the key members, explaining, educating, informing, helping them understand what you are seeing and what you are proposing. You may also want to slow down the change process."

Bob quickly responded, "Don't worry. I can persuade my Board to approve this. I know it is right and they trust me." Unfortunately, the two of us let the issue go and continued our work, rather than working harder to dissuade Bob. The months following the Florida meeting were filled with growing tension between Bob and the Board. Less than a year later he was asked to resign.

Despite the excellent work Bob and his Executive Team had been doing, the major change process was aborted and the System reverted to "business as usual." But this didn't last long. Unfortunately, within two years, the entire System no longer existed. Some hospitals were sold, others merged into different Systems. The Board ceased to exist. Had Bob successfully dealt with the Board and Sponsors, his excellent vision might still have come to naught, because the client system wasn't ready. But we will never know.

What we do know is as consultants, we can only provide our best advice and be there for our key clients in both good times and not so good. We have to stay up to date on what's going on in a variety of fields including business, healthcare, education, manufacturing, transportation and telecommunications. Still, the close relationships we develop with our clients make situations such as the one with Bob, very painful. Our conversations in the weeks following Bob's resignation turned into some excellent learning moments for all three of us.

This story is illustrative of some of our experiences in working with healthcare systems in four different states over a decade. It reminded us how fragile life can be for leaders when powerful stakeholders fear change. While many of our consulting assignments in healthcare had positive outcomes, this is not the only case where a healthcare leader we knew lost her/his job for attempting to do what was needed to prepare the organization for the future. It was the right thing but the wrong time for that particular health system.

∝ ∝ ∝

We've had the opportunity to work at close levels side by side with healthcare teams who became long time friends. We remember one assignment that found the two of us, plus our FGI colleague, Gene Morton, in a rather interesting hands on situation.

We were gowned and waiting as scheduled at the Emergency Entrance of the medical center as the ambulance pulled up. The patient was rushed through the admissions process and taken quickly to surgery prep. The three of us were following closely behind the action, taking notes: How many people interacted with the patient? Where did he have to wait and for how long? Was he asked the same information more than once?

Our goal: to chart different clinical care paths in order for the Hospital to improve those paths for greater safety, improved patient outcomes and lower cost. Using the findings from our observations, we worked with teams of healthcare professionals in order to develop new critical paths for patient care.

Soon the three of us were in the student viewing room, behind the glass window, staring into the operating suite. The surgeons and nurses were busy preparing to do a heart cath. The doctors began the incision. Soon the cavity was open. The three of us wondered as blood began to spurt. Is this what we expected to see? What were we doing there? We calmed down and reminded ourselves the reason behind this: to learn, to observe and capture the process. We went back to gathering our data.

We watched with awe and amazement what our clients considered their routine day of work. Once the surgery was complete, we followed the patient to post-op, then to the doorway of his room. We stayed there for three hours, noting when and how often nurses and other caregivers provided care and what they did. We then checked on his progress the next day and did additional data gathering. When the time came, we stood a discrete distance away as he completed the discharge procedure. Once we compared our notes, we felt we had as complete a record as non-healthcare professionals could create. It was the process we were attempting to capture.

For several days, the three of us followed many patients, usually one-on-one. We observed a variety of different processes and procedures. After all those observations, the real work began. Gene joined us at the office for weeks of analysis of all we had seen and heard. We were able to distill hundreds of pages of handwritten notes. Gene brought great professional expertise in the technical aspects of clarifying role accountability.

The three of us had a great time deciding the meaning of the many things we experienced. Because the technical aspects of healthcare were not our area of expertise, we had to be very careful in our examination of the data and the preparation of our findings and recommendations.

Our information became input for a team of nurses and other healthcare professionals who would map the path of these procedures and many others. The goal was to identify and control observed variances in order to develop effective critical care paths that could be used for each procedure. There were hundreds of such procedures in the medical center. We offered the teams a process and facilitated their work. It wasn't easy, and each critical path took weeks of fact-finding, discussion (often heated) and decision-making by the teams.

Many of the clinical leaders on these teams understood the process and became real champions of improvement. Especially key to the success of this work was the nurse manager from surgery who could get the attention of everyone in the hospital because she was known for great clinical excellence. When we met with her, she came to understand the technology we were bringing to the hospital as well as we did.

There was a pharmacist who clearly understood one of the major shortcomings in patient care was the ability of the pharmacy to provide accurate and timely service to patients. He was dogged in tackling the reasons for the gaps in service. A head of hospital housekeeping was able to point out the many ways her employees' work was sabotaged by clinical professionals who then complained about the quality of housekeeping.

Sometimes we felt as if we were running interference between the teams and the stakeholders in the hospital who were not sure about the work. We began to meet with groups of physicians, plus leaders of many other professional disciplines in order to include all those who were involved in each path. We often came face to face with the hierarchy in healthcare.

Because we were from "the outside," we could say things to physicians that "insiders" would never be willing to say, fearing retribution. We found our sessions with the doctors among our most enjoyable. It seemed to us they desired direct communication with accurate and reliable information about the future. Often, our key client, the hospital CEO, would wonder how we could "be SO straight" with physicians. We would wonder why some CEOs were afraid of the doctors. However, we also worked with some CEOs who lost the support of their physicians by being too assertive with them. Not being a part of the System was at times useful to us.

After many months of work, it was time to prepare a final report summarizing all of the role clarification and accountability decisions the teams had made. We both believe the report was one of the most difficult we ever prepared. It was also one of the most satisfying and one of which we are most proud.

The results from our clients' implementation of the System Redesign Report outlining critical clinical paths and accountability management were very positive. Outcomes and patient satisfaction improved; cost was reduced; professionals worked in interdisciplinary teams. We and our clients learned a great deal about negotiation, job clarification, system integration and outcomes management.

We both realize now each one of us also learned to be discerning and critical users of healthcare when it was needed for one of us or for our families.

∽   ∽   ∽

In many healthcare assignments, our being outsiders meant some practices in hospitals did not make sense. For instance, there was little standardization even within the same hospital concerning gloves, bandages and other supplies used on the patient floors. In one situation, we found big stockpiles of these items kept on the floors, rather than in a central materials storeroom.

When asked, we were told different physicians often wanted different brands and types of supplies and the hospital provided whatever the doctors wished. Also, it was believed by many that the materials management staff could not be trusted to have needed supplies on hand. So some nurses felt forced to stockpile on each nursing unit. In the hospitals where we worked, materials or logistics management were foreign concepts. Hence, well meaning professionals did not have processes for dealing with supplies effectively.

It took little research to determine that standardizing similar items and purchasing them in larger quantities would reduce unit cost. It was also easy to determine a Materials Management group able to provide supplies whenever needed would eliminate the need for unit stockpiles and would save a lot of money. However, getting the parties involved to agree to try a new approach took nearly a year of negotiating inside one hospital. As in most change efforts, it wasn't about the quality and validity of the new approach. It was about different professional groups learning to trust one another and believe they could count on the others to deliver on promises they made. It was all about trust.

In the two different Systems where we supported better logistics management, the savings on basic supplies were in the hundreds of thousands of dollars a year.

Thus, another important learning in healthcare as in other

industries was how to serve groups in developing respect and trust. Of course, we had to have processes client groups could use to effectively bring about healthy change. We had to be able to study and recommend appropriate actions for organizations to respond to future challenges. We needed the understanding of business and organizations. But all of these were secondary. Most important was providing insights and offering processes so different individuals and groups learn to value and trust one another.

As it became more apparent that healthcare costs need to be controlled, our clients sought our help in reducing costs while improving outcomes and patient satisfaction. While this was sometimes a daunting task, in others it came fairly easily. In one Health System, we were able to see examples of collaboration, patient focus AND cost effectiveness. At a hospital in south Texas, the Practical Nurses (LPN), Nursing Assistants (CNA) and Phlebotomists were being trained to do more of the tasks previously reserved for RNs. This allowed the RNs more time to do case management, coordinate all aspects of the continuum of care and increase quality of outcomes.

There was enthusiasm for these changes because it allowed all three levels of nursing as well as other professions to take on higher order tasks than they had in the past. The hospital was able to improve quality and reduce cost by having tasks done by professionals in lower pay grades, once they had been trained.

In this particular hospital, the Medical Staff had been a part of the decision to cross-train and more effectively utilize all members of the care team. We were working with the Corporate Team to find effective ways to turn this "pilot" into a process for all the hospitals in the System.

One of the great frustrations in working with healthcare was when clients wanted to become more patient-health focused, but this desire was thwarted by the way in which payment came to providers. Both insurance and government payment plans incented procedures regardless of their efficacy. Patient outcomes were not important to the reimbursement equation. The consequences were often increased payments for the volume of services provided whether the patient became healthier or not.

Because our clients always had high capital and human investment costs to cover, they sometimes resisted improvements that would jeopardize those payments. It was and is clear to us that there is substantial waste and inefficiency in the Health System in the United States. But this waste and inefficiency will remain until the reimbursement system is changed.

One of the great strengths of the US Healthcare System we admire is that the various professional groups focus on continuing education to maintain and upgrade their excellence. However, in some of the healthcare organizations, there was little or no focus on leadership and management development. Effective development of key leaders is critical to dealing with future change. The positive result: we were often invited to provide specific tailored programs to fit the unique needs of healthcare that could be used with both existing and high potential future leaders. It was impossible to simply substitute a program meant for a business-focused corporation because the nature of the work was very different.

We have always loved designing and tailoring creative leadership development programs for specific client Systems. One of our favorite FGI programs continues to hold a significant place in our memories. We were asked to design a leadership development program for a leading hospital. We gave the program the name *Moving Beyond Boundaries: Building High Performance Individuals and Organizations.* It was aimed at the development of high potential healthcare professionals representing all the disciplines in the hospital. It brought management level pharmacists, nurses, housekeepers, planners, nutritionists, medical records specialists and others together for six two-day sessions over a period of six months in an intensive development experience.

We designed the program along with two internal professionals, Kathy and Ginger. We spent many hours with them talking about the possible alternatives for design.

We led the initial groups in order to train Kathy and Ginger for future groups and also to fine-tune the design. Following the first two groups, they led the other offerings of the program. Two hundred fifty professionals were developed in ten separate groups over eighteen months. Graduates of the program continue to confirm the value of their experiences with comments and letters now fifteen years later. It made a significant difference in our understanding of and appreciation for outstanding health professionals and the challenges they face.

We thoroughly enjoyed our time with the first two groups. They were great students, incredible professionals and wonderful people. While the learning environment was serious, the learners had great senses of humor and we often had fun. As we look back on our years of working with this particular hospital, serving to develop a successful approach to leadership development is one of our proudest achievements.

Perhaps the most gratifying work we were invited to do was design and then facilitate sessions where large mixed groups of administrators, doctors, board members and key health practitioners could develop large System change efforts.

Such sessions included: assisting two Health Systems to identify issues and begin work on a merger; helping another large System re-design its corporate services so that the hospitals and clinics in several states could be effectively led through a process of change; helping a hospital determine key accountabilities and performance measures for each and every management position. In these cases, we worked with groups that ranged in size from 50-100. We were invited to be part of new and exciting creative approaches to organization design and organizational development. Just the kind of work we love. What could be better?

In each case, content included an assessment of the external environment, clarification of mission and vision, plus dozens of activities for mixed small groups of professionals to grapple with the often very contentious issues of change in healthcare.

It was not only exciting, but also incredibly satisfying to see large groups from multiple professional disciplines come together and create both plans and promises for the future of their organizations. We became true believers in large group design interventions. In truth, working with a group of seventy-five is not much more difficult than working with a group of a dozen – if those present are truly committed to the organization and its future.

Many of the wonderful women and men with whom we worked in those days remain close friends today. Our lives have been enriched by our work with them. It is important to mention that our colleague, Gene Morton, was very important to the success of our healthcare work. He brought both his personal energy and also valuable approaches to accountability management.

Our perspective on healthcare reform has been aided greatly by our experiences. And our learnings continue to this day. We look forward to the positive changes necessary for US healthcare in the coming decade.

Because healthcare is the subject of much national concern today it's easy for the two of us to reflect on what we've learned. First, we found more gifted, committed professionals and leaders in healthcare than in any other business area where we worked. These are women and men who gave 120% every day to insure positive patient outcomes and a successful delivery system.

Secondly, the US Healthcare System uses a paradigm so rooted in the past that significant change will be very difficult. This is especially true of any change that reduces delivery costs or improves outcomes.

We have seen amazing efforts to provide outstanding patient care. We have also witnessed scary examples of patient service failures. Finding a way to consistently provide outstanding care is very difficult but essential to the future of our country.

For us, our many years working in a variety of US hospitals as consultants was a constant period of learning and growing. That our work was recognized as useful and making a positive difference confirmed us. Additionally, what we learned from our healthcare work in theory, has often been transferable to other work settings.

## CHAPTER TWENTY

# A Deeper Dimension: FGISpirit

Restless, both of us were restless. We felt as if something was calling us, encouraging us to expand our work. We were given many opportunities, deep learning experiences and enormous thrills during our US and international travel of the past many years. We did what we often do when we need rejuvenation and insights of any kind: we sat silently. Each one of us meditated in our own way. After some time it became clear.

Meaning, it's time to bring more meaning into our lives and those of our clients and friends. The year 2000 was just around the corner. It was time to create again.

In the business sector, after many years of working mergers, downsizings, re-engineering projects, we sensed both organizations and their employees somehow felt our country was losing its way. The last ten years changed the work lives and even the work status of millions of working adults. We were grateful for excellent clients who were doing well. Our efforts were appreciated.

Work flowed to us more than we needed. But the human toll we observed in our client systems was obvious. Many of the "old rules" for being successful were no longer applicable. We could see capable and successful women and men losing energy, working under greater stress, while not feeling they could take the time necessary to have balance or satisfaction in their lives.

The days of "reengineering" were stressing human systems far beyond what was considered healthy. The growth in outsourcing to foreign countries was beginning to have significant impacts on US employers. Fear, even before 9.11, was already apparent in some of the companies who were our clients and others who were not. Many capable leaders shared that they wondered, "What does the future hold for me and my family? How hard must I work and for how long in order to be one of those who still has a good job?"

Clients confirmed our work in accountability management, successfully merging large organizations, downsizing, setting strategy and marketing plans. The leadership development programs INFLUENCE and FOCUS seemed to have been made for these changing times. The same was true of our work in Moscow. Programs were full and vibrant.

However, the human cost of the times kept calling out to us! Women and men were finding it more and more difficult to renew their own positive energy. If the US economy was to remain successful, it was important for talented leaders and professionals to be able to do their best.

Our path became clearer. We understood our new work must focus on renewing the essence of leaders who were daily giving so much of themselves. It was not about spas or vacations, it was about bringing meaning, self-love and consciousness back into their lives. It was the need to feed Spirit. This was always a part of our executive coaching work. However, it was not yet an overt part of our leadership development offerings.

It was clear to the two of us: without our work in Russia, we would not have understood this as readily. In so many ways, it was our Russian friends and clients who inspired us to give more of our intention and energy to creating lives full of meaning, lives with peace, lives with deep periods of silence. Both of us felt such a strong spirituality in the Russian people which then caused us to reflect on our own country. Why did spirituality emerge from the Russians more than those born and raised in the United States? It certainly wasn't about religion. The US is a country where religions are plentiful, active and supported. So, if not religion, then what was the source of the Russian spirituality we felt?

Two answers came through most strongly for us. From its earliest history Russians were people of the forest, engaged with the Divine through nature. Thus, every part of nature reflected the Divine and was infused in the Russian people. This preceded the beginnings of the Russian Orthodox Church, which was a primary guide of all classes of people for over a thousand years.

The second reason, we attributed to Soviet Communism during its 75-year history in Russia. Because Russian people were formally denied the practice of religion during Soviet times, something had to hold them together through those long, grueling years. It was their Spirit and connection to Nature, to one another and to the belief there is something deeper, something larger. This gave millions of people the ability to survive and remain whole. They survived persecution, poverty, starvation, the horrors of war and oppression by the government. We were keenly aware of that Spirit from our first day in Russia.

We made a few early efforts in sharing the concept of spirituality when providing short programs for INFLUENCE and FOCUS Alumni groups in Omaha and Denver. Initially, there was some hesitation and surprise. This turned into a few cases of resistance as we encouraged people to think about their spiritual (not religious) essence. This concept was quite new and there was a question about the relevance of spirituality to their work. However, most leaders seemed to appreciate taking time to think about themselves and what brought meaning to their lives. We encouraged them to read and reflect on works from spiritual teachers as well as read about the major spiritual traditions. We initially found it easier to introduce people to the five sacred elements or to the twelve *chakras* than to jump in with the essential question: "Who am I?"

We practiced short meditation, sacred silence and Reflection. Reflection and developing the Reflective Voice are used in every session of our INFLUENCE AND FOCUS programs. We asked participants to select one significant incident that happened to them since we last met, then tell us what they had learned about themselves as a result. The practice, while very simple, has profound influence on developing the individual. Many researchers say it is the biggest key to truly knowing oneself and thus to developing the individual as leader.

We introduced the concept of spiritual discipline to these groups of alums. Eventually, this approach took root. As people spent time clarifying, they began to feel a new sense of peace and meaning. Many asked for more ideas, more time to study and share together.

People expressed growing appreciation and began to share correspondence about their insights and new, more peaceful selves. There were a few, however, who were not happy. They seemed unable to accept religion and spirituality as two different things. In most of us, they may exist at the same time. Our intention was never to question or challenge religion. This is something very personal and has not been a part of our public work.

On one occasion, a professional woman we had known came to our office to criticize the work. "What right do you two have to be talking about Spirit? You aren't trained in Theology. You are not experts in comparative religions." Our response was fairly direct and simple: "Mary, we have no intention of teaching leaders about religion. Our goal is to invite leaders who wish to join us. Our shared goal is that each one of us will learn more about Self, discover aspects of our spiritual essence and find ways to enhance our lives by nurturing that spiritual essence." Mary left unsatisfied.

Suddenly, after dipping our toes in the few short workshops with alumni, we were ready to jump in at a deeper, larger level. It seemed only natural to invite our colleague, Geil Browning, to join us. We decided to design a longer program for a larger group.

We called the new program, *Finding Our Spiritual Path: Reflecting and Connecting (FOSP)*. *FOSP* was offered in Spring 1998. When we announced our plan, we had no idea whether it would attract participants. The three of us initially agreed twenty participants would be the minimum for us to hold the program.

Our uncertainty must not have been too great, however. The Universe began to provide. We were looking for the perfect location.

Carol, in her usual way, said, "Let's just put our clear, present tense intention out there and the right location will make itself known."

Within days, the US Mail delivered to the FGI offices, a brochure for a small, charming hotel outside Santa Fe, New Mexico. Sight unseen, Carol called and reserved the entire Bishop's Lodge with its 80 rooms!

Our intentions were clear, but there was still some trepidation as we sent out program invitations. To our surprise and delight, we had an immediate positive response. Over the weeks, this turned into one hundred twenty individuals who came from fifteen states and three countries! The demand for this program was evident.

We agreed the agenda would be crucial to the program's success. It would need to balance some proven activities with a number of new techniques and approaches to stretch and grow the three of us, the individuals and the community which would form. We were ready to receive the design tools as the vision became clear in our minds.

As always, all three of us, Carol, Geil and Tim, had many ideas. One of our many themes for the "work weary" participants who joined us was to reorient our participants' lives so that work became an expression of Spirit. Our belief was this allowed a person to express her/his intention for being present in all aspects of life. We believed this makes it easier for us as humans to attract and select work congruent with what brings inner meaning. The finished product included presentations, open space group work, singing, dancing, silence, meditation, individual and group art, drumming and much more.

With a certain amount of trepidation, we awaited the arrival of the first guests on a Thursday evening in April. Most were old friends or former participants in our programs. However, a significant number were new to us and were attending on the recommendation of someone else. The loving, genuine greetings we received as people arrived soon diminished our apprehensions. These old and new friends expressed gratitude in being able to find a place where they could really reflect on themselves as humans, as leaders, as family members, as citizens. And, they did this with joy, energy and a true depth of Spirit for the next three days.

Prior to this Santa Fe experience, Carol asked an expert in Sacred Dance from Creighton University to come to FGI to teach us how to lead large groups in Sacred Dance. The response from the *FOSP* group after the dance also surprised us. We planned to dance with the group once. However, due to the overwhelming requests, we ended up dancing at least twice a day to the song, "Morning Has Broken."

The three of us made opening comments every day as well as provided significant program pieces. We also asked several of our friends to work with us to take the program to deeper levels and to add to the richness of the experience. All of those people together added great value and understood our shared goals.

We asked Steve and Sara to provide music daily. Sara accompanied on the piano as Steve, his deep, beautiful voice filling the room, caused special energy and connection to something deeper. When Steve invited everyone to sing along, several of us commented we had never sung so well. Many people later told us just hearing Steve's voice took them to a new place of peace and joy.

Marcia and James began each day at the center table or "altar." They led a ceremony of sorts in which each person present placed an item of meaning in their lives. This provided positive energy and love for the group over the program days.

Our dear friend, Tatiana Ignashova came from Moscow. She spoke from her heart about Spirit as a Russian. The group went silent and deep. There were many tears of understanding as Tanya told her story and shared about her life and her beliefs. Her life had been tested. She emerged full of depth, wisdom, Spirit and love.

Our long time friend, Dave came with his beloved drums. As he led the group in drumming at night, the sounds were magical and went deep into the rhythms of our bodies and souls.

Additionally, our dear client and colleague, Carol, former Chancellor of the University of Nebraska Medical Center, was bold enough to share her own story of very personal struggles, speaking deeply on many levels. A huge group gathered around Carol after she spoke. It took a while to get the group back. The days were full of love, joy, connection and a true depth of collective wisdom and Spirit.

Results exceeded our wildest expectations – though we had entered with quite ambitious expectations. It has been many years since *FOSP*. Amazingly, people still share with us about the benefits they received. One of the special follow-up letters we received was from our dear friend and former client, Phil, who offered this commentary on the experience:

> "I thank you for having the courage (and that's what it is) to take the risk of putting on such a program, to reveal yourselves without the guarantee anyone else would

reciprocate, and taking the enormous amount of time to plan such an endeavor. I left Santa Fe feeling strong, confident in my path and excited about the new dimensions of my life I am exploring . . . You have touched my soul and kept alive my struggle to be honest and true to myself."

Buoyed with all that flowed to us as a result of this Santa Fe experience, it wasn't long before we took our second public step. We were invited to take part with Tatiana and her colleagues in presenting at the International Conference on Attitudinal Healing in Moscow, Russia. We worked with a group from several countries around the theme, "*Attitude, Stress Management and Healing; Reducing Life Stress.*" It was equally exciting, energizing and meaningful. Once again, Carol led the group in Sacred Dancing. There were several requests to repeat this throughout each day. As in all of our many experiences in Russia, we came home filled with joyful Spirits ready for the next adventure. Dreams filled our heads and hearts with what might be possible.

&#8766; &#8766; &#8766;

We both agreed our intentions were confirmed. We successfully engaged others in exploring the meaning of spirituality, not necessarily religion. Our participants were willing to consider how to bring true meaning into all aspects of life. It felt daunting when we realistically acknowledged our primary client base had always been corporations. Was it even possible for a larger public to understand bringing Spirit to leadership would in fact result in more meaningful, capable leadership? We were ready to find out.

We moved forward and decided it was important to create a new legal entity to enable this work. Within a few short months, we incorporated FGISpirit International as a 501(c)3 not-for-profit organization. The not-for-profit status would allow us to invite others to make tax-free investments in the work we would do in the area of spirituality in leadership. This would help get us started with our new "arm" of the FGI work.

We expected some of our current client organizations would be reluctant to sponsor participants for programs about Spirit. Initially, some may have been. However, we were delighted to find many were more than willing to sponsor participants for our programs.

It was essential to raise money from outside donors in order to keep fees low and to assist with scholarships for those who could otherwise not participate. We were blessed with generous investments by the Col Ro Mora foundation in Colorado, the Steele Foundation in Phoenix, the First Data Foundation in Denver, plus gifts from the Omaha Community Foundation and many generous friends. Gifts continue to this day. We, in turn, continue to give thanks and do our best to serve.

A new question now arose. We wrestled with what would be our first offering under the new banner: *FGISpirit*.

It was early 1999, the whole world was having Pre-Millennium Anxiety. Would something awful happen when the year 2000 arrived? Would computers stop, airplanes crash, all communications systems fail? Would people begin to realize the world was in a flux perhaps greater than at any time in history?

None of the negative predictions occurred. Still, not enough people had yet realized the world was and is in a tremendous flux in terms of becoming a whole new reality. However, the pre-Millennium focus inspired us to create the first FGISpirit offering: *The Millennium Project*. Our intent was to begin a conversation that would simultaneously allow participants to more consciously live as leaders of Spirit while exploring how they would actively influence the world of the future.

Part of the inspiration for *The Millennium Project* came from our experiences with the late Willis Harman. We were active in the early years with the Institute for Noetic Science (IONS) meetings. Willis' quote still inspires us, "Something as quiet as a change of mind is bubbling up . . . spreading around the world, changing everything." We intuitively knew this to be true.

The FGISpirit *Millennium Project* was actually two separate programs, both designed around one common theme: to consider the world of 2050 and prepare participants to contribute to the creation of a world that would truly work for all by 2050. It was our dear friend and colleague, Sharif Abdullah, Ph.D., who first used the phrase "creating a world that works for all."

The first part of the *Millennium Project* was a program, four sessions long, held in four different locations in the United States over a six-month period. This program, *Bringing Spirit to Leadership (BSL)*, began in 1999.

The second program was the *Millennium Pilgrimage*. It would be offered as a form of "pilgrimage" to visit sacred and historic sites in Russia, so long considered the enemy of the US. The Russia program also would include an intensive three-day gathering with Russian leaders to go deep on many subjects. We sent out formal invitations to one hundred former clients and participants in our FGI programs.

Twenty-four Americans from nine states joined us for *The Millennium Project Part I: Bringing Spirit to Leadership.* In designing the program, we wanted something never before offered. This required considerable time and complexity to create. What emerged was a unique world simulation, *"The Global Interaction (TGI)."* This simulation challenged participants to take a realistic look at various countries in the world and then "become" those countries as they "interacted" with other nations. The goal was to give our *BSL* participants time to experience living with the program's goal of creating a world that works for all. It was both a grueling and exciting undertaking.

When we created *The Global Interaction* in 1999, we wanted to develop a way to engage others in thinking more about global issues. It seemed it would also offer a new and different way to allow leaders to learn about the world and themselves. What better way to learn about leadership and the world than to give people the current facts about key countries and then ask them to be "leaders" of those countries and to work together solving significant issues. Just as we had long used the Center for Creative Leadership Looking Glass,® Inc. simulation, we found we can use *The Global Interaction* for leadership development.

Developing the simulation was simple: We selected fifteen countries in various parts of the world that seemed to have strategic roles to play in the future. Then we wrote a profile of each country, using actual financial and other statistical sources to ensure the profile was real and current. Based on those profiles, the major challenges facing each country were added to the respective profiles. Each country was given tokens of value reflective of their actual economic situation. These tokens represented raw materials and manufactured products for export plus knowledge and money that could be traded for things needed to meet the country's challenges. The goal was for all countries to work together to solve the problems of the world.

Program participants were assigned to represent the countries. Each delegation size was based on the relative sizes of the real countries. For example, China always has the largest delegation, Zimbabwe the smallest.

We assigned participants to the delegations, gave them information about their assigned country and asked them to prepare their goals and their strategy for how they would work and actually interact with the delegates from other countries.

In every case the participants have taken the work very seriously. When they are told to begin interacting, it is almost like the starting pistol had been fired signaling the beginning of a race.

Poor countries sought out help from rich countries. Rich countries decided whether they wanted to help the poorer countries or simply look to their own needs. Countries with similar traditions, religion or language often attempted to coalesce in dealing with others.

The United States, which is both large and very wealthy, was initially seen as the place to get help in solving problems of poverty or unrest. But the United States couldn't figure out how to meet the needs and/or demands of so many countries' requests. As a result almost every delegation decided that the United States didn't care for them and the US was then seen as "the problem" rather than "the solution."

After nearly an hour of attempts to negotiate, rejections, conflicts, several members decided that the world really needed to treat its problems globally. Paul, a delegate from one of the non-aligned nations asked the entire group to come together in a circle to consider a new way of managing the world. He was convinced that only by some reasonable sharing could the world be effective for the future. The response he received from most of the others came as a shock. The United States delegation was adamant they weren't getting involved in any redistribution of resources. Others agreed. The efforts at a form of world sharing collapsed.

When we finished the time of the simulation, participants were asked first to discuss what happened and then to decide what they learned about themselves.

The conversation was rich and very animated. Each delegation had opinions about the behavior of the others and why things had not worked out. Every delegation had words of criticism or blame for the United States – and sometimes for other delegations.

The three participants who had been the United States were visibly shaken by reactions to how the US had acted. They could not believe they were seen in such terrible ways by individuals who had liked them only hours earlier. These three from the United States were still talking months later about how they had been misunderstood and mistreated by the group.

The participants who tried to get the world leaders to meet and find ways to pool resources for the good of all were also dismayed at the reaction of the others. They couldn't understand why this approach was so quickly and decisively rejected. As Paul said during the debrief, "This is what I deal with daily: there is a large pool of money that if used well would do a lot of good for everyone. I have unbelievable patience for the process. Because I could see (that countries sharing would work), I thought all would."

Those who represented rich countries felt misunderstood. Those from poor countries felt ignored or abandoned or abused by the wealthier countries. As Steve, the delegate from Zimbabwe said during the debrief, "I knew that my country was nothing when even the delegate from Bulgaria refused to talk with me."

When we finally turned to personal learnings, they were both rich and powerful. Individuals discovered their behaviors during *The Global Interaction* were much the same in their normal lives as leaders. Some preferred consensus and became frustrated that other delegates totally rejected that approach. Some wanted to engage in win-lose negotiating. They found it worked sometimes and other times did not. Some believed in following the rules, others thought it was OK to break the rules. Just about everyone saw how she/he responded when under stress. And all agreed it was most important to learn much more about the world.

An unexpected benefit from *TGI* was an on-going discussion about what happened for the coming five months of the program. The learnings remained alive.

The United States team ended feeling no one appreciated their good intentions. They were right. No one did appreciate them and believed the US had acted selfish, aloof and disinterested. However, this was certainly not the case from our observation. All of us present for *BSL/TGI* 1999 understood clearly: those without enough resources to feed their people, to provide medical care or education, could easily believe countries with "plenty" were self-serving.

After that first simulation was over, Paul added, "We are in an apathetic stupor. We respond to the needs of others in a tribal manner. If we choose, it will happen. The distribution of resources has to coincide with some equality in the distribution of knowledge."

However, *TGI* continues to teach us and others even today.

*The Global Interaction* has been a regular part of our program *Bringing Spirit to Leadership* since 1999. Over the next fifteen years we observed exactly the same behaviors exhibited – though with one new twist. When we added more Islamic nations, we saw a tendency of those delegations to align with one another against countries like the United States and Germany. We continued to marvel at the ways in which American participants could so quickly act the way that countries from other parts of the world tended to act in real life.

That first *BSL* session also introduced participants to creative visualization, meditation, intention-setting plus a review of Spiral Dynamics.® According to the National Values Center, "Spiral Dynamics® is concerned with why we cooperate, collaborate and come to conflict over differences in values and the deeper value systems that form them." As FGI and FGISpirit, we have used Spiral Dynamics® with every INFLUENCE and FOCUS group and every *BSL* group. The theory has informed our lives and guided our work for over thirty years.

In *BSL*, the second, third and fourth sessions are each different from the other. In most cases, they are also different from anything participants have experienced before. The sessions include discussions of readings on leadership, development of spiritual disciplines from experts such as Thomas Merton, Wayne Muller, Roger Walsh, Deepak Chopra, Angela Arrian. We also introduce the practice of Sacred Silence to calm, center, as well as receive insights. A 360° feedback tool on elements of leadership often offers direction. And there's much more.

After completing the initial four sessions of *BSL*, we were both amazed and delighted by the responses from participants. The depth of sharing, the openness to learning new things, the quality of the learning community plus our genuine pleasure in working with this group brought us deep satisfaction.

In Sedona, the last formal session of our first *BSL*, participants would not accept the idea of *BSL* "being over." The result was their creation of The Wisdom Community, a leadership group in existence since that time, which continues to meet twice a year.

After the first *BSL* program, there was no time to bask in success. In five weeks, we were off to Russia for *The Millennium Project Part 2: The Russian Pilgrimage*. Twenty-eight Americans from six states came with us on the *Pilgrimage*. Nine of those had also been a part of *TMP-1*.

Phil Cousineau, in his book *The Art of Pilgrimage*, gave us these inspirational words: "Pilgrimage is a transformative journey to a sacred center. It calls for a journey to a holy site associated with gods, saints, or heroes, or to a natural setting imbued with spiritual power . . . Pilgrimage is a spiritual exercise, an act of devotion to find a source of healing, or even to perform a penance. Always it is a journey of risk and renewal . . . A journey without challenge has no meaning; one without purpose has no soul."[19]

With this definition in mind, selecting Russia as the destination for *TMP 2* felt perfect. We already experienced the spiritual power of Russia countless times in our seven years of work there, prior to the 2000 *Pilgrimage*. There were certainly a multitude of holy sites, saints and heroes. Additionally, since the Soviet Union had been the mortal enemy of the United States for nearly fifty years, there was a great opportunity for healing and for destroying preconceived stereotypes and outdated beliefs. All these factors offered each individual pilgrim vast opportunities for renewal.

The *Pilgrimage* was nothing short of life changing. Within a day of arrival, all of the Americans were amazed at the condition of Moscow. It was a glorious, modern city full of historical as well as modern conveniences. As Foster said during Reflections one evening, "I thought the Kremlin was the Headquarters of an enemy. I imagined a huge, ugly fortress. But instead, I find it is a place filled with beautiful churches. It really makes me think about all we were taught about the USSR as the evil empire."

It was true that as a country, the US considered the USSR and Russia our enemy. However, once in Moscow, those who traveled with us were learning every day and understanding how things had changed. Even by 2000, many consumer goods still were in short supply. The infrastructure was still clearly challenged. Despite the concentrated efforts of the Soviet Union to stamp out religion, Moscow by 2000, had returned to being a city of newly transformed churches. In fact, we learned one of the lovely, soft pink churches near Red Square had it's dome removed during Soviet times and was used as a wheat storage unit. However, upon our arrival it was an inspiringly beautiful church.

The two of us remembered the Russia we first encountered in 1992. In 2000, we saw through the eyes of others a whole new, shining, beautiful City. Were we too busy doing our work to have noticed? Or had it been a very gradual process and we were now seeing this changed Moscow through the new eyes of those who accompanied us to Russia? We felt homesick for those early days of first adventures in Russia.

Our US friends saw the Russian people as true magnets. The Americans sought them out, laughed with them, had long and deep conversations into the night, sang and danced with them and found deep meaning in their experiences. It was simply joy and Spirit flowing.

With the group, we visited one beautiful, meaningful site after another in five different cities: Moscow, St. Petersburg,

Vladimir, Suzdal and Sergei Passad. We quietly prayed, meditated or simply listened inside churches that were over 1000 years old. We saw jewels that belonged to Catherine the Great, experienced a wonderful opera at the Bolshoi Theatre, slept in cabins in a monastery in the woods and visited churches of The Old Believers (a sect outlawed for centuries). Many in the group sang in several beautiful Orthodox churches and all of us had lunch with the priest rector in the oldest monastery in Russia. A few "Pilgrims" even managed to get lost on the Metro. The experiences were never-ending.

What were the outcomes beyond an amazing trip to a very special country that had been virtually closed for seventy-five years? The outcomes were personal to each individual. They emerged from our daily Reflections. They appeared from alone-time jogging, walking or meditating. They returned from conversations with another American or with another Russian. For many these were life changing. For others they were affirming. Some received new and valuable insights about their present life intentions.

For us, the *Pilgrimage* confirmed our earlier intention to begin FGISpirit. We saw how the spirituality of Russia sustained the people of that country through seventy-five years, when religion as such was outlawed through the oppression and hardship of Soviet times. We observed how this experience allowed Americans to focus and deepen their own spirituality. We witnessed talented and successful US business leaders develop entirely new perspectives about the world beyond US borders. We also understood from many of the Russians we met how they developed new and quite positive impressions of the United States through their experiences with our group.

Nine months after we all returned from Russia, the American Pilgrims held a reunion to reflect on their Russia experiences and takeaways. Throughout the two and a half days in the Omaha FGI offices, we laughed and we cried. We told each other about actions each had taken in her/his life as a result of our time in Russia.

At the end of 2000, the two of us reflected on the first two years of our dedicated work on Spirit and leadership. There were still a few in our network who did not understand. There were some companies who could not see the connection to business. There were even two or three participants who decided, after a session with us in *BSL*, this wasn't for them. But overwhelmingly, people continued to discuss the countless benefits which came to them as a result of their *BSL* experience. In fact, there are now women and men who have been with us in the program more than once. They say it is always new because of where their lives are. We are privileged and blessed to be able to offer and partake in this meaningful work.

The restlessness we described at the beginning of this chapter has long been gone. Our work with FGISpirit seemed to enhance and also make all of our other work more significant. The management consulting and executive coaching became even more effective and meaningful. Our work with Geil in the INFLUENCE and FOCUS programs has continued to go deeper and have greater impact.

In our work in China we began to include the carefully articulated consideration of Spirit though the word was seldom used. Since our first year in China, some Chinese clients and friends have wanted to talk with us about Spirit by referring to developing one's essence, expressing care for others and giving back or making connections with a Higher Power.

Finally, the non-profit organization FGISpirit allowed us to begin a number of other programs in the US, China, Russia and India. Without FGISpirit, these would otherwise not have been possible. We continue to give thanks.

## CHAPTER TWENTY-ONE

# Once Around the World

Certain years stand out in one's memory. What makes this so? As we mature, the moments which stand out are often times of key learning. The learning is not always about a new concept, new information or a new adventure, though all three have usually been involved in FGI experiences.

Our work in Moscow moved forward with amazing experiences, plus a marvelous partnership/collaboration with Dennis Hopple and the Center for Business Skills Development. Contrary to the usual "dreaming forward" of Carol and Tim, we continued to delight in all of the excitement, learning, friendships and the new work opportunities Moscow offered FGI International.

That it is a very small world was impressed upon us over and over. It was never a surprise to have a new "Ah Ha" hit us in the face or in the gut on a regular basis.

The first eight years of our work in Moscow flew by quickly. The number of clients and/or organizations were now in the hundreds. Dennis smiled each time we offered a new program and CBSD grew some more.

We were enjoying our newest client, Mary Kay Russia, as they brought us a new set of experiences. The first to join us came in June 1998. The enthusiastic, young entrepreneurial women impressed us with their quick minds, driven work ethic and determined approaches to continued success. They surprised us with the news that Moscow was the Headquarters of Mary Kay Europe at the time. The market in Russia exploded for Mary

Kay!

We celebrated with them and planned our next trips to Moscow for the year 2000 and beyond. However, prior to our return to Moscow, Dennis's phone call came to us in Omaha.

With his usual, smooth delivery, Dennis asked, "How would you two like to go to China?"

Interestingly, in 1997, we decided to practice what we preach and immediately began to voice out loud our clear intention: "We are working in China within five years." We clearly believed by 2002, we would be in Shanghai or Beijing. We were inspired by Yi Fong Cai, at that time an INFLUENCE woman from Johns Manville in Denver, originally from China. During her INFLUENCE year, Yi Fong Cai took her first trip back home to China after ten years. Her stories upon her return only confirmed this was an important destination for us. We decided China was to be the next "frontier" for our FGI/FGISpirit work. Because it was only the year 2000, we were at first amazed when the invitation to China had come prior to 2002. However, both of us fully accepted and believed the Universe can be a powerful force in manifesting for those who have a clear intention.

The next chapter of our work in China was about to unfold, with no bidding, no planning, no strategizing. The Universe was at work on our behalf. We asked Dennis what he had done.

Dennis told us happily, "Oh, I did nothing. It was your students, the Mary Kay women, who did something!"

Yes, networks are amazing! In theory, they sound interesting, but not at all as amazing as they can be in real life!

What was the path of this unfolding intention?

Our Russian Mary Kay women clients in Moscow attended a larger conference of Global Mary Kay leaders. Bless their hearts, our dear Mary Kay friends and clients shared about "TimanCarol" and our FGI work. Chinese Mary Kay women also attending the conference, like young entrepreneurs everywhere, wanted more education, more knowledge. They wanted whatever the Russians experienced to become a part of their lives in China.

We both knew Dennis and Denny Aron would of course be a part of the FGI work. We four were a Team who had fun together, learned together and supported each other without anyone having to say a thing. Each one of us did whatever was needed to insure successful and meaningful experiences for our clients. Dennis had the contacts through his Thunderbird sponsored Center for Business Skills Development (CBSD) in Moscow. As fate would have it, the Arizona based Thunderbird University also had an extension in Shanghai. They were delighted to bring in a new company to their client groups and some new offerings for their markets. We began within a matter of weeks to correspond with the late Diana Last, at the time Director of China's CBSD and Dennis' colleague.

By this time in Moscow, the Center for Business Skills Development was a thriving business under Dennis' direction. The parent organization, Thunderbird University, Glendale, Arizona, saw the real benefits our work was bringing their clients. We were delighted to know there was also a CBSD, Thunderbird in Shanghai with a client list of Western Multi-nationals. Support was already on the ground, experienced in bringing US professors and teachers to China.

Once again, the two of us became students in order to serve as teachers in a new country. The preparations for our first trip to China required what Russia had required in April 1992. An important way the two of us learn is through reading. The Internet was alive but nothing like it is today. It was books about China: non-fiction and fiction that became our teachers. Though we read many books about Russia, we quickly learned from our long reading list that though it was impossible to believe, it seemed China could be a much more complex reality than Russia.

We set to work preparing for what might come our way in China. Our learning and reading took on new depths, new avenues of investigation and a new, deeper excitement than we knew possible.

The wheels were set in motion and life began to speed up. There was much to do prior to actually leaving for our first trip to the CBSD offices in Shanghai. We knew there were no guarantees this trip would bring work. Diana Last and the other CBSD staff in Shanghai were waiting to see how we did with our marketing meetings. We were just as eager to find out how it would all unfold.

Things seemed to fall into place in an amazing flow. We had a previously planned trip scheduled to provide our Looking Glass Leadership Experience in Moscow again in April 2000. Probably because we were eager to make things happen in China, we came up with the idea of making the trip to China part of an "FGI Around the World" April trip. Everything seemed possible to us.

Immediately following our last program in Moscow, we were ready for China. Flying from Moscow to Beijing was really quite an experience. As always, each one of us was exhausted from a long, demanding program with Dennis and Denny in Moscow. The past couple of weeks included the 40+ new Russian friends we worked with in our programs, plus the delightful outings offered to us by our dear friend Tatiana Smirnova with lovely family dinners with the Smirnov family.

Somehow, our energy stayed high with the thought of this first trip to China. Looking forward to our new experiences planned for both Beijing and Shanghai, we knew we would be exposed to an entire new country, culture and life experiences. We were ready to go!

At Sheremetyevo Airport in Moscow, April 2000, the two of us boarded the midnight Air China flight. As we stepped onto the plane, the heavy smoke entered our nostrils. Oh my! This was different!

In the Business Class section were about 15-20 Chinese Generals, in full dress uniforms with many medals on each chest. They spoke loudly, drank vodka and smoked non-stop, standing throughout the entire long flight. No one took any action to ask them to sit down. This was how it was. The two of us were literally invisible to these military men. We began to wonder how our first China trip would unfold. However, the experience with the Generals was a once in a lifetime thing.

Arriving in Beijing on April 4 was a delight! No matter how tired and exhausted we might be from our previous work in Moscow or the long, smoky flight into Beijing, the two of us each seemed to begin to run on adrenalin, ready to experience our first taste of China.

Diana Last met us at the airport with grace and warmth. It was daytime and though we should have been exhausted, the adrenalin continued to keep both of us going for another five days. Diana was eager to share her many years of experience working back and forth from Arizona to Beijing/Shanghai. She had a great group of corporate contacts and wanted to get us out to meet key players. Together, the three of us would determine how viable the plan was for FGI to offer our work through CBSD/China. We were excited and already seeing ourselves returning to China.

Diana loved Beijing and knew it like the back of her hand. She had so much to share and teach us. On that first day, Diana welcomed us to China with a fantastic lunch at the famous and historic Ritan Gardens. It became a favorite of ours also. The restaurant was almost an icon in Beijing, with such a colorful history and beautiful surroundings. Our conversations were informative and exciting right from the start. Diana's knowledge and experience in China were just what we needed to dive in and begin our new work. Diana felt it was important for us to have a day of experiencing Beijing prior to our marketing trips. With her driver, we were taken on a marvelous driving tour of Beijing.

Once Diana gave us the quick tour of Beijing, we headed out of the City to visit the Kohler factory – our first marketing call in China.

Diana told us it was imperative we see the Great Wall. The Chinese clients would find us more dedicated if we were able to speak about our new experiences and first positive impressions of Beijing. This would be important in making lasting relationships. Trusting Diana's years of experience working in Beijing, we accepted her advice and planned for the next trip to include the Great Wall.

The drive through the lovely countryside was amazing as the two of us sat as if we were school children experiencing a whole new world. The countryside was lush, the variety of transportation methods was nothing short of amazing and our heads were turning from side to side constantly. At one point at a fork in the road, Carol spotted a sign, in Mandarin, and a small cage of puppies along the roadside. In her usual exuberant way, Carol said, "Oh look, a little pet store here on the road." Diana, turning from the front seat to face the two of us, simply said, "Not quite a pet store. Just remember many people in China eat different things than we do." Oh goodness! Carol's stomach turned and an unfamiliar quiet came over her. It has taken some years to get over the full shock of that moment.

Luckily, the scenery was magnificent and thoughts soon moved away from puppies to just enjoying the new experiences. We saw the farmers in their fields, the herds of sheep being moved along the sides of the highway, the three-wheeled wagons being pulled by donkeys. We also saw the modern, Western-looking new automobiles driving alongside a large number of bicycles carrying more than one person. Traffic on the Beijing highway had a very different feel from the modern, buzzing highways we knew in the US. Each new sight and experience kept each one of us awake and alert.

After about ninety minutes, we arrived at the Kohler factory –

only to discover it was closed for the day and only security guards were present. A wasted afternoon? No. We experienced a wonderful introduction to China.

All three of us took naps on the drive back into Beijing. The driver treated us with care as he drove through the bumper-to-bumper traffic back into the crowded Capitol City. It was indeed a long couple of days. Still, the excitement returned as we drove into the City. Diana told us we were going to the Holiday Inn. What? Somehow, this was a surprise. We were expecting some Chinese hotel. However, everything was comfortable and enjoyable. This was a good place from which to make our many marketing visits with both delicious Chinese and American meals and service-oriented people who were happy to help us in our first days in Beijing.

The next morning, each one of us was ready to start the marketing. Diana lined up some amazing marketing calls with her contacts in Beijing. During one day, the three of us together visited five different multi-national companies doing business in Beijing. In each case, we were welcomed and accepted with lovely Chinese hospitality. People were interested in us, our history and work experience plus our lives in the US. Their questions were deep and insightful. Diana seemed delighted and told us we would have many more exciting experiences when we flew into Shanghai the next day.

How we kept up with this schedule is nothing short of amazing as we relive it now. And yet, we did keep up and felt as if we were on top of the world. Energy and adrenaline were flowing.

Over dinner that night, Diana reminded us we were scheduled to fly to Shanghai in the morning to continue the marketing. She shared some information about the clients we would see and gave us more history about CBSD/China.

It was a bit of a whirlwind for us as these first days in China sped by. Before we knew it, we were on the flight to Shanghai. Neither of us could even remember how many days ago each one of us left our homes in Omaha to fly to Moscow! Now we were in our third major world city and still filled with that buzz.

As we landed in Shanghai, it was clear from the runway views that this city was nothing like Beijing. Shanghai seemed a more modern, vibrant city. Once we were in a cab, how amazed we were to see a perfect replica of the Stalin Wedding Cake buildings we had become so familiar with in Moscow. It was rather like déjà vu, to see a somewhat smaller version of one of the same buildings we saw again and again during our drives to work in Moscow. The world history we read about as students many years ago was now showing up before our eyes. Apparently, this building was a gift from Soviet Russia to China. It was originally built in 1953, for the exhibition of the Soviet Union in Shanghai.

Yes, it was still China, but it was to be another new adventure. Diana was along to continue the marketing visits. No matter how exhausted we were, the old "buzz" of new experiences and learning set in. We were both ready to go!

Each one of us was to accompany a CBSD Chinese saleswoman who would introduce us to 3-4 new companies and their key Human Resources people. Within two days, we would have a minimum of 12 new person-to-person Shanghai contacts for FGI International. These bright, young CBSD Chinese professionals were key to our being able to jump in quickly because they knew these clients and worked with them for some years.

Tim went with Helen and Carol went with Penny. Both Chinese women chose "Western names" as have many Chinese business professionals who work in Western companies doing business in China. This was not for the women, but to make it easier for those from the US. Sadly, we learned few Western professionals are interested in learning Mandarin, let alone even learning the Chinese names of their Chinese employees and friends. Thus, during this visit, we committed we would learn the Chinese names of our new Chinese clients and friends whenever we were given them throughout our tenure in China. It was always very appreciated. At the same time, our use of their Chinese names amazed them. Some believed Americans were not able to do so. We believed if we could learn and use Chinese names, any American could. However, the sad truth was only a few Americans ever even attempted.

The days turned into a true whirlwind. With every new meeting, each of us became smarter and more able to comprehend the enormity of the opportunities put before us. The key people in the companies such as Emerson and Polaroid were eager to learn more and happy to meet new US consultants for the development and coaching of their talented key leaders. They were literally hungry for new resources. This was a great time to be in China.

Our many years as adjunct faculty with the Center for Creative Leadership (CCL) were considered a true asset. We very much valued our past experience, but did not understand just how much stock these bright, mature Chinese HR leaders put into the CCL connection.

The meetings went amazingly deep and the questions we received were no different in China than they were in the US or Russia during our early marketing calls. All of these leaders were looking for the best development opportunities they could offer the company's key leaders. They wanted to make sure they received true value for their money. We felt grateful the stories of our experiences and the companies with whom we had worked in the US and Russia seemed just what our Chinese contacts wanted to hear. The conversations were easy, exciting, very warm and friendly. Though we were providing these potential new clients with information, we were the ones who were really learning in the moment.

The connections were made and all involved seemed pleased. Over these five days in Beijing and Shanghai, we learned more about China and Western multi-nationals doing business in

China than we expected. It was also very beneficial when we were able to offer the plus of working for some of the same multi-nationals in Moscow as we were calling on in China.

Suddenly, it became crystal clear to us how small the world really is. More than one of these new Chinese contacts knew his or her counterpart in Moscow and was delighted to hear we had already done business with the company. The previous experiences of learning deeply about new companies in Russia had served us well.

We were also taking in incredible amounts of information and knowledge daily. Our brains were fully alive. These experiences felt as if we were gulping water after being parched and thirsty. We just could not get enough of the new China experiences.

Our visits set in motion the FGI International work that has thrived and delighted us for 13 years, back and forth from Omaha to Beijing and Shanghai. We were eager to return to the US and set up calendars for possible work with the many new friends we made. The two of us were flying high and ready to see what would unfold.

We were told that the program manager for our FGI programs in China would be a woman named Rui Shujie. We met her briefly but had little time together during this first trip. She was working away from the office that week. Little did we know how important she would become in our lives; not only as a business partner but as a lifelong, treasured friend.

We boarded the flight to the US, looking forward to arriving in Los Angeles. Our experiences as well as our dreams for the future work in Beijing and Shanghai were filling our heads. Exhausted as we were, we were pleased with the success of the trip and each one of us was eager to return home to family. However, there was to be one more surprise.

This was the first time we had flown into the Los Angeles Airport from an overseas trip. We were expecting to feel the easy comfort and familiarity of the US again. As the two of us came off the plane and into the security area, we pulled out our passports and flight information. Immediately, each one of us was harshly pulled aside by Security. Though this was in the days prior to 9.11, we were "man-handled" and pushed into a corner. Things became quite ugly. Guns were drawn and as each one of us tried to speak, the officers became even more intolerant and accusing.

Finally, each one of us settled down. We did our best to answer questions without inferring they were wrong about whatever suspicions they may have had about us. Carol was the first to be interrogated by a large man with a gun. Tim, apparently feeling a need to be protective, walked over and began to speak. Tim was soon being held against the wall, told to not speak and not move.

One by one we were interrogated with harsh and accusing questions. It took quite a while to understand what had caused the "Red Flags" around the two of us. This was the year 2000. It was less than a decade ago the Soviet Union dissolved. In the minds of US Security, apparently, this menace and danger was not really to be forgotten.

The travel patterns indicated in our two passports, showed we had been traveling regularly to Moscow, two or three times a year. Now we had just returned from a trip around the world, from the US to Russia, from Russia to China and now back to the US.

Who were we?

What did we know?

What were we hiding?

This pattern of travel was just not the norm.

Most travelers did not make this kind of trip to these destinations in a three-week outing!

Though it was frightening, both the Security officers and the two of us were able to settle down and talk to each other. Finally, we made it clear we were only teachers, trying to make a positive difference in the world. But we were also students, learning as we went.

We had been around the world in a three-week period. We were teachers and students. We met new friends and colleagues and continued our work with other long-time friends and colleagues. To us, we thought this was NORMAL . . .

## CHAPTER TWENTY-TWO

# The China Work Unfolds

Before we knew it, our first China offering of the Looking Glass Leadership Program was scheduled for October 2000, and the class nearly full. Although the learnings were many, they only increased in number as we prepared to convene our first groups of Chinese business leaders.

But, as is always the case, there was more for Carol and Tim to learn. Any business leader who has been our student in any country over these past thirty years, knows we begin with participant pre-work that always includes some self assessments. Upon receiving the first results from the Chinese participants we were soon to meet, we found the numbers startling. In our own minds, set against our own assumptions, the numbers did not make sense.

A call with Rui Shujie was in order. Rui would be our program coordinator for CBSD in Shanghai. Little did Rui know at the time, she would provide us with one of the most significant and key understandings of our many FGI experiences. Rui was in her twenties at the time. We were almost twice her age. Yet her strength and courage served us in amazing ways. To prepare for her role, she came to Moscow in June 2000, to participate in our FGI program. Rui and Nina Liu were the first Chinese Nationals to be with us in Russia. They more than held their own with the Russian participants.

We called Rui to ask some questions about the pre-assessment results. We were hinting the numbers were not correct. In perfect, "Ugly American" style, we suggested our new students perhaps did not understand the directions. Rui, always seeking excellence and learning for everyone, began her questions.

"What was the assessment measuring?"

"What did not fit?"

"What were we expecting to see?"

"How did you develop these expectations?"

And then, the key question, "How many Chinese have you known well in China?"

Courageous and brilliant, Rui heard in our silence the important response.

"Carol, Tim, is it possible you only knew a few Chinese in the United States? If this is the case, then there is no way you can compare the few Chinese you meet or even read about with these Chinese business leaders. These leaders were born and raised in China, working here now with much excellence and success."

As the saying goes, "Bazinga!" Her words of deep truth hit both of us in the gut with a real thud. Of course she was correct.

Rui went on to share more: "You are suggesting by surprise that you believe Chinese and perhaps all Asians to be more quiet and reserved than Americans. However, it must be true you have never been to a Chinese wedding here in China, right?"

With her gentle, loving, respectful approach, Rui Shujie allowed us to recognize our Western stereotypical assumptions. She taught us a new kind of humility that would serve our many years of work in China and for the rest of our lives. This learning would prepare us for our later work in India!

Life was good! We were blessed beyond imagination with this bright, young woman who had courage to speak her truth, to be our teacher and become our dearest friend in China. Brilliant, young, kind, beautiful, Rui would very soon become an FGI International staff member and founder of our China business. Rui is the one who brought the "business in the door" in the form of clients for our work. More important, Rui brought wisdom about China both to us and many other "foreigners" we brought to China.

As a graduate of the highly esteemed Fudan University in Shanghai, Rui, though very young, was and has been one of our greatest teachers. Rui lives in Shanghai which was the hub for almost all of our China work. Over the years we learned to know and love Rui, her story, her family, her children. We consider her part of each of our families.

The learning for us: Sometimes, it's the teacher who is more important than the actual learning. Or, both may make the important difference in our lives.

The weeks flew by. Soon the two of us met Dennis Hopple and Denny in Beijing. Before going to Shanghai, we followed Diana's advice to make our first trip to the Great Wall. Diana had told us it was best to start with the Badaling section.

As we approached Badaling, the roads were very crowded with buses, cars, trucks and people on foot. Oh my, we soon understood this day was a Chinese Holiday. Probably not such a good idea to come to Badaling today, but we were there now.

The closer we drove to the official parking lots for Badaling the crazier the traffic became. After parking the car, our guide procured our tickets in a long, long line of people. Literally hundreds of people were in front of her. She asked us to stand over by the bus stands to wait for her.

She might as well have asked us to move to the front of the stage so we could watch Chinese life up close and personal. And watch it we did. The people who were ready to leave for their trips home were very eager to get onto the buses. Thousands of them pushed and shoved to enter the already crowded buses. There was a finite number of spaces on each bus, including sitting, standing and squatting. We came to life as we watched one skirmish after another take place as people, exhausted from waiting, literally fought for the seats and the standing room.

Having recently come from Moscow, we entered into a rather interesting conversation about how the street fighting seemed to be different in China than in Russia. Yes, it seemed to be true, the rare street fights we had seen in Moscow seemed more like Russian bears, rolling around on the ground, hoping to overpower the adversary. Here in China, the street fights were more active and energetic, like Chinese tigers. Amazing to us that these images were now a part of our own life experiences. Every new sight provided us with learning, deep thinking and new "Ah ha's," not to mention the wonder of such gifts in our lives.

Our guide was a bright, young woman who spoke excellent English and seemed truly delighted to be showing us the Great Wall at Badaling. She had grown up at the bottom of the mountains and seemed to know every turn in the path as we climbed the wall and walked along the parapets and various guard and viewing stations built long before we could even imagine.

The Badaling Great Wall is located in Yanqing County, over 43 miles north of Beijing. We were told it was the most well preserved section of the Great Wall and was built during the Ming Dynasty (1368-1644). This section has an average altitude of over 1,000 meters (3,282 feet). The mountain slope is very steep and the roads are difficult. This is what made it such an important military stronghold. Looking along the tops of the Great Wall at Badaling, we could see the imagery of how the wall is like a strong dragon winding its way along the tops of mountain ranges. It was amazing! Later that evening, all four of us confirmed we had each had the feeling we would visit the Great Wall again. We were hooked on China!

Once off the Great Wall, we four knew we had to get ready for our adventure. We were no longer tourists. We were marketing FGI in China! Off we flew to Shanghai.

∼    ∼    ∼

The next day we boarded a large van to PepsiCo's Frito Lay factory in a suburb of Shanghai. We, included the two of us plus Denny and Dennis Hopple. Additionally we had Diana Last of CBSD China and the woman who would quickly become a dear friend, Nina Liu, the Director of HR for Frito Lay China. What a day it would become.

We believe preparation is essential before offering programs for the first time, especially in another country. Nina thought we could learn a lot by seeing how multi-nationals manufactured in China.

Soon we donned white coats and hats to tour what was then the newest Frito Lay chip factory in the world. Amazingly, in little more than a year it had become the second most efficient plant in the Frito Lay system.

The plant manager was proud to show us his new facility. He was very proud of the young women and men who were doing such fine work. We went onto the assembly line floor to watch as hundreds of thousands of potatoes went down the line. They were washed and then inspected as they moved forward. The workers would trim off bad spots and cut out eyes by hand. Then the potatoes moved past a scanner that searched for defects. The operator waited until he identified a bad potato. Then with a touch of a wand to his screen, the potato would literally fly off the line into a waste container. It was amazing to watch.

The potatoes went through a number of automated steps as they were peeled, sliced, flavored and then fried. The next step was for the hot new potato chips to be fanned dry and then blown out on their way to the bagging station. As we approached this station, the plant manager hurried to give us plastic gloves, saying, "I only give these gloves to Americans, because they can't help themselves and often catch the chips with their bare hands and eat them. I want to keep the rest uncontaminated. Please enjoy yourselves."

He was right, the fresh chips right out of the fryer were unbelievably delicious!

After the tour we asked the plant manager questions. Our biggest was to understand what made it possible for this plant to be so successful. He told us there were two factors. First, he selected as employees local women and men whose only work prior to this had been as farmers. The result was workers who were highly motivated, but required no "unlearning" from previous manufacturing experiences. Then the employees worked in self-organizing teams without direct supervisors. There were clear goals and they were responsible to each other for attaining those goals. There was only one supervisor during each shift at the plant in case of emergency. The actual work was done without supervision.

We left very impressed. If all Chinese manufacturing was like this Frito Lay plant, it was no wonder they were successful. We would later discover not all Chinese manufacturing was like this plant. Chinese workers were highly motivated and did excellent work. But Frito Lay had the advantage of what is called a "Green Field." In other words, they built a brand new plant and hired new workers and were able to organize in the best possible ways to begin. Most leaders everywhere love a Green Field opportunity.

❧   ❧   ❧

Once we were able to do some marketing and visit the potential client Frito Lay, we were now going to offer our Looking Glass Leadership Program in Shanghai! Our opportunities in China were often similar to those in Russia. There was a huge difference, however. In Russia, Dennis Hopple and his team at CBSD did the marketing, handled the logistics and took care of us. In China we had to create most of the opportunities ourselves. Though we began there by working with CBSD China, after our second program we were on our own. This led ultimately to us chartering a business in China to represent FGI and FGISpirit. More on that later.

We were very excited to begin our Looking Glass Leadership Program. The day before, we set up the meeting rooms at the Shanghai Regal Hotel. This was to become the most frequent site for FGI programs in China.

The two of us, plus Denny and Dennis, greeted the five women and fourteen men who were about to have a totally new experience of leadership development in China. We had some apprehensions about how this all would go. After all, China had to be different from our experiences in Russia and the United States. Didn't it? It was so far away; the history was so different and it was still a Communist country. Wasn't it? Hopefully our advance study would serve us well.

As they introduced themselves, one by one, our apprehensions began to dissolve.

The first participant to speak was educated in the US, and was division head of an American manufacturer. He talked about how rapidly his business was expanding. "Sometimes this growth," he said, "is not good. With change people have to rethink how they manage. Some of the people don't like this. I need to learn how to help people leave who don't want to change." Sounded like a typical American manager!

The second person worked for a large French mobile phone company. His job required him to work on a major restructuring to determine the strategy for the China market. He told the group, "I am reluctant to be here. Is there a need for this training? I have to learn from real life." We heard this sentiment many times in both the US and Russia. It would be interesting to see how he felt at the end of the program.

Four participants came from Mary Kay. In Russia, our Mary Kay participants had all been women. Here in China, all were men. One of them, Yao Yu Shan, the Mary Kay plant manager from Hongzhou, introduced himself as Vincent. Vincent told us his biggest issue for Mary Kay China was to decide which products to import and which to make locally. Another Mary Kay manager said with their rapid growth, the challenges were mostly about supply chain management.

PepsiCo companies sent the most participants – seven. They came from Bottling, Frito Lay, Marketing, Finance, IT and HR. In this group were three who became friends of ours for life: Nina Liu, SC Toh and Peng Hai Tao.

Yang Weihao told us her English name was Loretta. She was just beginning her career with the Municipal Government of Shanghai. She was required to have an "English" name so that she could interact with foreigners. Having a person from the government would add a very different perspective to the group.

Finally we were ready to jump into the program content. As usual, our FGI approach looks at major trends shaping the world of the leader. We then invite participants to discuss these trends and add their own opinions and ideas to what we have said.

The conversation that followed was lively. Some of the participants immediately understood how these trends impacted the life of a leader in an organization. Others found it much more difficult, perhaps because the whole concept of leadership in an organization was still so new in China.

The reality for many of our participants both in 2000 and succeeding years was that of working for multi-nationals who tended to give the Chinese limited freedom to act, believing the multi-nationals knew what was best. Our participants often left feeling good about new knowledge and skills they had, but also frustrated due to feeling their parent company restricted their freedom to act.

The core of LGLP is "running" the Looking Glass Company for a day, followed by additional days of debrief and feedback. Participants begin, however, by working with one another to select the leadership roles that each will have in the company, whether President, Vice President, Sales and Marketing, Manufacturing, etc. Following an overnight to prepare, the simulation was suddenly underway.

The President met with his Vice Presidents first thing in the morning at 9:00 AM. Here is how the conversation began:

President: "There was a lot of preparation last night. But what stood out for me is that I need to know what you see, because the person at the top has the least information in a company. I see no company vision in the materials"

Vice President #1: "It seems to me we are behind in international expansion. We have an urgent need to consider expansion in South America."

Vice President #2: "I found it hard last night to figure out where action is called for in the memos I read."

Vice President #3: "I agree that there is no strategic direction for the Company. We will need to determine it."

President: "I promised the Management Team that I would offer guidance to them at 9:15. I know that the Chairman of the Board wants us to have a greater global presence."

Vice President #1: "I think we have company-wide problems with customer service and product delivery."

Vice President #3: "We have some severe waste and environmental problems plus HR problems in Affirmative Action."

Vice President #2: "I will need to talk with my team first to prioritize our problems."

President: "I intend to challenge the Company to have US dollars one billion within three years (a 40% growth)."

This was a great start and not a bit different from the typical beginning of a Looking Glass no matter where we were offering it. Next the Executives met with the Management Team. The President set an inspirational tone for the Team. He talked about the need to expand global presence, develop Division Synergies across the Company, improve customer service as well as grow to US dollars one billion in three years. We wondered how they would respond to his challenges? Would they get caught up in tactical issues?

For the next six hours we watched the nineteen talented young leaders sort through hundreds of issues, set agendas, solve some emergencies as well as more strategic issues and ignore other problems either because there was no time or they failed to recognize them.

As a day in the life of the Looking Glass Company, this first group in China was certainly above average in performance when compared to groups in the US and Russia. Most of the participants were fully engaged and did their best to work with others.

When we held that first LGLP, it was less than ten years since Deng Xiaoping had announced the beginning of a socialist market economy and had given substantial freedoms to businesses, domestic and foreign-owned, to grow and develop. So leaders and managers had to do a lot of improvising because precedent was often not available. We could also see this as we debriefed LGLP.

≈    ≈    ≈

For the next day and a half we debriefed what happened, how each person contributed to, or detracted from, the success of the team and what each person learned. The sessions were lively, intense, introspective, genuine and very meaningful.

At the end of the debriefs we asked each participant to tell the entire group key learnings she or he would take away from the experience. The conversation kept us involved. Here is a sample of some of those learnings along with the position the individual occupied in the simulated Looking Glass Company:

Plant Manager: "I am poor at planning for the long term. I only work on what's in front of me. As a result I may make decisions that offend others who are looking at the bigger picture."

President: "I have a tendency to talk with my head. I need to more often talk with my heart. I make assumptions people understand what I am saying. I found out I am often not clear."

Dir. of Manufacturing: "Not all my colleagues back at work are as energetic as at Looking Glass. Leadership is an art from your deeper heart. Management is more of a science."

LGLP had a number of other elements including 360° feedback from each participant's co-workers plus time to consolidate all learnings and create an action plan for what each individual intended to do after the program ended. At the end of the fourth day, we asked each person to give a final comment to the rest of the group. Here is some of what they said:

Yang Weihao (Loretta): "This is the most exciting school I have ever experienced. You are the most wonderful teachers I have ever known."

Hai Tao Peng: "I have been attending trainings for many years and will remember this the rest of my life . . . I hope each of us will make a positive change."

Yao Yu Shan: "After this course we can make a more beautiful human life, each of us."

We finished LGLP feeling pretty great. The Chinese found it valuable to them. The program was a success.

That first LGLP was a great teacher for us. We learned Chinese managers and leaders deal with the same problems as those in every other country. For those from multi-nationals, it's common that greater distance to company headquarters makes decision-making more difficult and usually much more inconvenient. Those who worked for American companies had midnight phone meetings with peers or supervisors at US headquarters at least weekly. These midnight meetings were for the convenience of the headquarters without regard for the local leaders.

The Chinese often found the headquarters' holiday practice was followed rather than the holidays celebrated in China. In most cases, the Chinese leaders were given little autonomy in decision making, needing to clear things with expats in China or else with headquarters. In the Looking Glass simulation we observed, most participants delegated decisions up rather than down, reflecting their everyday reality.

Our second learning was that the programs we offered were just as relevant in China as they were in the US or Russia. The Chinese were enthusiastic learners as well as grateful participants.

We also learned there was much the Chinese were able to teach us. They were survivors of great suffering. The suffering gave them courage, strength, resilience. Watching those characteristics play out in a business setting was very valuable. They were representatives of over two hundred generations in this sacred land. The cultural heritage was in their DNA. It is easy to feel the difference between that kind of heritage and the very short heritage of those of us who live in the US. Throughout most of human history, China has been the most prosperous and successful country.

Rui had told us months earlier: "After our first program in Shanghai, we will have a party to celebrate our work." She had been right. We took a two-day outing with the four of us plus Rui and the other three CBSD staff members.

The outing began with a train ride from Shanghai to the beautiful lake city to the south, Hangzhou. There we were able to relax and celebrate our success in one of the most lovely cities in China. Built around the beautiful West Lake, Hangzhou has a sense of beauty, proportion and calm, even though it is home to over eight million in the City and some twenty-one million in the metropolitan area.

The trip to Hangzhou turned out to be much more than a celebratory outing. It became the basis for a new and very different program. While in Hangzhou, we visited two treasures of China's past. The first was the beautiful West Lake and the Three Pools Reflecting Moon shrine near the center of the Lake. The second was the Ling Yin Si gardens home of the ancient Temple of Inspired Seclusion.

It was while standing outside the Temple of Inspired Seclusion that Denny and the two of us – each standing in different locations – simultaneously had the same feeling: we must bring Americans to this magnificent, sacred and deeply spiritual site. This feeling, at this site, would inspire us to bring twenty-eight American friends to China in 2003 for what became known as the China Pilgrimage.

When we finished the trip to Hangzhou we returned to Shanghai and then back to our homes in the US. We were with Chinese in their environment. The stereotypes from Chinese we met in the US were irrelevant. Our Chinese participants were gregarious, funny, serious, charming, fun loving and intense. Before we left for home, we were already planning our next trip to China.

❧　❧　❧

The chance to return came sooner than we expected. The PepsiCo participants from the first LGLP returned to work convinced more of their colleagues would benefit from participating. So they asked us to do an LGLP program just for Pepsi the following year.

As you might expect, we were quite excited. Our work during 2000 was paying off with a return engagement the following year. FGI has always had as its performance standard: *Our clients refer us!*

We would have a chance to return to what we were discovering was a beautiful country with magnificent people to offer one of our favorite programs to an intact group from the same company. Now, however, the challenge was not to learn so much about Chinese participants as it was to learn about PepsiCo China. We eagerly began the study.

A year passed quickly and it was time to return. We read in the US papers that the Asia Pacific Economic Conference was to be held in Shanghai at exactly the time we were to offer LGLP for PepsiCo. This would be the first time China hosted leaders of the twenty-one member countries for their annual summit meeting. In Shanghai, it was a big deal.

We first experienced how big a deal it was when we arrived at the PuDong International Airport outside of Shanghai. The two of us and Denny were mistaken for delegates to the Conference. We were treated as dignitaries, whisked through passport control and then customs. The normal forty-minute process was accomplished in fifteen. We could get used to such grand treatment!

When we arrived the sky in Shanghai was a familiar gray. Air pollution usually kept the sun from shining through or the sky visible. We thought little of it and each of the three of us went to our respective hotel rooms at the Regal to rest.

When we awoke the next morning we could see blue sky and sun from the windows of our hotel rooms. We each expressed surprise at the transition over night. When we met Rui that morning to begin final preparations for the program, we learned that overnight the government seeded the sky with some type of chemical that first induced rain and then cleaned out the remaining pollution. The *Shanghai Daily* confirmed this and added that most polluting businesses were closed for the week of the Conference. We began to see what a strong central government can accomplish.

The newspaper also told us the Conference would open with an elaborate fireworks display that very evening down along the Huangpu River near the historic Bund area, across the river from the APEC conference center. We asked Rui if we could go to see the fireworks – after all the Chinese had invented fireworks!

She told us the Government had limited viewers on the Bund to those holding special tickets – and of course we had none. But, Rui thought we could get down into a nearby older residential neighborhood close to the Bund if we walked a few blocks from where the streets had been closed for the celebration.

That evening, after dinner, we walked through the restricted area until we reached the neighborhood she selected. And there we were, Rui, three Americans and a growing number of Chinese. By the time the fireworks started nearly twenty thousand were filling the streets in the two-block area. It was like a stadium concourse in the Big Ten during a football game, or like a Moscow Metro platform at rush hour.

The crowd, though daunting, was not as surprising as was the reaction to the three Americans. It was like we were visiting celebrities. Parents came to have us appear in pictures with their children. Those who knew a bit of English wanted to have conversations. One elderly man brought his grandson and asked if we would help the boy practice his English. This all was totally unexpected. We feared intruding in a Chinese neighborhood might be seen as inappropriate.

Rui told us in this neighborhood, probably many of those who lived there had never met an American. We were clearly welcome. That evening we also saw things that were surprising to us. The most significant was seeing the many men – mostly those of middle age or older – who appeared on the street in their pajamas. We asked Rui about this and she told us that although Shanghai was the wealthiest city in China, most people had very low incomes. In Shanghai, having pajamas to wear at night was a symbol of wealth. Those who could afford to own pajamas would wear them on the street so neighbors could see they were doing well.

Soon it became dark enough the fireworks began. For the next forty minutes we were treated to perhaps the most beautiful aerial display we had ever seen. Many of the Chinese around us, however, were more interested in us than in the fireworks. When the show was over we bid good-bye to many new acquaintances. Last minute pictures were taken with small children as we walked back to where we could find a taxi. It was the end of a wonderful day.

The next morning we began the PepsiCo LGLP. It was another wonderful group and a great experience. As in our first China program, we had the privilege of meeting and working with some very special young women and men. Three of them stand out because they remained friends and gave us the chance to learn more about how young professionals grew their careers while caring for children and parents as Chinese society began to change.

The first was Richard, a young marketing professional. A decade later he was still at Pepsi and was promoted several times. It was unusual in those days for anyone to stay at the same company for more than two or three years. Headhunters were constantly making offers to talented young women and men to take jobs in different companies, usually for great increases in salary. Many left and followed the money. Richard was the exception. He enjoyed his work and his company. He chose to stay.

More important, he and his wife were focusing their attention on raising their baby daughter. When we had dinner with Richard a dozen years later, we talked about his job for five minutes and his daughter for an hour. He is like many Chinese parents who believe the development of their child – most families are limited by the one child policy – is essential because their child is their future and the future of the culture and society.

The second was Molly, a young public relations representative who worked for Pepsi in Beijing. Before Pepsi, Molly worked for Ford. A couple of years after we met, Molly accepted a position with Volkswagen. Her position required her to learn German, which she accomplished in about six months. Within a couple of years, she was promoted to being the only woman and only Chinese national to be a part of the Managing Board of Volkswagen China. Today she continues to travel across the globe as a senior leader of that very successful company.

The third person was Janet. In 2001, Janet was a Human Resources representative for Pepsi in the Beijing offices. Several years later she was Vice President of HR for Alcoa Asia Pacific. Today she is head of Human Resources for the GAP China. Janet married an ex-pat who was from Canada. They have a son, Matthew, who is clearly one of the brightest children we have ever met. At age three, Matthew spoke three languages, moving from one to another seamlessly during a conversation. On one occasion we were talking with Matthew in English when his mother would ask a question in Mandarin and he would immediately answer in Mandarin with no pause. He was able to recognize all the instruments in an orchestra by hearing the sound only. His vocabulary, self-confidence and intelligence were amazing.

It has been a true gift in our lives to know Richard, Molly, Janet and their children. And while these three are good friends, they are not atypical of many other women and men that we met during our years in China.

≈   ≈   ≈

The second LGLP in China was just as successful as the first. PepsiCo hired very talented women and men to lead their Chinese operations. Because it was a single company group, they rather quickly turned the culture of the Looking Glass Company into the culture of PepsiCo. All of the difficulties built into Looking Glass, such as problems with customers, raw materials, product quality, developing markets, competing in a rapidly changing global marketplace, mirrored similar challenges facing PepsiCo China. The participants jumped in and did great work.

We learned so much in our first two years working in China. Working in China was easy. The participants in all our programs were happy to be there, were great learners and delightful humans. Chinese civilization has such a long history that we often felt in awe of the depth and breadth of the Chinese spirit. Their hospitality had no bounds. People everywhere made us feel welcome, honored and special. The Chinese desire to succeed seemed greater than Americans' desire to succeed. One of the positive consequences of a strong central government is that logistics of all types are very well organized. The Peoples' Republic of China is Communist. Most of the Chinese people with whom we worked were deeply spiritual.

We offered over twenty programs of various types in China. After LGLP, the most fun was a program called *Leadership, Teamwork and Productivity*. This program used the Emergenetics theory base developed by our colleague Geil Browning. The Chinese loved the experiences built into that program.

Most of our offerings were public; some were provided for specific client organizations. One of the most special aspects of work in China was similar to that of Russia: our participants came from many different countries. As an example, in one LGLP we offered for Alcoa Asia Pacific, we had participants from Singapore, Hong Kong, Japan, Korea, Canada, United States as well as China. What a rich experience that became.

How blessed we were to have been introduced to China by Mary Kay leaders from Russia. Our lives are permanently enriched by the myriad of experiences we have had with the wonderful women and men in China.

Tim enjoying Chinese dumplings with CBSD colleague Helen Zhao • Bicycles and motor scooters were primary transportation in Shanghai, 2000 • The Smiling Buddha was always a welcome sight whenever we went to China from 2000-2012.

The first FGI *Global Interaction* simulation for *BSL*. Representatives wrestle with world problems • *BSL* 2010 Medicine Wheel, Sedona, Arizona • A recent *BSL* group in Santa Fe, discusses the role of leader in the future.

Tim with some men of FOCUS 30 • Carol visits with Rod about his 2% initiative • Paul Koch, Tim, Sharif Abdullah and Carol prepare for *Omaha Commons Café*, 2001 • *Omaha Commons Café* participants celebrate a joyous moment.

Tim and Foster Harding in conversation, *Denver Commons Café*, 2002· Carol surrounded by school children during a stop in the Deep Mountains north of Beijing · Leaders of the *Talking Together Commons Café* in Shaghai: Tim, Rui Shujie, Carol, Denny and Lori Zahm · Rui and Carol observe multi-national table groups at *Talking Together*.

At the base of the Great Wall, American Pilgrims pray and dance for Geil Browning after receiving word of her stroke in Denver • Carol "walking" for Geil's recovery • Bo Hai Suo school children entertained us.

Tim presents Spiral Dynamics® *New Maps for Leaders* program, Moscow, 2004 •
Americans and Russians who represented Turkey during *The Global Interaction*, 2004 •
Russians, a New Zealander, a Chinese and an American working together during *NMFL*,
2004 • Enjoying our dear friends Tatiana Morskaya, Gennady and Tanya Smirnov at the
dacha, 2006.

Leslie Rill, FGI, with participants in our *LTP* Emergenetics program, Shanghai, 2006 •
Dear friend, Nina Liu (center) helped make the *Women's Leadership Program* in
Shanghai a success for five years • Participants in the first *Women's Leadership
Program*, Shanghai, 2004, came from China, Indonesia, Russia and the US • Women in
INFLUENCE 49 have a light moment.

Sacred cow, India • Carol makes a new friend • *The Global Interaction* in Hyderabad, India, 2009 • Indians loved to take pictures with us, here at the ruins of Golconda Fort in Hyderabad, 2009.

Carol presents Spiral Dynamics® to *New Maps for Leaders* participants from India, Argentina and the US, Hyderabad, India, 2009 • Marty Malley and Tim ride an elephant up the mountain to the Amber Fort outside of Jaipur, India, 2010 • View of the bus terminal in Charminar District, Hyderabad, from the offices of Prajwala.

Abbas Be, our student in the Prajwala leadership program • Dr. Sunitha Krishnan at the new Prajwala Ashram for recovery and rehabilitation of the survivors of sexual slavery • Meeting some of the bright, healthy girls who have been rescued and are now living in the Ashram, going to school, 2011.

Tim meets a new friend. The youngest rescued vistims of sexual slavery have been as young as three years old• Prajwala women discuss leadership characteristics, 2011 • Participants, FGI second leadership program for victims of sexual slavery, now Prajwala managers. Sunitha is at the far left.

# The Legacy Years

## 2001 - 2014

# 2001 - 2014

**2001**

US unemployment rises from 3.9 to 5.7%.

Explosive BRIC countries (Brazil, Russia, India, China) growth continues.

Outsourcing to China and India growing rapidly.

Experts say "Multi-Polar" World is rapidly replacing the "Unipolar" world that followed the collapse of the USSR.

9.11

US/Afghan War begins.

Asia Pacific Economic Conference meets in Shanghai.

**2002**

Euro becomes legal tender throughout the European community.

**2003**

US economy growing again but unemployment reaches 6.3%.

Operation Iraqi Freedom begins.

Hu Jintao becomes President of China.

First Chinese astronaut orbits the Earth.

**2004**

President George W. Bush defeats John Kerry.

Beijing Summit/Forum on China-Africa Cooperation

## 2005

Hurricane Katrina devastates Gulf Coast.

South East Asia Tsunami final toll number 282,000

## 2006

Democrats win back both houses of Congress.

Iran announces success in enriching Uranium.

## 2007

US economy enters recession. 1.9 million jobs lost in US.

Surge in Iraqi War

Mortgage crisis in US

## 2008

US unemployment reaches 7.3%.

2.6 million US jobs lost

TARP passed to save faltering banking system.

Loans extended to GM/Chrysler to prevent bankruptcy.

## 2009

Barack Obama inaugurated as President. Majority Democrats win both House and Congress.

4.7 million jobs lost in US. US unemployment rate increases to 9.9%.

Congress Party victory in Indian Elections; Singh continues as Prime Minister.

European Debt Crisis begins.

Recession in US officially ends.

Tea Party founded.

## 2010

Affordable Care Act becomes law.

Afghan Surge/Osama Bin Laden killed.

Republicans re-take majority in US House of Representatives.

Arab Spring begins.

## 2011

"Don't Ask Don't Tell" is repealed. Gay Marriage legal in 6 states and District of Columbia.

Non-white births become the majority in US. Non-Whites to be US population majority by 2042.

Syrian Civil War begins.

Last US combat troops leave Iraq.

## 2012

Over 2000 US troops die in Afghanistan.

Identified Radical Right Hate groups in US exceed 1,000.

African Union Summit in Beijing

Xi Jinping new President of China

US unemployment falls to 8.1%.

## 2013

Supreme Court decisions legalize gay marriage in California and rule Federal Defense of Marriage Act unconstitutional.

States, many reluctantly, prepare for Affordable Care Act implementation in January 2014.

Jobs that are suitable for the poor and under-educated continue to disappear in the US.

Nelson Mandela dies. The world mourns.

US unemployment falls below 7%.

## 2014

Syrian Civil War begins its 4th year.

President Karzai, Afghanistan, says no foreign troops needed after 2014.

President Putin, Russia, annexes Crimea.

*Before Our Eyes* by Carol Hunter and Tim Rouse, first edition offered for sale in US.

## CHAPTER TWENTY-THREE

# Bringing Spirit to Leadership

*"You have to leave the city of your comfort*

*and go into the wilderness of your intuition. What you'll*

*discover will be wonderful. What you'll discover will be yourself."*

*- Alan Alda, 2006*

Looking back on all the programs and wonderful adventures in which we have been involved in, *Bringing Spirit to Leadership* (*BSL*) has been the most meaningful and satisfying. Begun as an experiment in 1999, *BSL* has grown and increased its effectiveness year after year.

Developing leaders is mostly about starting from the inside. When talented women and men are willing to go deep and truly answer the questions asked by author, teacher and pastor, Wayne Muller: "Who am I?" "What do I love?" "How shall I live knowing that I will die?" and "What is my gift to the family of earth?" remarkable things happen.

We remember participants such as Phil whose career went from HR to the CEO role in a small international firm, or Shirley, a senior leader in a nuclear facility, now charged with the largest nuclear waste clean up project in the world. John went from being a middle level officer in an urban police department to deputy chief and subsequently to elective office. There have been dozens of women and men who took part in *BSL* and gained the clarity that allowed them to take on greater leadership accountability in their organizations. There have also been several who decided as a result of *BSL* that being less obsessed by their work lives would be good for them and bring them more time to find peace, joy and meaning in life.

Equally significant have been those who decided during or after *BSL* that they needed to identify and embrace different careers. Gladyce, a CPA and corporate controller, has become a hospital chaplain. David, a director of communications for a large corporation, has recently been ordained into ministry. Marty, who led hundreds of IT professionals, is now responsible for on-site education programs in India, Tanzania, Sri Lanka and Nepal.

Many colleagues through *BSL* were able to truly find themselves, or to work through old wounds or increase self-confidence or discover gifts they were unaware of having. Today they are making major contributions all over the US and in our world.

At a certain level, some credit for the success of the *BSL* program flows to the two of us. After all, we designed and provide it annually. However, it is quite clear it is an issue of timing. The world was more ready for what *BSL* had to offer in 1999 and since, than ever before. Much of the program's success resulted from the ever-accelerating rate of change that is swirling about in the lives of each of us across the globe. The women and men who joined us for *BSL* came because they desired ways to be more authentic, to increase meaning and purpose in their lives and to lead in times of great change.

The late Willis Harman described the present period of history as a "change of mind." As one of the most prescient thinkers of the 20th Century, Harman knew that whether we liked it or not, the human race early in the 21st Century would have to envision life in fundamentally different ways if we were not only to prosper, but to survive.

As the new millennium dawned, issues emerged that have called for a "change of mind." Technology has changed most assumptions about work. Outsourcing has changed locations of work. Many traditional jobs and career fields have been replaced with new ones which require different skills. Tensions with the Islamic world and concerns over China have left Americans unsettled about the world. Many young people have become disenchanted with the economic and social paradigm, previously the key to our US historic success.

On the world stage, influence is rapidly shifting from the US and Europe to countries in Asia and South America. Air and water pollution are damaging environments everywhere, and experts suggest there could soon be a global shortage of drinking water. Finally, other experts are increasingly predicting the future of global development will more and more require leaders to have and use attributes that have been traditionally described as "feminine." These would be a more caring, considerate approach with an overt sharing of appropriate emotion and intuition as well as quick, bright minds.[20]

For years during our FGI consulting work, we have been aware of the pressure building for our client US companies. Many leaders were working harder and harder, yet feeling less satisfied and less at peace. Younger leaders were/are asking whether the drive to earn more and consume more is worth it.

During our work for over a combined 20 years in Russia, China and India, we were able to feel a different kind of pressure growing. In emerging markets, young leaders were incredibly motivated by the chance to create a better life for themselves and their families. They were willing to make great sacrifices. They were ready to share in their life decisions, to have their successes confirmed and understand that learning from a failure is a precious privilege.

Fareed Zakaria, writer and commentator, captured it well in 2006 when he stated, "No workers from a rich country will ever be able to equal the energy and ambition of people trying to move out of poverty."[21]

However, the sacrifices made by our clients in other countries did not always translate into doing work the way we did it in the US. From 1992 -2007, young Russian managers often expressed to us their fear Russian business would become too much like business in the United States. When we asked what that meant, they would tell us Russians cared about family, people and community. US businesses, from their perspective, were uncaring about people and existed only for profitability. We were somewhat surprised by the intensity of feelings that accompanied some of the comments we heard. But as Denny and the two of us would talk late into the nights about our experiences with these young Russians, we began to understand the reasons they felt this way. We could understand what they were saying by thinking about some of our most driven clients in the US.

In China, from the year 2000 - 2012, the story was similar, but with two little twists. Chinese women and men not only had to attend to their own success, but also had to provide for the care of their aging parents. This has been a part of the culture for thousands of years. As a result the whole notion of extended family was of great importance. The ways many Western multi-nationals treated Chinese employees often felt demeaning. And though business and material success were important, due to the culture, other priorities including family and community were still seen as greater for these fine business professionals.

We had the benefit of wonderful experiences working with leaders all over the world. It was easy for us to see the conventional wisdom about organizations, societies and leaders changing. This was true whether one was in Russia or China or India or even in the US – all countries where we have had important life and work learning and experiences.

It was often emotional for us to examine assumptions about life that were a part of our US reality for decades. People in other parts of the world were saying, "Wait a minute. The US doesn't have it figured out. The US is out of touch with reality. Some new priorities for life need to be added."

Our most enjoyable and yet, eye-opening moment was an animated conversation in Moscow with a group of business leaders taking part in an FGI program. As we talked about subtle differences in culture, the young, bright Russians began to speak about how difficult it was to have the world being led by such a young country. "Just a teen-ager, really, in terms of the world development." said one bright Russian friend, as he referred to the US.

The growing trends, by themselves, would not have prepared us to offer the *BSL* experience. Fortunately, we had access to some of the best spiritual leadership thinkers of our time. From Wayne Muller, we learned the essence of Leadership. Deepak Chopra and the late David Simon invited us to see the ways in which all the great teachings converged in a world of pure potential. The late Angeles Arrien helped us to understand the development of collective wisdom. Sharif Abdullah anchored in our hearts the goal to create a world that works for all. Richard Rohr offered us ways to have truly authentic spiritual lives.

Our minds were challenged by the waves of change that were everywhere. Our spirits were stimulated by what we were learning. Our hearts were eager to experience life and leadership in deeper, more meaningful ways.

So the experiment with *The Millennium Project, 1999-2000*, convinced us that our most important work, during the balance of our professional careers, would be contributing to spiritual development of leaders who would enable the creation of a world that can work for all. This was not about religion, but about the essence of being human. Our efforts manifested in a variety of programs in China, India, Russia and the US, with *Bringing Spirit to Leadership* the most important.

We began the design of *BSL* with two questions:

1. What will it take to ensure that our lives, our organizations, our society, our communities and neighborhoods are effective as we move into this new century?
2. How can we co-create a world that works for all?

The content of the program, which was described earlier as the first offering of *The Millennium Project*, invited each participant to ask and answer four questions for her or his life:

1. What should be the "Central Project" of humanity. In other words, is economic success enough for our lives tomorrow?

2. What should we expect from leaders who are living in this time where the business environment is driven by speed, expanding borders and wealth creation?

3. How do we develop leaders for the new society when the present political and social structures are not working? How can we each live and work in ways that will make a positive difference?

4. How do we each align and integrate our reasons for existence with all aspects of life and so enable Spirits to thrive?

With these questions, we had to wonder, "Will corporations pay to have their key leaders participate in *BSL*?" The answer was "yes." In spite of our initial concerns, we were able to begin *The Millennium Project: Bringing Spirit to Leadership* in 1999, as an experiment, but with a full group of bright leaders from around the US.

*BSL* quickly became a part of our annual offerings with a positive, supportive response from most of our long-time sponsors. There were a few who decided the content sounded too "out there." Perhaps it was not understood that even in business organizations, the aspect of leadership is often enhanced by bringing spirit to the workplace. This is seen in caring about other people, in speaking honestly and with care toward others, in providing support and respect for colleagues at all levels.

Our sponsors continue to send excellent leaders with new organizations joining us each year. When companies are not able to sponsor, many participants have decided to pay their own tuition to join the program. They have confirmed later this has been a worthwhile investment for career, family and life in general.

We could never have imagined that *BSL* would attract participants from dozens of states in the US and even from Russia. Many have never taken part in other FGI programs. They come to us through recommendations of our clients and from their friends and co-workers who have attended *BSL*.

These *BSL* women and men have ranged in age from thirty to sixty-five. They have been leaders in every kind of work one can imagine. They have had incomes ranging from less than $30,000 to over $500,000 per year. In addition to Euro-Americans, the groups have included African Americans, Hispanics, South Africans, with others originally from Brazil, India, the Sudan, Russia, Poland and Japan. Graduates of the programs have also joined us for additional learning experiences in India, China and Russia. The stories we could tell of our *BSL* experiences could fill a book by themselves. The lessons for leadership development have been touching and confirming.

We remember the day a particular *BSL* group was reflecting outdoors in a rainstorm near the Pacific Ocean. The rain poured down for hours, but the group was so focused on what each person was saying that we didn't even notice we were wet until we finished. The depth of true connection among this group made weather a non-issue.

Another occasion, a *BSL* group was walking through a beautiful forest in the Oak Creek Canyon of Arizona. One member was wheel chair bound. Two of the men in the group picked up the wheelchair with Marty in it and carried her nearly a mile so that she could be with the group in the circle near the rushing water. Such love and commitment!

Pam, a very successful executive, said she "didn't get it" the first time she came to *BSL*. Two years later, Pam joined us for *BSL* again. She began to understand and announced she now found value. Over that same time she left her huge corporate role, returned to college to earn a Ph.D., became a college professor, and today holds the COO role for a major non-profit. While Pam was the first to "repeat" *BSL*, there have been a number of others who have returned. Each has reported the second time experiencing the program has been even richer.

Perhaps our most significant learning moment came when Sally, a Muslim born in the Sudan, and Hal, a Christian from Colorado, sparked a conversation about religion. Fear, anger, love, understanding, friendship all resulted from that conversation. An entire group of *BSL* participants developed one of the deepest bonds we have experienced. The ability to disagree, to understand another's point of view and to learn to really listen makes an incredible difference in the world. That the two of them, in front of the entire group worked through issues alive for thousands of years, gave each person present a chance to learn and grow.

In 1999, when we designed the program, one of our most important considerations was the careful selection of the places where each of the four sessions would be held. Because *BSL* depends so much on deep consideration of life topics, the setting must be conducive to rest, reflection and deep interaction. We began each group in Nebraska City because it is an ideal place for grounding. All but one group ended their time together in Sedona because the beauty and energy is magnetic. Other sessions have been held in Colorado, New Mexico, California and Illinois. In each case, physical locations that are sacred and inspirational have been key. True leadership development requires the leader to get away from familiar environments.

*BSL* has also been a place where many participants have experienced healing. Cancer survivors have regained their confidence and sense of self as they returned to their full potential as leaders. Victims of incest and abusive relationships have come to terms with their abusers and found paths to healthy lives. Victims of discrimination against homosexuality have found comfort and support from their *BSL* community. Individuals isolated or persecuted for their ethnicity or religious beliefs have been supported, encouraged and valued.

🙞   🙞   🙞

*BSL* has exceeded our fondest dreams. We learn at every session with every group. There is something profound about the simplicity of convening women and men of depth and encouraging them to teach and learn from one another.

It often feels as if the most important contribution from *BSL* has been to the two of us. Each one of our lives has been enhanced by the opportunity to serve as both program leaders and participants in the curricula. Our own individual intention setting, our times in Sacred Silence, the personal time for Reflection in the group, the readings and most importantly, the depth and value of the deep and real discussions as a part of the group have grown us and added true meaning for each one of us. Taking an active part in all aspects of *BSL* curricula has also allowed us to be fully present participants, engaged in deep personal and spiritual growth.

Sitting by the creek in Oak Creek Canyon, Sedona, the depth of reflections and the genuine connections among each group, have touched us beyond explanation. Time stands still. The circle becomes sacred. The stories become honest and deep. Mutual acceptance becomes a loving gift. To understand that it is possible to create such an experience with blessings and inspiration from some Wiser Source, has confirmed we are never alone.

We spoke earlier of the Wisdom Community, created by that first *TMP: BSL* group in 2000. It has continued as a forum for all who have participated in *BSL* or other FGISpirit programs. The Wisdom Community is a self-organizing community that hosts a web site and discussion group as well as offering two meetings a year to continue the *BSL* experience. The two of us come as participants not as leaders or presenters.

Some recent meetings have included Oklahoma City where we examined the causes and consequences of violence; Philadelphia where we reflected on the foundations of our nation and the blessings of our freedoms; Omaha where we studied examples of ways that single individuals can make a big difference; Whidbey Island, Washington where we considered issues of sustainability and the beauty of nature.

For us, the Wisdom Community allows the learning to continue indefinitely. It also permits members of different *BSL* groups to create a single community of learners who act as support and challenge for one another. Finally, the Wisdom Community allows members to expand their reach across the country.

In retrospect, it's easy to ask what made us jump into this? It was not a long considered business decision. We can truly say for us, *Bringing Spirit to Leadership* has been a calling. We give thanks.

## CHAPTER TWENTY-FOUR

# Focus Leaves a Legacy

Through these years of FOCUS, we have been blessed and learned so much. We have seen incredible transitions and changes in the world and in the men with whom we work.

It really began with 9.11. Since then the men in FOCUS have been "different" as have almost all Americans. 9.11 was actually the first day a new FOCUS of Denver group met. Men were driving up the mountains to Emerald Valley Ranch outside of Colorado Springs, where we held the opening FOCUS retreat. On the way they heard on the radio about the first attack on the Twin Towers. When they arrived, they joined the others, all huddled around the only television available, to watch the news coverage. Before we began this first meeting, we cried, screamed, sat in stunned silence. It changed not only FOCUS of Denver, but also FOCUS of Omaha, which would begin the following week.

There was one, and only one humorous incident connected to that FOCUS retreat on 9.11. We gave the men a thick readings book of global and national news and opinions articles, which they were to read before the retreat. Most did. One man, upon arriving, met Carol in the parking lot. Ken said, "On the way up here, I was listening to a radio show that was interrupted to tell us about an attack on the United States. I am so impressed you are able to prepare us for this retreat by getting something like that put on the radio station." It took Carol several minutes to convince him we had done nothing to influence the radio news. We hadn't even tried. The 9.11 tragedy was real.

Just as the terrorist attacks on the United States changed life for our Country, it changed the FOCUS program permanently. Never again would a participant tell us he did not understand the importance of learning about the world beyond our borders.

But there were factors beyond 9.11 that created a new set of realities for the FOCUS men which mirrored our larger society. Careers in a single company were by 2001 almost non-existent and change was a given. Most of the women in their lives had active and meaningful careers and some men had another man as life partner. The FOCUS men were coming to us from all over the country as well as the Midwest and included Euro-American as well as Asian, African, Middle Eastern and Hispanic men. Fewer since 2001 have been motivated by "getting-ahead." Many see the well-being of the world just as important as material success. The realization has grown that White males are already the minority in the workforce and all White people in the US will be a minority of the overall US population within fewer than 30 years.

We were part of a self-made laboratory witnessing how the transition of our world was being experienced by men month by month. It has been a very special privilege and great opportunity for learning.

The growing diversity of the groups also expanded the learning opportunities for all who were open. In 2003, a man whose partner was another man, decided to adopt a child from Guatemala. The group shared in his experiences that year as he and his partner made multiple trips to Guatemala to go through the process of adopting in a foreign country. They brought their son home near the end of the FOCUS program. The little boy came to the end of program celebration and was the hit of the party. Recently he entered junior high school. His fathers could not be happier.

A few years ago a FOCUS group was having an intense conversation about the world. The issue of whether we should be afraid of Muslims or not, brought much emotion. However, one of the men said, "I don't know how I feel because I have never met a Muslim." Another man across the room responded, "Yes you have. I am one." Although it was clear the second man was either from India or Pakistan, some in the group did not imagine he could be Muslim. A lot of learning ensued. More learning is still needed.

While most men may see career as upward mobility and big rewards, a growing number now measure their success by the time they spend with their children and their life partner, or the ability to make a difference in their community or an even bigger stage.

Some of the stories of the men of the 21st century include one who was a major stockholder in a successful small business. This business was sold to one of the US giants. He took an executive position at the acquiring company for a few years, then left to find work that would *feed his soul.*

Another FOCUS man left a high-ranking position in City Government to run for public office and serve in a different way. He subsequently ran for a higher office. Because he is an African American in a very "White" city, his courage and dedication to his country is continually tested by others.

The stories are endless.

Some recent FOCUS men express fears they may not be as successful as their fathers. These feelings are quite different from those we described as a part of FOCUS men in the 1980s and 1990s. In the '80s, they knew they were living in a world controlled by White men and that prospects were very positive, especially as the Cold War was winding down. In the '90s, they were exploring what it means to be a man and how to deal with a more inclusive environment and prospects were still quite positive. After all, the US was now the only world Superpower.

Of equal greater importance, there has been concern among

some FOCUS men that the United States may no longer maintain its world leadership dominance. And if that should happen, what will it mean for us and our children? A typical question might be: "How can we prevent that from happening?" For other FOCUS men, any assertions the US will not remain as the dominant world power are disregarded or rejected. However, some are willing to consider a multi-polar world – in which the United States is not the most powerful – but one of many powerful. This has been an acceptable, even desirable, organizing principle for many.

Participants since 2001 have included more men from small and medium-sized businesses, many who have changed employers multiple times. There have been a number of entrepreneurs, far more IT experts and some who travel overseas regularly as a part of their work.

Today over 80% of participants come from organizations who have international operations. All of these demographics suggest a group more aware of world dynamics and better able to respond to change without fear.

These men are bright, good learners and great participants. The range of acceptable emotions they show is quite broad and includes sadness and fear as well as love and tenderness. Tears have been quite acceptable. Sensitivity is not a sign of weakness. They still love the good business topics, but are often just as interested in exploring spirituality, parenting, life-balance, caring for parents and grandparents. They are representative of the emerging American man who is quite different from preceding generations and at the same time influenced by those who came before them.

It is important to remember we work with men who are successful as leaders or managers in traditional businesses or non-profits. We do not see people who lack ambition or motivation. Almost all fit into what would be described as high achievers in "mainstream America."

The most challenging conversations with recent groups have focused on sexual trafficking. Because the two of us are involved in educating others about sexual slavery and human trafficking (see Chapter 31), we bring it up wherever we are. Making others aware is part of our work.

Some of the men are uncomfortable with the topic of sexual trafficking. They assert we must be exaggerating the extent of this terrible crime. Some want to know why we insist on talking about it. And even when faced with the research statistics, a few have attempted to dismiss the topic as irrelevant to being a leader. By contrast, others in the groups were appalled by the information and became active themselves in educating others and in contributing financially to the work done to fight against sexual trafficking and to support recovery.

Recent groups included men with education and jobs similar to the early days of FOCUS though with more in high tech and entrepreneurial enterprises. They came from a "start up" in North Dakota, packaged goods manufacturers in North Carolina and Wisconsin, insurance executives from Ohio, a quality manager from California, a utility leader from Arizona. As individuals and as FOCUS groups they all inspire us.

Over the past thirty years, the men grew in more ways than we could imagine when we began. Spirituality, not religion, has now become a topic of interest to many. Developing real friendships has become a goal for many of our FOCUS graduates.

Granted, we are privileged to work with very special men, who in most cases have chosen to be with us, whose companies believe they are of such value that they paid the tuition and travel associated with this nine-month program.

As men experience the huge transition occurring in the world, many of the men realize the old paradigm for "being a man" is not working any more. The projections that say people of Color will soon exceed the number of European Americans in the US is disconcerting to some. The expectation China will soon pass the

US in Gross Domestic Product violates what we have been told since birth – that the US will always be the largest. Some FOCUS men struggle with these realities, as there are not yet established models for how American men can be successful in the emerging global economy. Additionally, a small but growing number of men are saying women may have more of "the right stuff" for tomorrow's world.

As we reflect on the national education statistics, we know more women than men are receiving college degrees or even graduating from high school. We also know more of the occupations that were traditionally male, such as construction or manufacturing, are ones experiencing the most shrinkage in our economy. Increasingly some men are facing a more challenging future than women. These trends do not affect our FOCUS men directly because of their education and career experiences. However, they are recognizing the seriousness of this reality as they think about raising their own children and about what is happening to the US economy.

As leaders of the program, we have not changed our approach. But the approach receives a more and more ready group of learners with each new year. We model openness, sharing at a deep personal level and developing close friendships with other men. In the '80s, not everyone saw these as important or even appropriate. Today there is recognition by most that these traits, while perhaps unfamiliar, produce great benefits to the individual and greater productivity for his organization.

So how has FOCUS been different in the 21st Century? The level of career success and expectations FOCUS men had in the '90s has declined in the years following 2000. It seems to have been a combination of fear provoked by 9.11 and what is happening since: uncertainty about the future of the US economy with the world changing so rapidly, what globalization will really mean and how it will feel as a white guy to be a minority. In some ways we find our emphasis in FOCUS shifting to some of the themes we explored with the women of INFLUENCE over the years.

The various changes affect FOCUS men in different ways. Some are excited at the change the world is experiencing and are looking forward to a time when the US no longer has to be "in charge." Other men insist none of these trends are real and the US will very soon be back in charge of the world.

The pace of change since 2000 has been more rapid than in the '90s and '80s. It's hard for us to appreciate the rapid growth of countries such as Indonesia and the Philippines. Americans were just getting used to the successes of India and China. Thinking about how rapidly other countries are growing can still be mind-boggling. Even the most uninvolved Americans are starting to realize that our national debt, the cost of being the policeman for the world and the continuing acceleration of health care costs, are creating a new reality that has never been experienced. A new reality must be met with new ideas and new responses.

We see more men are taking a longer view of the future and are increasingly feeling the value of connecting with others of different ethnicity, country of origin, religious beliefs or sexual orientation. We can see in the population at large there is both fear and discrimination shown against Islamic Americans, Gay Americans, African and Hispanic Americans and many other groups. We feel hopeful, however, because the men we work with are much healthier in their understanding of and acceptance of those who are in some way different. On a positive note, the understanding toward homosexuality is becoming more open and accepting.

The FOCUS program has been provided annually now for twenty-seven years. Working with so many wonderful men has provided us with an education. It has given us a wonderful window into the transition that both Euro-American men and men of Color are experiencing in the US. It also allows us to continually understand how companies across the nation are dealing with this time of rapid change. Finally, FOCUS has given its graduates the opportunity to think through how each man wants to be in a positive, healthy manner in our challenging, exciting, opportunity-filled world. It has been and is an honor to share the journeys of so many wonderful men.

## CHAPTER TWENTY-FIVE

# Creating a World That Works for All

*"WOW! Congratulations! This is an indescribable experience for which I am*

*beyond grateful...Please know that you have given many a new sense of hope.*

*Also thank you for graciously giving "college kids" the chance to be here.*

*Inviting us says much to me about your sincerity in trusting us with the*

*future and seeing us as essential in your goal to build a better world."*

-Participant in the *Omaha Commons Café*

It was September 7, 2001; we just completed the first evening of the FGISpirit *Omaha Commons Café* on the Creighton University campus. Three hundred women and men, young and old, rich and poor, of many different races and spiritual traditions were gathered to share conversations, food and entertainment while discussing issues that ranged from experiences growing up to how to enable world peace.

While others were preparing to go home, a White woman physician approached us. She began by telling us she really liked the purpose of the *Café*. But, she said, "I need to be at another table tomorrow. One of the men at my table has upset me so much with his anger toward White people." We asked her who it was. She pointed to an older African American man who was a Pastor in the Black community. Tim knew him well for his many years as a strong voice for justice in Omaha. We both knew he carried a lot of anger, much of which was aimed at White people and the racial injustices that existed in Omaha for decades.

We encouraged the woman to commit to the process and get to know the Pastor as a man. She was very skeptical, but she agreed to try. When we began again the next morning, we were able to see she was doing her best. As the day unfolded, we felt a different energy at her table. By the end of the second day, the woman came back to say she appreciated our encouraging her. Getting to know the Pastor was an amazing experience for her. She now understood he was a beautiful man and she learned so much from being with him.

We have multiple photos of their table group. On day one they all looked very serious. By day two they were animated and joyful, proving that the *Commons Café* process can work when participants are open, committed and decide to take down their barriers.

*The Omaha Commons Café* was one of our first and most powerful offerings of FGISpirit, the non-profit organization the two of us created in 1999. People sometimes wonder what prompts us to do things that seem outrageous or impossible. *The Commons Café* would be one of those things. We knew it would require much work, but we never felt it would be impossible.

Most of the three hundred participants would never have met each other without the *Café*. One of the participants summed up the experience by saying the three most positive benefits were: "Connecting with people I would never have met; talking about matters of consequence; and seeing the possibility of what our society could become." So what was *The Commons Café* and how did it unfold?

As often happens, we are inspired by what's possible, though not easy. Carol returned from a conference of the Institute of Noetic Sciences in 1999, full of new ideas. During the conference she met and worked with several people who would have permanent impacts on our work. The most significant of these was Sharif

Abdullah, an attorney, peacemaker and author. His book, *Creating a World That Works for All*,²² radically changed the way we describe our work to this day.

We have believed in the idea of "a world that works for all" for over forty years and express similar ideas in our work. Sharif coined the phrase and has offered some excellent ways in which such a world can be attained. We committed all of our work to this goal – whether with corporate America, women recovering from sexual slavery in India and everything else we do.

One of Sharif's beliefs is that if socially and racially diverse people could meet in a café and get to know one another over coffee or tea and food, they could break down barriers and find ways to come to value each other and eventually create a healthy society. Sharif began in the '90s by offering a series of such encounters, or "commons cafés," in different parts of the United States. Typically the cafés lasted two to four hours and attracted 30 to 50 people. We loved the idea; and thus, the FGISpirit *Omaha Commons Café* was born.

As we began to visualize such an event in Omaha, we were thrilled and excited to envision dozens of tables with truly diverse people talking about important life and leadership questions. It would surely be a first for our City. At the same time, we couldn't imagine how such an event would be possible, since Omaha's history up until then was one of segregation and discrimination.

Tim grew up in Omaha where most White people had limited interactions with People of Color. Tim personally knew few People of Color until he served on the Omaha Board of Education and later the Omaha City Council.

Carol, by contrast, grew up in Southern California where there was constant immersion in diversity. As an adult, she was involved many years with the US Air Force where again there was great diversity. Early on, Omaha was a challenging place for Carol to live since there were so few non-Whites in the area and almost no mixing of ethnic groups.

It seemed to us a "Café" would be more effective if it attracted a larger group and thus offered greater chances for diversity. It would also be valuable to have the experience last over two days, allowing one to learn far more as s/he reflected on the experience overnight and then continued the learning. The challenge, of course, was how to get a very diverse group of people to come together and have the conversations.

Sharif confirmed a larger group for a longer time period would be desirable, but wondered whether we could pull it off. After only a few weeks of implementing our plan to recruit participants, we wondered if Sharif was right. Would we pull it off?

Prior to this, we had not sponsored a program where we were given the opportunity to recruit such a large and very diverse participant group. Moreover, we needed to convince this group to participate in something never seen before in Omaha, being sponsored by a small organization with almost no community presence. We were way beyond our zone of experience and expertise. This didn't stop us. Many with whom we spoke praised us for having such an ambitious goal, but still told us they didn't think it was possible.

Those skeptics included some who knew the Omaha Community well. We considered their concerns, but ultimately decided we would give it our best effort and see what was possible. As is often our practice, we began to "see" our positive, present tense intention. We imagined the *Café*, saw the diverse group gathered and talking at tables, heard what was being said and felt pleased and grateful at the outcomes.

Then, we also looked at the actual numbers. In Omaha at the time, 84% of the population was White, 7.7% African American, 5.2% Hispanic, 1.5% Asian, .4% Native American. Our goal for the *Café* was our participants would be more than 30% People of Color, doubling their actual representation in the City. It sounded a bit crazy, but we pushed on to bring our goal to life.

The tasks we needed to complete in order to make the *Café* successful included the following, in order from easiest to most challenging: find a location and co-sponsor, make a budget, design the program, get friends who would help, recruit three hundred women and men who would be as diverse as possible. As we tackled these challenges, we had the good fortune to encounter wonderful people in all walks of life who helped us make the *Café* a reality. Each one of these encounters convinced us we were doing what needed to be done.

We talked to our friend, Pat Callone, then a Vice President at Creighton University. She arranged for us to meet with Rev. John Schlegel, SJ, then President of Creighton University. He was known in Omaha as one who strongly advocated for a more just and inclusive City. After confirming the value and benefits of our proposal, he quickly offered us use of the ballroom in the Creighton Student Center. Even more remarkable was his agreement that Creighton would be the *Café* co-sponsor.

He sent us to meet and work with Maria Teresa Gaston, then Director of Creighton's Justice and Peace Center. Maria Teresa welcomed us and gave much of her personal time to arrange the space plus purchase the meals at the lowest possible cost. During the preparations, we shared hours of great conversation with Maria Theresa about social justice, inclusiveness and virtually every topic under the sun. In addition to her work for us at Creighton, she introduced us to many in the Hispanic community in Omaha. She also helped recruit Creighton students to participate in the *Café*.

Others at Creighton who supported our efforts were Tami Buffalohead McGill who worked with Native American students and Ricardo Ariza who counseled minority students. Both had remarkable personal stories and offered their wisdom and encouragement. And then Pat Callone introduced us to the Creighton Community by hosting a meal with key campus faculty and administrators to let us describe the *Café*.

In our experiences with these women and men at Creighton, we received many insights from leaders who cared deeply about making our world a better place. It really confirmed the *Café* could succeed.

We felt we had a perfect site. Our intention was clear: to have 300 very diverse women and men seated at tables, engaging with one another in deeply personal conversations about life, work and the steps to creating a world that works for all.

Building a budget was easy. After we allowed money for food, entertainment, travel and a stipend for Sharif, marketing and administration, we determined that the *Café* would cost about $90,000, not including FGI staff time. This was roughly a cost of $300 per participant.

By the standards of corporate training in those days, $300 was a huge bargain. Where could you get over ten hours of content and process, three excellent meals and eight segments of entertainment that was also educational?

On the other hand, it would have excluded at least 250 of the people we wanted to have in the room. So we set aside funds for scholarships, better enabling those who couldn't manage the full price to attend. Later our decision was confirmed by many of those who joined us with a full scholarship. They told us in many ways how proud they were to have received a gift of such value.

With calls out to former friends and supporters plus a couple dozen corporate contacts in Omaha, we were able to raise over half of the budget. We trusted the rest to the Divine and went ahead with marketing. Subsequently we covered the balance of the cost with a contribution from our for-profit business, FGI International.

Initial letters and a few phone calls is all it took to fill the *Café* seats with over 150 White women and men. We probably could have recruited 300 White people at full tuition. They seemed intrigued or eager to have the experience. We were delighted several dozen came from outside Omaha, including Philadelphia, Phoenix and Denver. They further broadened the experience base of the *Café*. One of those from Denver summed up the experience this way, "This is the most wonderful event I ever went to. Let's do this in Denver. I want to help."

Identifying and recruiting the women and men of Color presented a different challenge. Bringing in those who were in poverty, had physical handicaps or were aged was even more complex. For several weeks, we crisscrossed the City, calling on women and men who were leaders in their respective communities. This included pastors of all-Black churches and churches with large Hispanic congregations. It involved the heads of social agencies who provided services to the poor and those who knew people in the various ethnic communities.

The response was always polite and usually quite interested. People told us how pleased they were we were undertaking this project. But when we reached the point of asking them to commit to recruiting people from their community or even committing to come personally, there was often some backpedaling.

We heard, "All our people work on those days." Or, "If I encourage our people to come to your *Café*, they will probably decide not to come to church that Sunday." "The people I know would never come to something so new that no one has ever attended before." "If you can't tell me exactly what will happen, I can't help you."

Anyone who believes that because Omaha has such a low unemployment rate there must not be poverty would be shocked to see parts of the City we saw. We sometimes had long waits for women or men who were so busy helping those in need that fitting us into their schedule was a real problem. In most cases we met people who inspired us as they told us their stories. In many ways, our recruiting visits were the *Commons Café* for the two of us.

After many visits to community leaders, we realized it would be possible to have the people we needed to be present. We identified 40 individuals, each of whom committed to bringing ten people to the *Café*. We called them shepherds because they were "shepherding" their little "flocks" to *The Commons Café* on September 7. The profile of the individuals they were to recruit was very specific. If they could do this, we would be successful. We offered them the freedom to adjust the program fee down as far as needed to insure the right people came.

It may sound odd to say we wished to have 300 in the room, but we had forty shepherds each recruiting ten. We "guesstimated" that if 400 agreed to come, 300 would actually show up. As it turned out this was absolutely on target. The week before the *Café*, we had 386 registered and 30 on a waiting list. When we began that Friday afternoon, there were 307 in the room. Those 307 included participants who came from local homeless shelters as well as a handful of Omaha millionaires. There were also teenagers, college students and people over 80. There were many who were able and others who were physically challenged. More than 30% were People of Color.

Working with the shepherds was not always simple. The number of calls and follow-up calls, reminders and gentle prods, assertive requests and begging took days and days of work. Tom Rouse, who was working with us at the time, took a big share of this work and genuinely enjoyed it. Because he spoke Spanish, he was especially helpful with the Hispanic community. Paul Koch also joined our effort. He was then Executive Director of the largest homeless shelter in the City.

The recruiting was a full time effort for three months from four of us at FGISpirit. At times, it seemed we would add a dozen people one day and lose as many the next. Because we were always mindful of the demographic mix, we had to turn some away while redoubling efforts for others. Lori Zahm in our office handled all of the logistics beautifully. Everyone at FGISpirit was "over employed" for about three months.

When we told Sharif Abdullah in mid-August we were on track to reach our goal of 300, he was genuinely dumbfounded. He was also intrigued by the prospects for seeing the group in action. We were excited to have the group hear him speak and feel the hope and inspiration Carol had felt when she worked with him earlier.

September 7th arrived. We decorated the tables, hung banners, checked the sound system and prepared to see who would come and how the *Café* would unfold. We felt a combination of positive excitement and fear. What if more people came than we were expecting? Where would we put them? How would we feed them? What if no one came after all this work? What if the program fell flat? What if people didn't want to sit at tables with those who were different? What if no one spoke? What if people hated it and walked out? What made us undertake this project?

Our irrational fears, fortunately, lasted only a short time and then people began to arrive. First came the forty women and men who agreed to be "Table Hosts." As Hosts they would welcome people to their table and then facilitate the conversations throughout the *Café*. They came early for some brief but intense training led by Carol. When we heard them asking questions, we felt much better. These were the ones who would make the table conversations actually happen. As a group, they were as diverse as those who would soon arrive.

Then our dear friend, the late Luigi Waites, came onto the stage and set up his vibraphone. He provided the music to welcome the participants. Luigi was a famous musician in the Omaha area. He played in several famous jazz bands in the '50s and '60s, worked with thousands of children in the Omaha Public Schools and was a fixture in the Omaha jazz scene for over 40 years. Whenever we had a gathering or party at FGI, Luigi was a part of the action. He was the perfect greeter to *The Commons Café*. Luigi stayed and became a participant.

Upon arrival, each person chose a table number from a large bowl. These numbers ensured *Café* participants would be sitting randomly with others whom they had not met. White participants drew from one bowl. Non-whites drew from a separate bowl. This ensured no table had a majority of White participants.

Imagine if you had come to *The Commons Café*. You enter a ballroom on a college campus you have most likely not visited before. You are coming with one or two friends, but know almost no one else as you come into the room. You draw a table number and realize it is different from the ones your friends have drawn. You tell your friends you hope they have a good time, then look for your table number.

As you approach your table, you see six others already there. Only one other at the table has your ethnicity, only two others seem to be about your age. You introduce yourself, sit down and prepare for the *Café* to begin. You are going to spend two days with these people. You aren't sure what is going to happen, but have heard there will be some open discussions of important topics at the tables. How would you be feeling? Are you excited or wondering why you came? Are you ready to do whatever is expected or are you thinking about how much flexibility you may have in terms of your participation? We suspect that most of the three hundred had that kind of conversation with self as it came time to begin.

Watching people arrive was thrilling for us. It was a true rainbow of ethnicity, gender and age. A woman over 80 arrived in a wheel chair. Several severely handicapped people came on crutches, often with help from friends. About twenty homeless women and men came from a local shelter. A few ministers and priests came. Some thirty Creighton students arrived, probably wondering why they had signed up. Native Americans from Omaha as well as a nearby reservation also arrived. Several very prominent Omahans were also present. FGI friends from other cities made the trip. Our colleague, Sharif Abdullah appeared and we were ready to start!

We understand, in retrospect, that the design of the *Café* process is what produced the magic. We alternated deep conversations, a few short presentations, plus entertainment and meals over the two days. Each table of seven or eight individuals had seven conversations during the two days. The first couple of conversations were fairly easy, with questions such as: "What brought you to *The Commons Café*?" "What would you say is a good life?" "How would you describe your economic class?" "If you really knew me, what would you know about my passions, what's really inside of me, who I really am?"

Then the conversations went deeper, asking participants to discuss with one another issues such as: "Why do Americans consume so much? "Do you believe there is an underclass in this country?" "What are the characteristics of an underclass?" "What was your earliest experience with race/ethnicity? How did you feel about it?" "How have your attitudes changed or deepened since those experiences?"

During the last conversation on Saturday, they were asked to consider issues such as: "Is it possible to use ethnic and religious differences to bring people together rather than to drive them apart?" "What is your vision of a society which would work for all?"

The entertainment throughout the three days included the choir from a homeless shelter, a professional theatre group which did a presentation in song and humor about racism in Omaha, a choir from an African American AME church, African drummers and dancers, a Mariachi band and dancers from the Ballet Folklorico Mexicana plus a Native American drummer. Between the table conversations and entertainment, the Café alternated meals and occasional comments by Sharif or one of us.

The stories from *The Omaha Commons Café*, as with all four of our *Commons Cafés* programs, were too numerous to recount. However, some do stand out.

There were two elderly men at one table, both 85. One was White and one was African American. In the course of table conversations about their lives, they discovered that in the 1940s they were each drafted into the US military. After basic training, they both left Omaha on the same train on the same day. Because one was African American, he was not allowed to ride in the same train cars as the White soldiers. They never met one another until *The Commons Café*. The realization produced a deep and heartwarming conversation about their two lives around this one, shared experience.

The college students who came were a great addition to the small groups. They brought energy and youth, optimism and compassion. They also felt the program was of great value to them. As one student said at the end of the *Café*, "It was very valuable to have the opportunity to participate in something like this at the age of 20, to be in the midst of such wisdom and yet be respected and heard as an equal."

Another college student summed up the experience with "Wow! This is an indescribable experience for which I am beyond grateful. Good luck in the future and know you have given many a new sense of hope."

Some of the wealthy White participants remarked at how wise and insightful others at their tables were – regardless of ethnicity or economic success.

Many of the professional entertainers whom we engaged were so taken with what they experienced in the room, they stayed after their performances and pulled up chairs to join table discussions. There was one such group, who had come from Denver to perform the skit about racism in Omaha. Known as The Performance Works, Chris Keener listened to the two of us talk about the local issues of race and discrimination prior to the actual *Café*. He then wrote a unique script just about Omaha.

They sent a draft to us. We were disappointed because we did not feel the messages were strong enough. So we asked for a re-write. They were afraid because they had never said things so strong in front of an audience. We reassured them and asked them to perform it anyway. Then **we** worried whether it would be too strong. We decided that if we didn't let people know how bad situations really were, we would not be true to ourselves. They went ahead and told through song and dialogue what it meant to live in Omaha if you were poor or African American or Hispanic or homeless or a victim of abuse.

Those of us who lived far from the inner city didn't experience the 19th century wooden sewers that backed up into basements after every hard rain. We didn't know what it was like to have no access to even decent groceries or a drug store near us; or that there was no decent public transportation to jobs. The Performance Works covered all of this and did it in a way that people could hear. During the break that came after their presentation, an elderly black woman came up to Carol and said, "Thank you, dear, for sharing our truth."

As the first day of the *Café* ended, people left feeling positive and in most cases deep in thoughts and feelings. The experience touched many very deeply. We finished the evening debriefing with Sharif and Paul and then handled a few logistics with the FGI team. Each of us left for our respective homes with feelings of *relief* – people had come, the *Café* was underway; *happiness* – the early conversations had gone well, energy was positive; and *apprehension* – what if people don't come back tomorrow?

The second day was even better. Participants arrived early and engaged immediately with others as they came. The noise level was loud and animated. As the table conversation questions became deeper, most tables had richer, more open and candid conversations. The day was animated, full of energy and deep conversation from 9AM-3:30PM.

There were a few tables that were exceptions. In those cases, it appeared that no one at the table took initiative to get others going. Consequently a few participants ended feeling the *Café* was not meaningful enough for them.

We continued the conversation process until late afternoon. The remaining entertainment segments included dancing throughout the room, singing and enjoying one another as well as celebrating the whole process.

Once people completed a brief evaluation, the *Café* was complete. Many, however, stayed to continue conversations, make arrangements to follow up with people they met, or talk to us or to Sharif. After the last left, we reviewed some of the comments. Here are five that stood out for us:

What was positive for me:

"The flow of the event, Spirit was definitely in the house!"

"The sea of faces, the beautiful differences."

"The opportunity to enhance the lives of a few and have them look at the world through your eyes."

"I continue to be truly amazed at how a group of strangers can come together and open their hearts to one another – it's about loving and valuing the human dignity of each others' lives."

And a final one from Sharif, "I have enjoyed time in cafés in many countries around the world, but this is the ultimate café. You have taken the curiosity, discussions and acceptance that can be found in traditional cafés to a new level and encouraged us all to accept the power of one."

There is one more very important issue to report about the *Café*. Earlier we talked about the desired participant mix. We stated that in Omaha, 84% of the population was White, 7.7% African American, 5.2% Hispanic, 1.5% Asian, .4% Native American. Our goal had been to have at least 30% Women and Men of Color in attendance. When the numbers were all in, the 307 participants were 55% White, 18% African American, 15% Hispanic, 3% Asian, 5% Native Americans, 4% foreigners. We exceeded our goal!

We finished the *Café* exhausted, but extremely satisfied. Little did we know that three days later 9.11 would occur in New York. The feelings of understanding and acceptance of differences were largely wrenched asunder for most people living in the United States. But those of us who had been a part of *The Commons Café* carried our feelings from the *Café* experience for many months.

Those who came to *The Omaha Commons Café* from Denver decided they wanted to hold a *Commons Café* in Denver in 2002. The process was the same, except there was a great committee of volunteers who did the legwork in addition to the FGI staff. Sally Anderson, Foster Harding, David Goldberg, GG Johnston, Laura Majors, Paul Moore, Theresa Montoya and Kistie Simmons were marvelous. Sharif joined us again. He was delighted in seeing his work carried on in this way. Denver University was the partner and host. The agenda was virtually the same. The total number who participated was smaller at 200, but the experience was real and again touched many people deeply.

Our greatest *Café* feat was accomplished in 2003 when we held our *Commons Café* in Shanghai that drew over one hundred from six countries. However, *The Omaha Commons Café* remains in our hearts as the most meaningful, partly because it was the first; partly because it was so challenging; partly because it was our home city, but mostly because we witnessed a true rainbow celebration that many thought would be impossible in Omaha.

What learnings did we personally take away from *The Omaha Commons Café*? There were many, but the ones that stand out today include:

- The author, Margaret Wheatley, is right when she said, "We can change the world if we start listening to one another again. Simple, honest, human conversation. Not mediation, negotiation, problem-solving, debate or public meetings. Simple, truthful conversation where we each have a chance to speak, we each feel heard and we each listen well."[23]

- The *Café* process has proven to us that when people who would otherwise never meet have the chance to know those with very different life realities, hope and belief in the future are enormously enhanced.
- It is true that "breaking bread together" can be wonderfully therapeutic as well as informative, enjoyable and educational. Sharing different kinds of ethnic entertainment together can be even more enjoyable and just as educational and therapeutic.

Having a successful *Café* was one of the most difficult challenges FGISpirit ever faced. But we would not have traded it for any other experience we can imagine. We personally learned so much and grew tremendously. The looks of hope and joy on the faces of the participants at the end of the second day will stay with us forever.

## CHAPTER TWENTY-SIX

# The China Pilgrimage

It was a beautiful October night in 2003. We were standing in the courtyard of the Two Springs Crossing Hotel outside of Bo Hai Suo Village at the base of the Great Wall. The night was clear and beautiful. A goat was being roasted on an outside fire for our dinner. It was feeling like life could hardly get better. For the past two weeks we had been in China with twenty-eight Americans on what we called *The China Pilgrimage*. To provide the experiences, we purchased seats in planes, trains, boats and taxis.

The *Pilgrimage* included hotels in four cities, visits to temples, gardens, palaces and the Great Wall. In Hangzhou, we were entertained by Chinese Opera Singers. In Beijing we saw a wonderful dinner show provided by natives of XinJiang, a Province in the far Northwest of the country. The previous night at our hotel we experienced a marvelous musical program offered by the children from the school in Bo Hai Suo, the deep mountains. In addition to these experiences, we convened a very successful leadership program in Shanghai which attracted one hundred seven participants from six countries.

The evening concluded with our own Chinese fireworks show provided by the Hotel owner, Mrs. Wang, after the goat roast.

Looking back on it a decade later, this trip still stands as one of the 3-4 highlights of our careers! After all, who would have believed that in 2003 we convened so many people in China to participate in a leadership program that took individuals deep on issues of life, spirit and work with people they had just met? Or that the thousand-year old village built for soldiers who defended the Great Wall would welcome outsiders, especially Americans, for the first time in history to walk their streets and even to visit the factory where they manufactured munitions?

It's amazing, even today, to re-live the story of how all of it happened.

We received the idea for the *Pilgrimage* in 2000, when the two of us and Denny visited the City of Hangzhou. We were standing in three separate locations on the grounds of the Temple of Inspired Seclusion, LingYin Si. Each one of us had heard the message *"We must bring Americans to this spot."*

Then in 2001, we convened *The Omaha Commons Café*. That incredible experience made us wonder what a "commons café" would be like if we held it in China with participants from multiple countries.

Finally, the women and men who worked with us in both Russia and the US kept asking us if we would take them with us to China. So in 2002, we said to each other, "Let's do it." Of course, without Rui Shujie, nothing would have been possible. With her, we were able to do amazing things.

In many ways the planning was more of an adventure than the *Pilgrimage* itself. We traveled two to three times each year to China over a three-year period. How could we give Americans or Russians a feel for this amazing country in just one short trip?

American media had convinced our country that China was a place where everyone was oppressed, living conditions were appalling and "the spiritual" was at best a distant memory. How could we make this trip reflect the amazing China we were experiencing, not the one reported in the US? Answering this question resulted in experiences with some marvelous women and men.

We knew the *Pilgrimage* would be centered in Shanghai, since this is the City where we had the greatest number of Chinese friends. But we did not want it to be a "sightseers'" experience. The first thing was to find the "right" hotel. We had used the comfortable Regal East Asia Hotel for our programs. It was a great spot, but more like a Marriott in the US than a Chinese hotel. Within several hundred yards of the Regal we found the Olympic Hotel. This was a small garden hotel where no one spoke English, where there was no Western breakfast and no foreign guests except a few from Japan. Rooms were not as nice as the Regal; air conditioning was only available part of the time. While food was excellent, menus focused on many dishes unfamiliar to Americans.

With Rui acting as translator, we met Mrs. Pan Jin, Sales Manager, who created a wonderful Chinese experience for us. Over the year and a half we worked with her, it was clear that she did many things on our behalf which were beyond her authority at the Hotel. We knew that Chinese hotels had fairly strict rules about what can and cannot be done. Additionally, the Olympic was State Owned. So the rules were even stricter. Mrs. Pan became our advocate.

There were little things such as our desire to have small round tables in the Lily conference center. The Olympic didn't have small round tables. Mrs. Pan went outside and borrowed some for us. The Olympic had one microphone for the stage in the conference room. We wanted at least six with audio mixers. The only newspapers in the Hotel were written in Mandarin. We wanted English language newspapers delivered to all the guests' rooms daily. Those who know us can imagine a long list of things we wanted that the Olympic didn't have and did not want to have. Mrs. Pan found all of them for us – and more. Over about eighteen months, Rui spent many more hours with Pan Jin. The results were a perfect experience.

The centerpiece of *The China Pilgrimage* would be the three-day Conference with Chinese and foreigners. We called it *Talking*

*Together: Business, Culture and Friendship.* Using the *Commons Café* model, we would have participants do most of the work in conversations at small tables that included both Chinese and foreigners. Our vision was there would be at least two Chinese for every foreigner. Also using the *Commons Café* model, we needed to have a rhythm to the meeting that included: input from the stage, small group discussions, multi-cultural entertainment, meals and then repeat.

The one big question became: how to find great Chinese cultural entertainment at a price we could afford? Rui identified some young Chinese entertainers with a combination of acrobats and martial arts, plus Jasmine Flower Dancers. We would later ask the Americans and Russians to each prepare some entertainment as well. It was a perfect complement to the serious work of the Conference.

The next order of business was finding the right guide to help us show Shanghai to the "foreigners" we brought along. There are thousands of English speaking guides in Shanghai, most controlled by several large travel agencies. We went with Rui to interview travel agencies and find the perfect guide. Most of the agencies had trouble understanding why the guide mattered. It was out of their understanding why we would care. But of course we did. We wanted a person who was knowledgeable both on what we were seeing and how it became that way. We wanted a person who would speak when needed, but would be quiet the rest of the time. We wanted a guide who laughed, interacted with our friends and worked with us to make things right. We were adamant that our guide not be one who carried a raised flag and herded us around like animals.

The travel agency we chose gave us Coco. And were we fortunate. Coco was a young, well-educated woman who spoke great English and did exactly what we asked of her. We fell in love with her and continued to engage her during the following eight years as we brought Americans and Russians to China. One year we asked CoCo to begin taking us and some Americans to

Xitang, a distant water village. Coco was unfamiliar with the place and certainly had not visited it. Before we arrived on the next trip, she visited Xitang, identified the most important things to see and selected a great restaurant for lunch.

With Shanghai activities managed, we headed off to Hangzhou to plan our days there. Here we decided to use a hotel that was more Western: The Ramada. We chose it because it was within walking distance of the most spectacular site in Hangzhou, West Lake. There we arranged for boats to take us to the island where a special pagoda and Buddhist worship site were to be found.

Our other Hangzhou destination was to be LingYin Si, the magnificent park which had at its center the Temple of Inspired Seclusion. This park and temple had been under the special protection of Zhou Enlai, the Premier of China during the Cultural Revolution. The Premier protected LingYin Si from the Red Guards who would otherwise have defaced the statues and most likely even destroyed the temple and the park.

We visited this site in 2000. During this earlier visit, the two of us and Denny were struck by the huge Buddha statues carved directly from and into the rocks. The two of us and Rui returned to make arrangements for the Pilgrimage group. We anticipated seeing those incredible statues once again and to share them with our friends. We purchased our tickets and walked through the turnstiles into the park. We walked but a few paces when all three of us gasped and shrieked. All of the giant statues of the Buddha were gone!

What happened? Where were they? We never found out. One of the many puzzling, sometimes maddening things about China is that often one cannot find any way to get answers to questions. No one seems to know. The only proof those amazing statues had ever existed were photos of our first visit.

The grounds were still beautiful; the temple was magnificent. We were still pleased to have come. And yet, this was quite a mystery – or in reality, a Chinese political decision?

A plane flight carried the group north to Beijing for our next stop on the *Pilgrimage*. Rui already found a wonderful hotel that we continued to use whenever our work brought us to Beijing. It was Traders, a part of the exclusive Shangri La hotel group. For whatever reasons, they were willing to meet our needs at a very modest price. The staff at Traders was incredibly well trained and eagerly looked out for our every need.

Rui arranged for a driver to meet the plane and accompany us during our work in the area. This is how we met the wonderful Mr. Rao, who owned his own car and worked directly with us. He spoke very little English, but with Rui present, it really didn't matter. Mr. Rao was ready to drive us whenever and wherever! We knew what we wanted the Pilgrims to experience in Beijing. So our primary task on this trip was to go to the Great Wall at Mutianyu and see if we could find a good place to stay near the Wall. Mr. Rao had a list of four hotels near the base of the wall, and so we set out.

The drive from the center of Beijing to Mutianyu is an enjoyable one, once out of the City. It is very hilly farm country, with many small villages along the way. Most of the steep hills have been terraced. The farmers have intensively planted every possible bit of space on those hills. As the road rose towards one of the villages, we stopped the van for a short stretch break. By coincidence we ended up next to a grade school. The kindergarteners had just been released to go home for lunch. In seconds they surrounded Carol. It was heartwarming to see all of them surround her laughing and smiling. They did not want to let her go.

After a couple of hours of driving, we came to Mutianyu and then the hotels Mr. Rao had found. The first was right at the Wall. The views were spectacular, but the hotel was filthy dirty and in great disrepair. The second and third were further away and were in the same shape as the first. They had been built some time earlier with heavy, probably Soviet architecture. None were acceptable. We were close to despair.

Then as we were going down the road to Mr. Rao's last choice, we saw what looked like a brand new, small hotel, nestled at the base of the Wall and accessed by bridge across a beautiful little creek. The sign near the road proclaimed that it was "Two Springs Crossing Hotel." Carol said that we should stop and see what it was. Mr. Rao was not so sure as it was not on the list. Rui and Tim agreed we should definitely stop. We crossed the bridge and parked our van on a lovely plaza outside the entrance. There to greet us – though she did not know we were coming – was the owner, Wang Xiurong. Mrs. Wang built the hotel two years earlier, after retiring from a career at China Telecom. The hotel had about thirty rooms plus a lovely dining room, a large meeting room and a karaoke room.

The rooms were simple, but quite clean. The shower in each bathroom was a hand held wand and a hole in the floor. There was certainly no air conditioning. The staff consisted of very young Chinese women and men, most in their late teens. They were all children who had grown up in this area known as the Deep Mountains. Of course, none of them spoke any English. Every one of them, however, was there to serve. This would be the perfect hotel for the last days the Americans would be in China.

The three of us agreed the basics were determined. We could return to the United States. Rui would follow up with all venues and work out the details as the *Pilgrimage* began to take shape. Now the three of us felt more confident knowing the specifics were being managed.

We headed back to the US to design the program for our *Talking Together* Conference. Once the agenda was clear, we started inviting specific Chinese, Americans, Russians and New Zealanders to be a part of the formal program of the Conference.

Recruiting the Americans was probably the easiest part of the project. Few of those we knew had ever been to China. They were eager to see and hear what we had been talking about since

2000. We limited recruiting to the number who would fit on one bus with their luggage. That became twenty-eight plus Rui and the two of us.

Recruiting is one thing. Managing all of the logistics before, during and after the trip was close to a nightmare. Lori Zahm, who was our FGI Business Manager in those days, took over the *Pilgrimage* logistics and finances. She worked with Rui to flesh out all of the specifics. Lori did a wonderful job handling individual requests for roommates/or not, foods eaten/or not, problems with visas, problems with airlines. And finally the problem with most FGI trips: those who sign up for our programs are so busy they often fail to read or follow instructions. Lori often had great patience in dealing with each of the issues that arose.

Lori was also working with Rui on recruiting those from China who would come. We used a system similar to the one for the US *Commons Café*. A dozen Chinese friends agreed to be "shepherds" and identify and recruit Chinese they knew. Though they very willingly accepted this assignment Rui was still left with a huge challenge in getting the desired number of Chinese to actually appear at the Conference.

One of the big learnings we had working in Russia and China is that in both countries, people tended to often live only in the present. It was incredibly difficult to get people to make commitments to anything in the future. It seemed that often "life" interfered with those commitments. In the United States it is not uncommon for people to determine something they will do a year in advance. In China, a week in advance was a long time.

As the dates for the trip came closer, it was clear to us that we would need more "on the ground" support than Rui could provide. So we asked Lori to come along at least through the end of the Conference. Although she was a single parent of two young girls at the time, she readily agreed. Lori's presence along with Rui and the two of us made the Conference possible.

However there was soon one more hurdle. Our closest advisors in Shanghai, Peng, Nina and SC, told us it was possible the Chinese Government (Communist Party) would think we were coming to China to preach religion or to spread American capitalism and democracy. None of these would be acceptable.

We needed a prominent Communist to be a part of our Conference. Rui made inquiries and soon had a name, Mr. Ming Ming Lu, then editor of one of the major business magazines in Shanghai and an important cadre in the Communist Party. But how to approach him? More inquiries and our friend, Nina, came up with the name of Christopher Zhu, a local entrepreneur and member of the Communist Party. We had to meet Christopher to help him understand we would not do anything during the Conference that was forbidden or in any way to proselytize. The meeting was scheduled.

We packed our bags for China with a huge concern: "What if Christopher doesn't like us and thinks we are a threat? We have all these foreigners from other countries coming. If there is no Conference, what will we do?"

As usual, Denny and the two of us arrived in Shanghai several days ahead of the other foreigners, to make sure that everything was ready to go. In this instance, our most important task was to convince Christopher Zhu that we did not intend to do anything that would be inappropriate from the point of view of the Communist Party or the Chinese government.

When we met Christopher, our fears were quickly assuaged. He was a delightful person who was able to "check us out" without any casual observer even noticing. He said he was confident that we would meet the requirements. However, to reassure both the government and the Party he would personally participate in the Conference. He said Mr. Ming Ming Lu would be pleased to offer the formal greeting on behalf of Shanghai at the beginning of our first evening. Because Mr. Lu was very busy, he would be present only to open the Conference.

It's hard to remember whether we were more relieved or more happy. The news was great: the *Talking Together* Conference could go forward.

The next day we were at the Olympic Hotel, working on details for the Conference. During the day we had two important experiences. The first was going to a conference room we were to use for the Conference. But in the room on that day was an English language class for workers at the Hotel. We sat down to listen for a few minutes and heard what we knew were very poor pronunciations of English by the instructor. He could see that we were dismayed and asked if we would help with the class for a little while. So there we were teaching "Hotel English" to those who would be serving us during the coming days. We felt honored that the Hotel employees were comfortable with us in that role, plus we enjoyed ourselves.

Our next experience was even better. In the Lily Ballroom where the Conference was to be held, we found about fifty Hotel employees practicing their choral singing. In a few days they would be competing against hundreds of choirs from across Shanghai in a Government competition. We discovered that this Hotel was a Government entity. This meant these employees were technically all part of a Communist Work Unit.

We found their singing stirring, inspiring and quite beautiful. So on the spot we asked if they would be willing to sing at the opening of our Conference the next evening. To do that meant some members of the group would have to come in on their own time since they were not all scheduled to be on duty at the Hotel. They quickly agreed and seemed honored.

The next morning the Americans began arriving in Shanghai for the *Pilgrimage*. Shortly after, those from New Zealand and Russia arrived. We were so excited that all of our work had reached its climax.

The Conference was to begin in the evening of October 10. During that day we had the Americans, Russians and New

Zealanders tour Shanghai to get a tiny feel for what it was like to be in China.

Tour highlights included a visit to Old Shanghai, a section of the City that was like the Shanghai of a hundred years ago. Here the foreigners saw an ancient garden, lunched at an historic restaurant and had their first experience in Chinese shopping. In China nothing should be purchased for the price that was announced by the shop clerk, as it would take the fun out of the whole encounter. Carol offered a great demonstration of this several times during the tour.

The most fun to watch was when she helped our friend, Marilyn, purchase a porcelain statue of a beautiful woman. The clerk was offering it for RMB1200 (about USD150). After a long series of offers and counter-offers, Carol was able to persuade the clerk to sell it for a little over RMB400 (about USD55). A small crowd of Americans and a few Chinese had gathered to witness the bargaining. The clerk shrieked and moaned about how Carol was denying her family food and ruining her life. She shouted at Carol, "you cutting my throat." But after it was all over, she hugged Carol and both smiled and then shook hands. The Americans were amazed. The Chinese who witnessed the scene were delighted and applauded. One said to Carol with genuine respect, "you very good cheap woman." All then applauded again. Here was an American who understood the process of buying and selling in China. The Chinese were pleased and considered this as understanding and respectful.

The final stop of the tour was at the Jade Buddha Temple, an ancient and beautiful compound, little changed in hundreds of years. During the day, foreigners saw both great wealth and great poverty. The skyline of Shanghai is filled with glittering skyscrapers and luxury shopping. But as one looks down the older, narrow streets and paths, it is clear that there are millions who struggle every day to stay alive. The contrast was very troubling for many of the Americans.

When we returned to the hotel in late afternoon, Lori approached us with tears in her eyes. She said the poverty she had seen this day troubled her so much that she wanted to return to the United States immediately. We sat together, hugged Lori and talked some more. We reminded her about all she could teach her children with the stories of China. We talked about how much we needed her during the Conference. Reluctantly, she agreed to stay until the end of the Conference. How we appreciated who Lori was for FGI and as our trusted, dear friend.

In less than an hour, Conference registration opened and Chinese began arriving. Shortly thereafter, the foreigners registered and people began finding their assigned tables. Like the earlier *Commons Cafés* in the US, each of the small round tables included Chinese, Americans and a Russian. Some tables also had a New Zealander, an Italian or a Singaporean. By the end of our time together on the 12th, people at most of the tables became very close. Some continue to email one another to this day.

Soon it was time to begin! Christopher Zhu and Ming Ming Lu joined Rui and the two of us on the stage. Christopher introduced Ming Ming who made the official welcome to the City of Shanghai. We were told that as soon as he had welcomed the group, he would leave. But Ming Ming didn't leave. He went to one of the tables where there was an unoccupied chair and sat down. He joined the table conversations and it looked as though he was with us for the duration. We became a bit nervous since we expected the conversations to go a bit deeper than what might be comfortable for a Government official.

Then the Olympic Hotel employee choir sang several numbers. We didn't know what the words to the songs meant as all was in Mandarin. What we knew was that they sounded great and those at the tables appeared to enjoy the performance. Later we learned they were singing patriotic Chinese and Communist songs familiar to the Chinese at the tables. In retrospect, it may be that those songs made any Chinese who were nervous feel like the Conference would be safe for them.

The *Talking Together* Conference was launched. The next two days flashed by as we alternated speakers, panel input, table conversation, entertainment and meal. There were more than enough touching moments to fill a separate book.

At the end of the first evening, Ming Ming Lu came to tell us he was so sorry he could not return on the second day because of a schedule conflict he could not change. Would it be all right if he came on the third day to join us? We said, of course, and then wondered! He did return on the third day. At the end of the Conference, he asked to have a few moments to speak. He came to the stage with gifts for Rui and then for each one of us. Surprising us, Ming Ming then spoke in perfect English his appreciation for our efforts. He finished his remarks with a poem. We were nearly "blown away."

At the beginning of the second day, our dear friend, Toby Curtis, from New Zealand was the opening speaker. Toby was an elder of the Maori – the indigenous people of New Zealand. He spoke beautifully about the plight of oppressed peoples everywhere and the opportunities we all had to make a positive difference. People throughout the ballroom were in tears.

At the beginning of the third day, a friend from Russia, Elena Florova, told the group how grateful she was to be there; that this assembly would have been impossible only a couple of years earlier. Americans and Russians would not have been welcome in Shanghai. Chinese meeting with them would have not considered sharing with one another at such a deep level. Finally she said a woman who was a leader in business would not have been allowed to address such a group. She challenged everyone to take the lessons of the Conference back to their respective lives as leaders and to make a difference for themselves and for the world.

As the *Talking Together* Conference ended we were almost

speechless. It surpassed our fondest hopes and dreams. How wonderful it felt to see and hear over 100 women and men of all ages, from six countries and many walks of life, share with one another at such a deep level on what it means to be a leader in this time of change and opportunity in the world. Once again we learned that having a positive intention and being willing to take a risk to realize that intention was well worth it. We knew that our success came from focusing on a positive outcome and enlisting others of like minds to help make that outcome possible.

Within minutes of the Conference ending, Lori came up to talk with us. She was scheduled to return to the US the day after the Conference. Again there were tears in her eyes. We asked her what was the matter? She responded that she didn't want to leave. The experiences with the Chinese had so positively moved her she wanted to see more of China. Sadly, she had to return because she had not arranged care for her daughters beyond a day later. We reflected on how much we were always moved when spending quality time with Chinese or Russians. The people from these countries who came into our lives were incredible and we have been so blessed – just as Lori was.

The following morning we Americans were off to Hangzhou by train for the second stage of our Pilgrimage. The time on West Lake, the afternoon at Ling Yin Si, the Temple of Inspired Seclusion was very meaningful. Then we were scheduled to fly to Beijing.

We arrived at the Hangzhou airport for a flight to Beijing. The time for the flight came and went and we were left sitting in the waiting room. Then a voice came on the loud speaker to announce that our plane was being held – as were all planes in the country – because China launched its first space flight that morning. The airspace above the country must be kept clear until the astronaut returned to earth.

The news was exciting. The wait was maddening as we planned

to visit The Forbidden City as soon as we arrived in Beijing. After two hours we were advised that the astronaut had landed, the space flight was a success. The Chinese applauded and we all joined in.  It was a moment of great pride for the Chinese to be in space. Now we could board our plane. Off we flew to Beijing where we just barely made it to The Forbidden City before it was scheduled to close.

Reflecting on the experience we both agreed that only in a country like China could the government shut down the airspace so totally. Only in a country like China would the people accept the delay and inconvenience. Over our years in China we experienced dozens of situations where the strong central government was able to do things impossible in a more open democracy. And yet, things seemed to work well.

The time in Beijing was very meaningful for the Americans. The old and revered Lama Temple offered a deeper experience of Buddhism. We also were exposed to a number of facts about the history of Tibet, quite different from the history we hear and see in the US.[24] We spent one afternoon at the Summer Palace of the Rulers of China. The splendor of this immense compound was offset by the realization that it was all a reconstruction a hundred years after the Western countries – France, Great Britain, Germany and the United States – destroyed much of the original Summer Palace. Every artifact that could be carried away was stolen. In addition to those countries listed above, Japan and Russia also took part in the terrible things that occurred.

The more we learn of Chinese history, the more we marvel at the ability of the Chinese people to forgive – or at least accept – those countries who so terribly pillaged their land in the late nineteenth and early twentieth centuries.

After fifty hours in Beijing, we boarded our bus for the last destination in China, The Great Wall. We arrived at our hotel, Two Springs Crossing, in late afternoon, checked in and had dinner. We then went to the large karaoke room to be captivated by the wonderful Children's Choir from the Bo Hai Suo Village School. Some two dozen youngsters ranging from fourth to seventh grades sang and danced for us in a program that we will remember forever. Their last number, sung in Mandarin, was "It's a Small World." When they finished, the Americans spontaneously stood as a group and sang "It's a Small World" in English. Then both Chinese and Americans sang together, each in their respective language. It was an amazing and sweet experience.

≈ ≈ ≈

The next morning we were to go to the Great Wall. As Carol came to breakfast from her hotel room, she said to Tim that she had a very disturbing sense that someone close to her was in trouble. She felt something was terribly wrong.

Within minutes of having breakfast, Carol ran to call her husband, Terry. Terry said, "I figured you would call." Geil had suffered a stroke a few hours earlier and her husband, Armistead, was asking for prayers.

Within seconds, it seemed, we gathered all the Americans out onto the plaza in front of the hotel. Carol told the group the news. We paused for a few moments of prayer and then joined hands and danced to the song, "Morning has Broken," a beautiful song to which we have danced with groups in the US, Russia and now China. Virtually every person with us knew Geil.

We set out to the Great Wall with some heavy hearts, but closer than ever. The majesty of the Wall quickly captured the attention of every one of us. We split up into small groups and spent the next six hours exploring this true Wonder of the World. The two of us were able to visit the Great Wall at least five times during our years in China and were profoundly touched each time.

It was while we were on the wall that we decided to call Armistead, Geil's husband, to ask how Geil was doing. Imagine using a cell phone to call a friend in the US while walking on The Great Wall in China. Armistead was so happy to receive the call and hear that we were praying for Geil. We were reassured that she was getting the best possible care and was expected to recover – which she did within months. We gathered together in front of the Great Wall for a photo for Geil. All of us sent healing thoughts and prayers.

We returned to our Hotel in late afternoon to rest and then enjoy the goat roast and fireworks described earlier. What a day and a wonderful experience the past two weeks had been! But there was still more to come.

A day earlier we asked if it might be possible to take the Americans down into the village of Bo Hai Suo to see a Chinese rural village. The initial answer was, "No. Foreigners are not allowed here. This is a special village built a thousand years ago. The inhabitants had the sacred duty of defending The Wall against invaders. This is an official Chinese closed village."

But because the children were so well received when they came to entertain us, the local village officials decided to consider our request. Three cadres (local Communist leaders) were sent to interview us and see if they felt we should be admitted. After a very lengthy interview they said, "Yes, you may enter, but must stay in a single group and will be limited to visiting the school. And no photographs except inside the school."

The next morning we walked to the village, eagerly imagining what we might see. We were taken directly to the school where teachers gave us a tour, explaining in detail the high quality of education that was given to the children. We were impressed. We asked many questions. We showed our respect. Then, as we were leaving the school, the local Cadre who was with us suddenly told Rui the village was open to us and we could go everywhere and see what was there.

After we walked through the streets and met both adults and children who were eager to see the foreigners, we were taken by bus to see the largest industry in the village, a munitions plant. We were driven past the guards and through the gates right up to the entrance to the factory. And guess what? We were allowed to take photographs everywhere.

Our learning was very significant. We were accepted to visit the closed village because the Chinese decided we were not like what they thought Americans were. We know we strive at all times to be open and loving with everyone we meet. Our hosts could feel it. Their fear of letting Americans get close dissolved.

The next morning, the Americans, except for Denny and the two of us, headed to Beijing's airport to return to the United States. The three of us, plus Rui, took some hours to just decompress and reflect on the two weeks. Mr. Rao, who was with us the whole time, told us there was something we should see. We went to his van and he took us on a trip back into the nearby mountains.

After driving for some time we came across several areas where caves were cut into the sides of the mountains. Mr. Rao stopped the van to tell us that on the earlier night when the children had entertained us, he provided rides home for those children who did not live in the village. He brought them to these caves where they lived with their families. We were dumbfounded! How could those young girls and boys travel so far to school each day from these caves? What were their life prospects? How wonderful they had been to us.

The next day we drove down to the Beijing airport. Rui took a flight back to her home in Shanghai. The three of us returned to the US. What a life experience!

## CHAPTER TWENTY-SEVEN

# New Maps for Leaders and a Rabid Bat

*"I believe the biggest benefit from New Maps for Leaders is that I developed as a human. So lead, leader! It is not about a matrix or spiral but about my experience with such people...Most important for me are the open hearts and sharing we experienced."*

*– A Russian Participant*

After over twenty years as FGI, we should have known great psychological challenges come when we least expect and when we feel least able to work them into our schedule. This was to be one of those times.

Denny Aron and Tim were in the International Terminal in Atlanta waiting for the flight to Moscow. We were on our way to prepare for the arrival of thirty-five participants for our *New Maps for Leaders* program at CBSD. The participants would be twelve "foreigners" from China and the US, plus twenty-two Russians and one New Zealander who was working in Moscow. It was a new program design which took us several months to develop.

The airport public address announced the flight to Moscow was cancelled. A Delta Service Rep told us not to worry, we could take a Delta flight to Zurich and then transfer to Aeroflot, which would get us to Moscow a half-day later than our original itinerary. We did.

Our colleague, Dennis Hopple, arranged for Dr. John Kotter, noted Harvard Professor and author, to provide a workshop in Moscow. The attendees were to be Moscow business leaders as well as the Americans and Chinese joining us for our *New Maps for Leaders* program. We needed to be there to meet with Dr. Kotter prior to his presentation and to brief him for the audience he would address. This briefing was to be held the morning after we arrived in Moscow. As we sat in the Atlanta Airport, knowing we'd be late for our esteemed speaker, there was nothing we could do except go with the flow. We boarded the plane to Zurich and then Aeroflot to Moscow.

Arrival in Moscow was a bit troublesome. Denny's luggage arrived, as did the two large trunks filled with materials for the programs. Tim's clothes and personal items, however, were nowhere to be found. When leaving Omaha, we checked Tim's luggage under Denny's name. This ended up causing Denny much grief the next day. However, there was nothing we could do that evening; so our driver took us to the hotel.

The next morning Dennis Hopple picked us up and we were on our way, along with several Moscow and CBSD leaders, to meet Dr. Kotter at the Grand Hyatt Hotel near the Kremlin. Since Tim had no clothes suitable to the occasion, Dennis loaned him a shirt, tie and sport coat. They didn't quite fit, but were much better than the tired travel clothes Tim had worn since leaving Omaha. While at the Hyatt, word came the missing bag would arrive in Moscow later in the evening. What a relief! Tim would be able to greet the American participants the next day with clean clothes.

By evening Dennis, Tim and several others were busy attending to last minute details for the Kotter presentation and then *New Maps for Leaders*. Denny returned to the airport to retrieve Tim's bag since the claim check was in Denny's name. He and the driver were gone for a long time. He finally returned to the hotel and Tim learned why he'd been delayed. At the airport, he'd been shown to a room about the size of a football field, with bags piled at least twelve feet high. The guard said, "It should be in there somewhere. Good luck!" Tim was grateful for Denny's diligence, but equally wishing he could have seen Denny's face at the sight of those thousands of bags.

Anyone who knows Denny Aron would know he would find that bag. It was not in any logical place, so the search took a couple of hours. Both Denny and Tim vowed to check luggage only under their own names in the future. Our hotel rooms beckoned and each of us went eagerly to our rooms to get some rest before the group of Americans arrived the next day.

Now you may be wondering where Carol is in this story? The answer is enough for a stand-alone chapter, but here are the highlights. Two days before we were to leave for Moscow, the two of us, Tim and Carol, with our colleague, Geil, were at a ranch in the mountains west of Colorado Springs, beginning the retreat for a new INFLUENCE group. We planned to finish the meeting, fly back to Omaha and leave the next morning for Moscow – typical, and sometimes crazy FGI "just in time" scheduling.

Near the end of the first day of the retreat, Carol stood on the porch of the ranch house, talking with several women before dinner. Suddenly, a small black object fell on her, grabbed her hand and bit her. It was a bat! After a few appropriate shrieks by the women on the porch, the bat was stomped to death. The owners of the ranch told us bats were plentiful and quite harmless. So Carol, being a committed professional, decided to do nothing and we went on with the retreat.

Later that evening Carol had second thoughts about the serious nature of the bite and decided it was best to call the Colorado Department of Health emergency line. She was told to find the body of the dead bat immediately. But the INFLUENCE women had not only stomped on the tiny bat, they had thrown it into the forest in defense of Carol! With flashlights and gloves, Tim and the owner of the ranch walked the pitch-black Rocky Mountain land with specific information from Carol regarding the arc on which the Influence women threw the bat into the forest.

Amazingly, after an hour in the pitch-black night, Tim did find the tiny, dead bat. Putting the bat carefully into his empty wine glass, Tim brought it into the kitchen and put it into the refrigerator.

The next day, after the retreat ended, we drove down from the ranch to Colorado Springs and the nearest hospital, where Carol visited the Emergency Room. After completing the necessary preliminaries, Carol was shown into one of the treatment rooms to await a physician. Upon entering the room, the doctor took one look at Carol's hand and said, quite assertively, "Based on what you've described, there is a good chance you've been bitten by what I believe is a rabid bat. We must begin the injections immediately."

When Carol questioned his statements, he answered, "Because the bat appeared from nowhere and flew directly to your ring finger, there was a good chance of rabidity because bats are not otherwise prone to attack or bite." What followed were sixteen shots of medicine injected all around the bite marks on Carol's hand. Shots are never all that pleasant, and sixteen into your hand and fingers where there is little fatty tissue are way beyond unpleasant.

The doctor told her it was very important she not bite anyone for at least a year after the shots, which assuredly she did not do! He said she should return the following day for the next series of shots. When Carol told him she had to catch a flight back to Omaha, he was not happy. However, he agreed to talk with her doctor in Omaha to make sure she could receive the same medicines. He said, "Now go home, see your doctor tomorrow and take it easy for the next two weeks."

Carol then informed him she was leaving for Moscow the next day, he became even more assertive. He told her she was not taking this seriously enough. If she didn't receive all of the treatments – and the bat tested positive for rabies – she would die.

With this sobering news, Carol thanked the doctor and raced off to the Denver airport to fly back to Omaha.

Carol's husband, Terry, as one might imagine, was quite concerned and advised cancellation of the trip to Moscow. The next day Carol missed the flight with Denny and Tim and went to see her regular Omaha doctor. Her goal was to figure out how she could go to Moscow and still be safe.

Her doctor said the medicine being used for the injections was not approved for use in Russia. A call to our friend, Dennis, in Moscow, confirmed what we suspected: if detected, the vaccine would be confiscated by Customs. Additionally, the medicine had to be kept at a constant cool temperature at all times or would be useless.

Carol was determined to go to Moscow while ensuring she was doing all necessary not to put her health at risk. Dennis advised there was a VIP service available at Sheremetyevo Airport. For a substantial fee, a traveler could easily use an "elite" route through Passport Control and Customs. Dennis and Carol decided this was necessary.

So with an insulated cooler filled with injectable rabies medicine, passport, visa and luggage, Carol boarded the plane for Atlanta and then on to Moscow. Because she was leaving the US later than planned, she found herself in good company, traveling alongside the ten Americans who were joining us. Upon arrival at Sheremetyevo, Carol and her cooler were whisked away to a VIP lounge where she had tea and sweets for over an hour. She was then escorted to the airport exit and rejoined the other Americans. We continue to discuss whether this was a "prestige" service or a fancy Russian approach to bribes.

In any case, Carol and her rabies vaccine arrived safely in Moscow, hoping this was the end of the bat story. The next day, however, the laboratory in Colorado confirmed the bat had indeed been rabid. Dennis made arrangements at the European Medical Center in Moscow for Carol to go daily for the balance of the injections. The lesson from this story is simple: not even a rabid bat can deter a determined Carol.

Once the Americans and Chinese participants arrived in Moscow and had checked in and left their luggage at the Alpha Hotel, we all headed to the Izmailovsky Park Metro station. Our destination was the center of Moscow so the participants could experience Red Square and the Kremlin in the evening. But first the foreigners would experience the Metro.

The Metro was and is one of the great wonders of Moscow. The original lines were built during the Stalin era. The stations are some of the most impressive works of Soviet art in Russia. Beautiful mosaics, statues, chandeliers, paintings adorn the underground stations.

Many of the early sections of the Metro were used as bomb shelters during the Nazi attacks in the Great Patriotic War (World War II in the US). Some of the stations were also used as conference halls for the Soviet Communist hierarchy. A tour of the Russian Metro is by itself a glorious experience. We were eager for our first excursion with this group.

Our many trips taking foreigners to Russia began with a visit to Red Square. This historic place generates many emotions. Growing up in the US from the '50s to the '80s, Americans watched TV scenes of military parades passing through Red Square while Soviet leaders watched from the reviewing stands adjacent to Lenin's Tomb. Always there were thousands of Muscovites cheering and waving signs.

Contrast that with our view in 2004. The busy square was filled with shoppers going to and from the large department store complex GUM; tourists posing for photos with St. Basil's

Cathedral in the background; Russians in costumes of medieval soldiers hoping to get tourists to pose with them for a price; children playing. There was no sign of danger or threat. And when the visitor looked beyond the Kremlin walls, Orthodox Cathedrals filled most of the view. Along one wall of the Kremlin and outside of Red Square were Alexander Park and the Tomb of the Unknown Soldier. We watched the changing of the guard along with many Russians.

After returning to the hotel in the evening, we heard the Reflections of each of the foreigners as we would most evenings in Moscow. Some of the first impressions of being in Russia were heartwarming; others reflected excitement and anticipation of what was to come.

The most memorable came from Marty Malley, a retired career US Navy officer: "I've been waiting for two years to be invited here. I'm here to find out why I was on patrol off the coast of the Soviet Union on the USS Nevada. I've seen Russia many times, but always from the periscope of a nuclear submarine. I'm eager to see it while on the ground."

Another significant Reflection came from our Shanghai friend, Nina Liu, "I am here for two reasons. First, my parents always wanted me to visit Russia. Both of them were in the Red Army, which was heavily influenced by the Soviet Union. I want to understand how the USSR influenced so many Asian countries. Second, I want to meet wonderful friends."

Everyone was happy to adjourn early for a good night's sleep.

As with our previous Moscow trips with foreigners, the American and Chinese participants spent the next two days touring Moscow, seeing the inside of the Kremlin, visiting the gigantic Christ the Savior Cathedral and many other sites. We also spent a morning at the Vernisage, an outdoor bazaar where the shopper can purchase virtually every type of Russian art object – new, used or antique – as well as inexpensive souvenirs of every description.

One of the Americans had a mishap at Christ the Savior Cathedral, stumbling on the way down a steep set of marble steps. Although she broke no bones, Lou Anne was in a lot of pain for the next week. She joined Carol on the visits to the European Medical Center. Hardly the way either of them expected to spend time while visiting Moscow.

The second day with the group in Moscow provided many deep Reflections. The words of our American friends echo in our heads even today:

"I was looking at the faces of the people we saw. I didn't see poverty. They are simply going about their daily lives. My family on my father's side were Nazis who ended up in POW camps in the USSR during and after the Second World War. It is really meaningful to be here and to be thinking of them."

"I am moved by the care the Russians take to collect things of beauty from the past. Humans for centuries have desired to create beauty. There was a great paradox in looking at so many beautiful treasures housed in the Russian Armory. I pray mankind can find ways other than war in the future."

"Today helped me think about my country, the United States. Russians have a deep love of their history. Our country does not seem to have a love of history."

"Today was a great day. I am really pleased with what I experienced of the Christian culture. I had always thought this was a Communist country. But the faith here is much stronger than in China. I am really enjoying the wonderful friends we met."

≈   ≈   ≈

With our initial orientation to Russia complete, the primary reason for our being in Moscow began. We left our hotel and walked again to the Metro where we boarded the train to the Radisson Hotel, across the Moscow River from the Russian

White House. Once there, we joined several hundred Russian business leaders to spend the day with Dr. John Kotter. It seemed strange then and still seems strange today: We took American friends to Moscow to hear a professor from Harvard. It was a little like the experience in 1992 when we took Americans to the Russian Bolshoi Theatre and ended up seeing a Japanese Kabuki Theatre presentation.

Because the foreigners enjoyed meeting Russian leaders, we knew Tuesday would be a new and exciting day for all of us. The Russian participants would be joining us at CBSD for the beginning of *New Maps for Leaders*. The two of us were very excited to start the program.

On Tuesday morning, we traveled to Izmailovo Island and the remains of Czar Alexey's summer palace. We entered the old Officers' Quarters, which were now the CBSD conference rooms. Entering the Officers' Ballroom, Americans and Chinese met the Russian, Italian and New Zealand participants and we all enjoyed tea and a few sweets. Our group sightseeing had given us a small taste of Moscow. It was now time to begin the actual *New Maps* program.

Our work for so many years in the United States plus over ten years in Russia and three years in China, had taught us much. We were convinced leaders for the future would have to look at different information and learn to process that information in quite different ways than had leaders of today or yesterday. This was our effort to begin that kind of learning in a global setting.

We felt very fortunate to have a group of thirty-five women and men to consider what the future would demand of leaders. They were coming from Russia, China, New Zealand, Italy and the US. This was the first time people from multiple countries had participated in *The Global Interaction*. This gave us a perfect opportunity to see how the simulation would work with leaders from other countries. We were eager to see, for instance, if non-American participants would assume the role of the United

States in a different way. We were curious to see if the dynamics between rich nations and poor nations would be different.

Because most of those present knew us, they quickly became a learning community. Individuals were very open with one another during the first half day as we began the program.

The time for *The Global Interaction* arrived. We divided them up into eleven country delegations, with size of delegation determined by the actual population of each country. The Russian delegation included a person from China, one from New Zealand and one from the US. The United States delegation included three from Russia and one from China. And so on! What a thrill for the two of us to observe leaders from four countries bringing our simulation to life.

When the simulation ended, we gathered to discuss the experience in a large group. One of the most profound observations was about the thinking of the countries other than the United States and Germany. Participants agreed that it was difficult to know when to trust or whom to trust. The summary statement was: "If you have more, you can afford to risk. If you have less, you fear to risk. If you have nothing, you have nothing to lose!"

The comments were the same as we experienced in the US. However, with an international group, the feelings were even more pronounced. People were furious with the US, despite the sincerity and best efforts of the four delegates, none of whom was a American. Nothing they attempted worked. They were seen as greedy capitalists even though they made countless efforts to be helpful. As one representative from another country said during the debrief, "The US was inward focused and scattered." The Chinese and Russian participants who served as US delegates felt helpless. They certainly did not feel THEY were greedy capitalists, so the reactions of others made them feel even worse.

Delegates from Kenya and Zimbabwe, who were both successful

leaders in their real world jobs, once again felt the situation was hopeless for the poor.

Here are a few of the participants' learnings:

**US:** "We became too concerned with our own tasks and needed to adapt to needs of others and get the whole picture first."

**Indonesia:** "I get too easily pulled into management thinking rather than being a real leader."

**Brazil:** "I don't believe it is possible to create a world that works for all, but that's not a reason not to try."

**China:** "My intentions as a great humanitarian conflicted with my actions."

**US:** "After a while, I started taking the initiative, stating opinions and others listened."

**Zimbabwe**: "I am very sensitive to the situation in Zimbabwe. This exercise makes me even more depressed. I know now how narrow I am as I think about global issues."

So we had our answer, *The Global Interaction,* whether done with only people in the US or with people from multiple countries and cultures, has an overwhelming number of similarities. It was confirming that our simulation had not only worked in a global arena, but had been very successful.

Different cultures may approach issues in different ways. But the bottom line: people with radically different national origins and cultures see the needs of our planet in quite similar ways. We have learned this again and again during our sixteen years in Russia, twelve in China and three in India. We have learned it from our participants who have come from over two-dozen countries on all six continents.

The debriefing was deep and meaningful. All participants marveled at the degree to which their brief efforts mirrored the real world. Many were amazed at how little they knew about countries other than their own. All agreed the leadership challenges were daunting if they desired to create a better world.

On the second day we followed the simulation with an exploration of Spiral Dynamics®, our long favorite theory developed by Dr. Clare Graves on how the human system responds to change. With *The Global Interaction* plus Spiral Dynamics® we were then able to spend the third day looking at specific skills and abilities to develop in leaders for success in the future.

In the post program Reflections of *New Maps*, participants told us:

- "I relearned the importance of learning person-to-person. I developed a new global vision and began to understand the Russian hearts. I feel it is going to change my life. It so exceeded my expectations – priceless! I could not imagine even 1% of it."

- "I am especially grateful for the sharing with those from other countries. This as an extra special dimension."

- "This was an eye-opening program. However some topics became too emotional. That made me reserved at first, since I'm not used to such intimate things in public."

- "I did not have specific expectations when I came other than to be bowled over, which I was!"

- "Regardless of expectations, I have been given the information, tools and insights to become a more effective human."

Over the years, we invited foreigners to work with us in Russia, China and India over a dozen times. We have also worked for client organizations that have convened participants from multiple countries many times. When a learning community includes people from multiple countries, the results have always been richer, deeper and much more enjoyable.

After the last day of *New Maps,* we took the foreigners and most of the Russians to a favorite Moscow restaurant of ours, Mama Nina's. About half way through our evening together, a small band began playing. Many of our participants were quickly on their feet and dancing to some wonderful Russian popular music. We doubt it was Vodka that enabled them to dance, as most of the foreigners did not drink or drank little. It seemed more like a final expression of gratitude for one another and the community they had formed. It was also a way to demonstrate appreciation for all that Russia offered.

The next day would be the last day we were with the foreigners. We planned a needed trip out to the countryside. After breakfast we traveled to the nearby Sergie Posad. In this small city is the oldest monastery in continuous operation in Russia, somehow continuing its existence throughout the Communist period. We had taken three other groups of Americans here over the years, but this visit would be different!

St. Sergius founded the Trinity Monastery in 1345. It is venerated in the Orthodox Church as one of the most sacred sites in Russia. The monastery is truly remarkable and beautiful. Several churches are found inside the walls along with wonderful grounds and the living area for the monks, priests and young men in training. The time we spent in the Monastery truly provided beauty, peace and reflection.

The most important learning for all of us foreigners, however, did not come at the Monastery that day. Instead it came at the home of an elderly Russian woman. Without our knowledge or agreement, the guide we hired took us to see what a "real" peasant home (izba) was like. He paid a local woman to allow foreigners to traipse through her izba in exchange for a small amount of money.

Thus, our group of Americans and Chinese, along with a few Russian friends, followed him through the small izba in the country. There we found an elderly woman, apparently quite frail, sitting in her chair, wrapped with many blankets. Her home lacked even the simplest of comforts.

It was a very awkward experience. Most of us hurried through the house, thanked the old woman and returned outside. A few stayed longer. One of the foreigners, Hal, attempted to communicate with the woman. Then after we left, he tried to return to leave her a small amount of money and to thank her. But she had locked the door. We can still see the foreigners in our minds, inside the izba, attempting in some way to communicate with the woman.

When we returned to our Moscow hotel that evening, we held our final group Reflections. As might be expected, everyone had much to say about what they had learned from one another and from their time in Russia. What was not expected was how much the foreigners reflected on our experience with the old woman in her home. Here are a couple of the comments:

- "I've learned so much this week from watching and listening…I am struck by so many Russians who have so little and yet are filled with passion."

- "I was so sad at the village outside of the Monastery. It makes me appreciate what I have today. We must help those with so little. They need food, clean water and medicines. In my China many are very poor as well. Today my boss in the US emailed me. He asked, 'How was it.' I told him I just spent days with the best community in the world."

- "I always learn something when I come to Russia, which I do often. I realize today my identification with my family and roots is stronger than I realized. My father and mother came from Eastern Europe and lived like the old lady... my journey continues."

The most important Reflections about the day, although not known at the time, came from Hal who said to the group, "I had a lot of emotion on this last night. I wrote to my wife this has been indescribable. I knew I needed something when I came on this trip. It was the countryside and the old woman. I don't know what God's plan is for me, but I thank Him for putting her in my life. My father grew up in a house like that. I did not have the courage to somehow connect with the woman. I left without saying what was needed. After I left the house, I desperately wanted to return and tell her I appreciated what she did for me."

Carol looked at Hal and was moved to say, " Somehow, she served you. In your near future, Hal, you will need to express your deep feelings when you feel them. She has served you to be ready."

Only two weeks after returning to the United States, Hal's son was in a terrible auto accident, which left him paralyzed in much of his body. Hal believes the learning community in Russia, especially meeting the old woman, prepared him for who he needed to be and what he and his wife needed to do for their son after the accident. Hal believes to this day the old woman was God speaking to him.

The next day the foreigners were off to St. Petersburg for two days. Then they would return to their homes in the US and China. The two of us and Denny stayed in Moscow, because in three days we would begin another program at CBSD with all Russian participants.

Now that we have the benefit of distance from this wonderful experience, what did we learn? Three things come to mind. First, each time we convene a program with participants from multiple countries, we believe anything is possible in the world. Second, when we host newcomers in a place which is familiar to us (by

2004 we had been to Russia over forty times), our senses become more acute, and we see things we had not seen before. And last, the success we have had over the years has been possible because the women and men we convene for our programs trust us and so learn to trust each other.

Building communities may sound daunting, especially international ones. However, for thirty years being able to create community has been a gift in our lives through our FGI work. Bringing groups of strangers together from different cities, states and even countries may be daunting to others. We've learned that as people are allowed to reflect out loud within a group, they not only know themselves better, but learn to trust and respect the others willing to share in the same way. It doesn't take long, therefore, to create community. At some level, this suggests hope for our world.

## CHAPTER TWENTY-EIGHT

# Grace, Wisdom, Strength

Our work in China continued to bring us marvelous learning, important experiences and added life meaning. It seemed the right time to expand our offerings. The idea to bring a woman's program to China continued one of the themes of Carol's life: The education and development of women could change the world for the better. Both of us were committed. Having seen the magic of sisterhood and feminine energy in nearly 25 years of INFLUENCE groups, we set out to begin *IGE: Influencing the Global Economy*, a women's leadership program in Shanghai.

It was 2005, our work in China up to this point included five years of building client groups in both Shanghai and Beijing. Leaders came from all over China and a number of other Asian countries. The idea of providing a leadership program dedicated to women leaders seemed to strike a loud chord with our many client organizations in China. They encouraged us to get started and were ready to become sponsors.

Earlier, the two of us, with our dear FGIAsia Partner Rui Shujie, agreed it was necessary to develop a Chinese company in Shanghai. It was not legal for a foreign company to do business in China except through a Chinese business partner or by registering FGI as a foreign company. The latter had a significant cost increase. Up until this time, our work required us to have a Chinese partner who could collect money and pay the taxes. But the partners always took a significant percentage. After several years of working in China, we decided that we were giving away too much revenue to our "partners" – all of whom we had never met. To us, they existed on paper and Rui handled the interactions.

Now we wanted something different: our own company. In order for us to start a government approved, small business in China, there were many requirements. To be incorporated by US citizens, the fee was going to be about US $100,000. However, if Chinese owners started the business, the fee was one-tenth that amount. It was easy for the two of us to decide with Rui that the new owners would be Rui and her father. Both were thankfully ready to take on these responsibilities. We also formed a small Board of Directors consisting of our long time friends and clients, Nina Liu, SC Toh and Peng Hai Tao. Originally a part of our first PepsiCo China programs, these three executives had the leadership experience and deep integrity of solid, credible business leaders we needed as advisors. Each one was now employed in a different company and this provided the diversity of organizational views we needed. Each one contributed in many ways to our thinking. Most of all, we loved and respected them.

The Board of Directors met with Rui in Shanghai and decided to name the new, little company, BoXu. They told us with love and respect that when the Mandarin was translated into English, BoXu means the "sun comes up in the morning spreading wisdom." How touched we were when we were told they chose the name based on who the two of us are and what we and the FGI work offered their lives. Thus, BoXu became a small Chinese business, operating in China as the extension of FGI/FGISpirit in Asia.

The prospects of offering a women's leadership program in China kept the two of us buzzed for many months. Though we would be responsible for the program design and content, Rui would carry the burden of recruiting and overall management of the program. Because she was always an excellent business leader, we knew we were in good hands with Rui beside us.

It was time to get the recruiting off the ground. A program for women only was quite a new concept in China. We immediately decided with Rui's strong recommendation, that our dear friend and strong supporter, Nina Liu, must be involved. It took only one phone call to Nina in Shanghai and we were on our way. Nina's network allowed good things to happen with seemingly less stress than usual in China. Nina invited a large group of key corporate women leaders from about twenty different multi-national companies doing business in China to join us. Our gathering, with Rui's leadership, was a lovely party with hors d'oeuvres, drinks, many great conversations plus some upfront talk from Nina, Rui and the two of us. We did our best to introduce this concept of a leadership program for women only.

As we talked to the large group assembled, there was a pleasant buzz in the crowded room. We could feel the excitement of this idea flowing and creating energy and buy-in. To have a leadership program for women only was very positive and exciting to these Chinese women. Several of those present made commitments that evening to support and attend the program. We were flying high and Rui could feel the energy of what was set before her. She was ready and able, always the most competent and dedicated partner we could have.

It was obviously impossible to take the entire content of INFLUENCE, our nine-month leadership program for women, and offer it over three days in Shanghai. Though Shanghai does operate at high speed in every aspect of life, this would have been impossible. The two of us spent many days deciding upon each module of the agenda. We customized some of our favorite parts of INFLUENCE, added others and focused on the essence of each. We were able to bring the current global discussions we believe are so important for leaders of all ages and in any country. We also made a commitment during the first years of our work as FGI to never provide an FGI/FGISpirit program without Reflections. So, this was an obvious, not to mention essential, part of the program.

In fact, we may have underestimated the deep impact Reflections would make in China. To share one's deep thoughts and feelings in a public forum was new for the Chinese leaders in all of our programs. They also did not realize how much one could learn from others Reflections. The most comforting aspect in any country is to discover one's own life is similar to other's lives. Sharing deeply in even a small gathering is not the norm in China. However, there is a connection made through this. When a woman understands this is the case, even if the woman has come from a totally different part of the world, it is even more significant: "I am not alone."

Preparing to recruit for participants was an exciting and seemingly overwhelming task. The good news was that we had great success recruiting in the US, Russia and China for our other programs such as INFLUENCE, FOCUS and the Looking Glass Leadership Program. The reputation of FGI with our Looking Glass Leadership Program and individual Executive Coaching work left good experiences in people's minds. Relying on what we knew, we used our networks to help us complete our dreams of bringing a women's leadership program to China.

Nina and Rui together were incredible in their contacts and networking. Chinese women were registering from many Chinese cities. We imagined it might be more difficult to recruit women from the US to go to Shanghai with us. It seemed to be something people could not believe. "What, go to China for a leadership program?" We did hear many women say they were concerned about leaving their families for a week or more. Some families were concerned about the women being so far away in China. "What if there is an emergency?" However, many were not concerned and built a support system for their families that made their own travel for their jobs possible. We soon realized we shared enough stories about our work in Russia and China to have "whet" the appetites of many of our friends and clients.

In spite of our concerns, the recruiting seemed to go well. However, it suddenly became clear this whole experience would be incomplete without also inviting Russian women to join us in Shanghai. Our love of our many years working in Moscow helped us understand the Russian Spirit added so much to any gathering. What excitement and new thinking this added to the possibilities of *IGE*.

American women joined us for our earlier Russian *Pilgrimage* and/or our *New Maps for Leaders* program in Moscow. Rui and Nina were with us in Moscow for *New Maps*. These connections made deep bonds and seemed to open up what was possible in China with *IGE*. Additionally, several of our male clients in all three countries were very supportive of the program and took an active role in sponsoring and/or recruiting women to attend the program.

The first *IGE* program started on April 19, 2005. Seven women from the US and two Russian women joined a woman from Indonesia and 17 Chinese women in Shanghai for a marvelous leadership development experience.

However, it was even more. It was a true coming together of women to understand what it means to be a woman. Not a woman in China, or a woman in Russia, or a woman in the US, but a woman who is working in a competitive, demanding role as leader in some kind of enterprise. The similarities and commonalities were touching. The differences were sometimes stark or depressing or thrilling. All of us grew together.

We loved the PuJiang Hall at the Regal Hotel in Shanghai. It was good to return. The room felt a bit like home to us. We used it for many years with other FGI programs. Our friend, Rupert Li, at the Regal, had already been our event coordinator for five years. He knew us and we knew him not only as professionals, but as also as friends. His goal was always to do whatever he could to insure our programs had everything needed from the hotel and that all hotel professionals were there to serve. This made the entire experience so much more pleasant as well as positive.

We were able to hold onto our excitement and energy in spite of the previous day's work coordinating with Rupert and Rui. The plan was that prior to the actual program itself, we would show those traveling in from outside China a bit of Shanghai so they could gain a feeling for the history, the city itself and the chance to see a few sights of this huge, crowded, constantly buzzing city.

The second day, we also rented a bus for the two-plus hour drive to the centuries old water village, Xitang. The term "water village" refers to a village where the main thoroughfares are canals. This ancient Chinese water village dates back to 700BC – 476BC. The more recent village buildings date to the Ming Dynasty in the 1700's. This outing took place prior to the *IGE* program. Our goal was to serve the "foreigners" in adapting to jet lag, tasting new foods, hearing the language and simply realizing they were in a totally different country. The bus trip to Xitang seemed to be a perfect way for the women from the US and Russia to get to know each other, gain a bit of a nap for some or to just sit and stare at the new world outside the bus windows.

Upon arrival, the thriving, ancient water town seemed to captivate our new visitors. Although, truth be told, some took a while to adapt to the sounds and smells of an ancient water village. Others jumped right in and began contributing to the Chinese economy.

Xitang offered every opportunity for Chinese goods. Small shops with friendly proprietors considered our US and Russian women to be just the ones for whom they had been waiting. Many large embroidery art/needlework pictures of various scenes in Xitang now hang in these women's homes across the US. Over the years, it became a tradition that the young proprietor of the needlework shop would be waiting for our bus in the parking lot upon our arrival. He was so excited to greet us and announce that thanks to our American women, he now had TWO shops in the village. We had contributed to Xitang's economic growth.

The bus rides back to Shanghai were always quiet and reflective. Often the women took quick naps or engaged in deep conversations with each other, those they had only met for the first time on this trip. The two of us sat separately, always looking for quiet and rest. We knew the next day would be the first day of the program and we wanted to be ready.

The group arrived back to the Regal Hotel, ready for a big dinner. We knew our work was just beginning. After dinner, the two of us plus Rui would hurry off to Pujiang Hall. We spent most of the evening before the program preparing the room with our wall charts plus other décor that seemed appropriate to us. We were ready!

It was a joy to be there early in the mornings of the first days of *IGE* to watch the women arrive. We loved to see them break into smiles when they saw from our room setup that this was going to be something special. Art, beauty, leadership quotes, lovely arm chairs, flower arrangements and other efforts made *IGE* something new and unique in terms of a professional women's leadership program.

Rui also always arrived early for these meetings. Being the main recruiter of the Chinese women, she introduced them to each other and to the two of us if we had not already met. Rui's way of being Rui seemed to always give people a sense of security and confidence in what would unfold, plus a lovely and warm acceptance. Several times a day, the two of us gave thanks for having such a talented, exceptional partner and friend as Rui Shujie.

It had been difficult to decide on the program content. There was so much we both wanted to share. Finally we narrowed the design to reflect some of our INFLUENCE content plus additional topics appropriate for these women leaders from countries such as China, Indonesia, Russia, Dagestan, Hong Kong, Mongolia and the US. We covered topics such as leadership, world events, assertiveness, power, communications, the FGI 360° Professional Development Questionnaire©, our "Mother's Stories" and whatever else seemed to emerge. We sang, we danced, we hugged, we cried, we laughed. It was healing, exciting, touching, memorable and for many of the women - life changing. They had never known, experienced or even imagined this thing called "Sisterhood."

To be a young Chinese woman from a distant province far away from Shanghai, now serving as a professor in a Chinese university, then suddenly be among women from two or three different countries turned out to be an overwhelming and life changing experience for one bright and dear participant. She did not fully understand who she really was until she was able to see herself in the mirror of these women with whom she experienced *IGE*. Our hearts were full of gratitude.

The most moving aspect of the program was in every case, the "Mothers' Stories." When we provide this in our INFLUENCE work, it is always incredibly special. We believed we were prepared to move forward with it in China. However, there was much we did not understand in the first years of offering *IGE*.

In the US, we experienced INFLUENCE women sharing the stories about who their mothers were and how their lives were shaped as a result. While these often produced emotion and even pain, the US experiences were nothing compared to China.

The two of us read stacks of books about China's history and culture. However, we were not prepared for the stories we heard. Additionally, even Rui was not prepared. Rui's life was different due to her younger age and to her having grown up a small village outside Tianjin.

Some of the Chinese women in our *IGE* groups were older than Rui, plus many had also grown up in Shanghai, Beijing and other large cities. The reach of Mao's hand in the Cultural Revolution shaped many lives of our dear women friends in *IGE*, often in terrible and unbelievable ways.

Most of the mothers of our Chinese women friends were expected to be a contributing part of the workforce. Thus, the children of these women were often cared for by their grandmothers or even some other woman. It was how it was from the mid-sixties into the mid-seventies and even beyond. Thus, the relationships some of the women desired with their mothers were never available to them.

From 1966, the beginning of the Cultural Revolution and into the next ten years, life was different in China than many of us from the US could easily comprehend. Many of the stories were heartbreaking and very emotional.

This caused us some concern. Were we asking our dear friends to experience pain in order to share their stories? Should we drop this aspect of the program?

After many deep conversations following the program, our Chinese women friends assured us this was important to continue. Many told us they had never before spoken to anyone about the pain they experienced in not knowing or being close to their mothers. They never thought deeply about how it must have been for their own mothers. With children of their own, many of these dear Chinese friends were able to imagine the pain their own mothers felt in not being able to raise their children. As a result of the program's "Mothers' Stories," many Chinese women whose mothers were still living, opened new, accepting, loving relationships with their mothers. There was forgiveness, joy, sometimes closure.

Life in China, as in the US and every country, had its beautiful moments and not so beautiful ones in terms of history and families. The stories of all of the women who were a part of our *IGE* experiences taught us so much. We give thanks. As women and students, we saw them as capable leaders and managers. Their inner strength and outer demeanor gave most who interacted with them confidence and courage in who they were. As they opened up and shared the stories of their lives, we saw the depth of their emotions, their caring as well as their strength and commitment to a better world.

We are also aware of how much we learned as a result of our experience with *IGE* and the marvelous women who shared it with us. Though the two of us have always been excellent students, we found our own learning was able to go even deeper. The experiences of being with women from two, three or even four countries in one room for three days seemed to provide us with some of the most deep and profound learning of our lives.

Some of this was really unlearning. We experienced first hand the depth of emotion, both joy and pain, so many held inside. We saw and felt their relief as they recognized themselves in each other. They were more able to feel proud of being women.

We confirmed again that our own ability to transfer our US methods, not only to Russia, but also to China, could be meaningful and useful to our clients. At first we wondered if it was a bit too much to use special decorations of beauty and artistic decorations in the meeting room. And yet, it seemed these small efforts, the arm chairs, the round tables – all somehow made *IGE* feel more like a gathering than a program. People opened up in ways we and they had not expected.

The use of Reflection was something totally new to many of the women. This built our small communities of women and brought all closer. That we danced and shared laughter also encouraged solid emotional bonds and deep joy. Chinese women went out of *IGE* eager to share more with their friends who were not present. In the past, we may have wondered if this dancing was appropriate, but here in Shanghai, we understood it brought new life to us all.

We learned more than we ever understood about the pain and suffering of the Chinese people over many periods of history. Some of these women had personally suffered during the Cultural Revolution when the Red Guards were persecuting millions. And for those women who were younger, their parents and grandparents had suffered greatly. We learned more about how resilient and strong the human spirit can be when faced with such pain. It's hard to imagine how our lives would have changed had we experienced the Cultural Revolution as these women had.

We found a different side of China when focusing solely on women's development and women's lives. We found a true calling which enriched our lives and taught us deeply.

## CHAPTER TWENTY-NINE

# Influence Leaves a Legacy

The day will come when we are no longer offering programs and consulting to organizations. When that happens, what will be our legacy? It feels the largest single component may be the remarkable women with whom we shared the INFLUENCE leadership experience.

By far the largest number of women with whom we worked were in the INFLUENCE program in the US. All that we learned with the groups in the '80s and '90s was inspiring, confirming, satisfying. It was less, however, than what we would witness after 2000.

With the dawn of the new century, we watched as change came more from outside than inside the organizations where INFLUENCE participants worked. The Millennium Effect, outsourcing, rapid globalization, 9.11, the Iraq and Afghan wars, the rise of China and then India – these and many other issues changed all the rules about how things should work.

The Unipolar World rapidly shifted to a Multipolar World. This development produced disbelief in many Americans who thought the United States would always be "in charge." While many politicians insisted to the contrary, it became clear that the Twenty-first would not be known as The American Century. This did not mean anything negative would happen to the US, rather that a world would develop in which multiple successful economies would be interdependent.

Interest in the global reality increased a great deal for those with whom we worked. While we had been talking about each of these issues for over a decade, it was still hard, even for us, to imagine how all of it would feel. The positive benefits of the new global economy were elusive, because most of them were not yet visible. But it was easy to begin recognizing and fearing what seemed to be the losses, because they were happening already.

The tragedy of 9.11 produced a fear in Americans that has grown steadily since then. And while the transition to the global economy has mandated that we draw closer to others, the exact opposite has occurred. As the United States experienced the prolonged recession that began in 2008, world opinion began to shift. In 2011, the Pew Research organization reported that more countries believe that China either had already or will soon replace the US as the dominant economic power.[25]

All of these factors resulted in women coming to INFLUENCE feeling more vulnerable than those who had come earlier. And everyone became much more interested in current events.

The week after 9.11, the INFLUENCE group in Phoenix had their opening retreat. Of course the two days included the expression of many emotions and numerous attempts at analysis of what had happened. One of the women, Canadian by birth, explained in great detail why Canada is better able to understand the world than the United States. She went through the entire year unable to understand the rest of the women and how they truly viewed the world.

Another woman, a native of an Eastern European country, told the group that Americans do not have concerns for any but the wealthy. She wished there was a greater concern for all. As the year unfolded, she realized that in this group of women was more than enough concern for all. She has since become one of the greatest advocates for INFLUENCE as well as other FGI programs. It is interesting that she was talking about the status of the wealthy in 2001. This theme has become even more pronounced in today's United States.

Organization change became a regular condition of work in the United States. It was just a part of daily life. One of the new developments people had to deal with was the rise of "teams." Increasingly, work was being organized around cross-functional teams who had to learn a new way of being together and accomplishing goals. Another development was managing people remotely. As outsourcing grew so did the challenge of managing the work done by the outsource provider. And finally, as offshoring expanded, there was the challenge of managing the resources of one's company in remote locations.

The women who came to INFLUENCE held more responsible jobs, were paid better and had much broader experiences than their sisters in the '90s and '80s. [26] They came from all parts of the United States and many traveled internationally for work. Heidi was responsible for many of the worldwide sustainability efforts of her employer, a premier shoe and sporting goods manufacturer. Karen from Union Pacific was sourcing from all over the world and visited vendors in countries such as China.

Other companies such as Cisco, Accenture, Western Union, First Data, Applied Communications, all sponsored women for INFLUENCE who were also traveling overseas regularly for work. Had women from the early years in the '80s been present, they would have been incredulous at the changes.

The INFLUENCE women had less guilt about career and family than in the '90s. Most were interested both in how to get ahead and how to make a difference in the world. A substantial majority of the participants were the primary income source for their families. The mean income rose to $140,000 with the range going from $50,000 - $350,000.

In 2005, Caliper, a national consulting firm, published "The Qualities That Distinguish Women Leaders." This report confirmed what we had been observing for the past decade as well as the research we had completed in 1998, reported earlier.

A summary statement of their findings included this quote: "Women leaders are found to be more empathic and flexible, as well as stronger in interpersonal skills than their male counterparts. These qualities combine to create a leadership style that is inclusive, open, consensus building, collaborative and collegial. Women leaders scored significantly higher than male leaders in ego-drive, (persuasive motivation) assertiveness, willingness to risk, empathy, urgency, flexibility and sociability."[27]

The world for women leaders was opening up rapidly. Would the women of INFLUENCE step up to the opportunities available? The answer is a growing Yes! In the past ten years we have seen a rapid increase in the number of women who are taking a risk, speaking up, tackling difficult challenges, abandoning safe corporate assignments for work that is more meaningful, making a difference both inside organizations and beyond.

Elizabeth is one who was touched by the absence of clean water in the slums of Kenya while traveling there with Geil. Upon her return she created her own foundation to raise money and drill wells. Everyone told her that she couldn't do it, that the corruption was too great. But Elizabeth was determined. A graduate of the FOCUS program helped her with the fundraising. Having raised money she returned alone to Kenya, drilled the first deep water well in the slum of Kibera – despite the corruption in Kenya.

Since then, her foundation has enabled two slum schools, each with 500 students, to become self sufficient by creating a bottled water business and a chicken business. She returned to the US to quit her job with a large corporation and headed AfricAid, a non-profit that focuses on empowering women and girls in East Africa, primarily Tanzania. Four months after the birth of her second son, she and her baby returned to Africa to continue the work. Recently, Elizabeth has returned to corporate America because the demands of the non-profit took away the time she needs to raise her family. Her commitment to Africa, however, is in no way diminished.

Deborah is a woman who has dedicated herself to others for a number of years. Her passion has been organizing and leading trips of health practitioners to Guatemala to improve health care in that poor and war-torn country. She does this while continuing her regular corporate job in a large financial organization.

Tanya, an African American woman, decided during INFLUENCE she would run for the Nebraska State Legislature. She was the first woman of Color to be elected to the Legislature from a majority White district and only the second woman of Color in the Legislature. She faced strong opposition in her first campaign, but was re-elected with ease in 2012. In 2014, Tanya went to Ukraine as an election observer, despite the civil conflict and danger.

Some of the traditional themes of INFLUENCE persisted in the 2000s, but with some new twists. Some participants continued to lack confidence. It appears, however, that much of the confidence issue was now stemming from what was happening in the broader world. Companies were downsizing. Two-income families were becoming single income families, the political rhetoric became more and more shrill on almost every topic from taxes to illegal immigration. Pressures at work became larger. The challenges of juggling career and family felt greater than they had earlier. All of this set the stage for a more intense INFLUENCE experience.

We have been thrilled that during the past few years, the INFLUENCE women are much more ready to "go deep" with their peers. The level of learning for most has become more intense and more valuable. Stories of physical abuse by spouses or parents and other relatives continued to concern us. Many women thought that physical abuse was something that happened to women in poverty or with less education. Our experience has clearly taught us abuse of women is boundryless.

The women who lived through such horrors and then regained their health and happiness with the support of their INFLUENCE sisters humbled us.

Women have increasingly recognized that self-understanding is critical to effective leadership. Answering the question, "Who Am I?" became the key for most to a satisfying and successful INFLUENCE experience.

Significantly, a number of women in recent years have followed the answer to the "Who am I?" question with the decision they have been chasing the wrong goals. Karen left her executive role in Sourcing, wrote her personal biography and is now an inspirational speaker and consultant. Sharyn, who was on a fast track at a large international consulting firm, is now the head of Information Technology for a large urban public school system. And there are many others.

A new content piece added to the program in 1998 was the consideration of Ethics. From the first year of that addition, the INFLUENCE groups were very thoughtful and concerned about the potential impacts of alternative ethics decisions. They took the discussions very seriously and often expressed amazement at the different opinions a group of capable professionals could reach. The time spent on Ethics is now among the most memorable of the program year. More than a few participants have taken the ethics cases considered during the program and shared them with colleagues and friends for debate and discussion. One woman in Denver began having "black and white" parties. She invited friends to her home for an evening, passed out the cases and had her guests reach ethical decisions in each instance.

The travels of the three of us have translated into international travel for INFLUENCE women as well. INFLUENCE participants and graduates accompanied us five years in a row to the women's leadership program in Shanghai called *Influencing the Global Economy*. There they worked for a week with women from China and Russia on the themes of INFLUENCE. Considering those themes with Chinese and Russians made for an even richer experience. We learned that women leaders have similar goals and challenges in the US, Russia and China.

INFLUENCE graduates also accompanied us on the *China Pilgrimage* in 2003, *New Maps for Leaders* program in Moscow in 2004 and most recently *The Global Leadership Exchange* in Shanghai 2012.

INFLUENCE women joined Geil on several trips to Africa where they were able to work with slum children, many of whom have AIDS. On all our trips with INFLUENCE women abroad, the American women have both learned from and taught the women from China, Russia and other countries. Most important however, is that these women easily connected across global borders.

In addition to travel organized by us or by Geil, a number of women found the attraction of other countries strong enough to seek jobs abroad. Graduates have ended up living in and/or working in countries such as Lana in Austria, Eva in Switzerland, Deb the UK, Marti in Indonesia.

Perhaps it is the time in which we are living; perhaps it is a result of the consolidation of programs. But whatever the reason, INFLUENCE participants since 2001 have drawn closer to one another in each group and have become even better coaches to one another. Members of recent groups tend to have greater commitment to staying together after the formal program was over. Alums get together for running events, hiking, skiing and volunteer work. They meet in many different locations around the country. The sense of Sisterhood seems the strongest it has ever been.

One recent memory is of Ginger who died from Lou Gehrig's Disease within months of completing INFLUENCE. She was in her forties. Her INFLUENCE sisters flew to her City multiple times to be with her and then at the end to celebrate her life.

Another memory is of Amy, who has MS. She was required to have very serious back surgery. Early recovery stalled and there was a fear she would never recover. Her group organized prayer for her daily at noon. Within four months she recovered from the surgery and was vibrant and active again.

Bringing women from all over the country provides the program with some important learning moments as well as many humorous ones. Several years ago, a December meeting was accompanied by an ice and snowstorm in Omaha. The participants who had come from Phoenix found themselves totally unprepared. So the evening between the first and second days of the meeting, a group of about eight women (four from Phoenix and friends from other places) were out buying winter wear for the Phoenix women. After a group dinner they shopped the City, ending up at Wal-Mart and finding items for everyone. The evening was the source of many great stories.

An important part of INFLUENCE is having the participants consider big questions of national or international policy and make recommendations to their peers. In the early years, INFLUENCE groups were often hard-pressed to have a good discussion because of their limited backgrounds in national and international issues. But since 2001, the situation has changed dramatically. Participants come to the opening retreat more knowledgeable about such topics than many earlier groups were at the end of the program.

The thirtieth year of the INFLUENCE program began in September 2012. This national leadership program for women has been offered fifty-six times. Over 1600 women from 25 states and the District of Columbia have participated in the nine-month long experience in leadership development. The latest INFLUENCE group of 30 women came from nineteen organizations and from Arizona, California, Colorado, Illinois, Iowa, Minnesota, Nebraska, plus North Carolina and North Dakota. They ranged in age from 27 - 55 and had incomes from $65,000 - $225,000 with a mean of $113,000. Four were from not-for-profit organizations. Collectively they held 44 degrees. They represent the best and brightest of their respective organizations.

One of the women who joined the 2012-2013 class offered a great answer on her application as to what ways she believed the program could serve her. She said: "From what I understand from other attendees, I expect that INFLUENCE will help me make a difference without doing more myself." INFLUENCE is not intended to have women increase the quantity of what they do. Most are too busy. INFLUENCE allows women to make a difference in the world by clarifying the meaning of their lives and acting on that meaning with a clear intention.

INFLUENCE is alive; its participants are bright, capable, ambitious and making a difference across the nation and beyond.

Watching bright, talented women wrestle with the social, economic and political changes of the past thirty years has been a great learning experience for us. We have witnessed them becoming stronger, more confident, more committed to make the world better for the generations to come. At the same time we have experienced them becoming more vulnerable, appreciating the free expression of emotions and loving themselves more fully. What a privilege this has been for us.

## CHAPTER THIRTY

# India Treasures

On August 8, 2009, the *New York Times Magazine* published a special issue called *Saving the World's Women*. The stories shared were incredible, hard to believe, gut wrenching, but inspirational. One particular article, written by authors Sheryl WuDunn and Nicholas Kristoff, was *The Women's Crusade*. This article was adapted from their book, *Half the Sky: Turning Oppression into Opportunity for Women Worldwide*.

On the cover of the article was a striking photo of a beautiful young Indian woman. She was dressed in a lovely yellow sari, sitting on some ancient steps, as if she had not a care in the world. The woman was Abbas Be. It was this picture and accompanying article that changed Carol's life and within a matter of days, changed Tim's as well.

In this featured article, Kristoff and WuDunn used their excellence in writing to capture our hearts, minds and commitment to increase our focus for FGI work: sexual trafficking and slavery. Though we spoke regularly in our INFLUENCE and FOCUS programs about the need to be aware of and work against sexual trafficking in the world, we did not have first hand knowledge or experiences, just research. We used the statistics as a way to share with our INFLUENCE and FOCUS women and men the horrors faced by those held captive, exploited and forced into sexual trafficking.

We understand these victims are most often women, but also children. The younger the child, the more she/he is worth. They have no ability to fight back, to speak out, to save themselves. Many victims often die as a result of AIDS and other diseases transferred to them by their captors and those who rape them. Sometimes, they die due to being abused by their captors until they can no longer survive. The abuser also fills the victims with fear, hoping they will not attempt escape.

As we read about Abbas Be, we learned about Prajwala, the organization responsible for her rescue, recovery and full rehabilitation.

At the age of 14, due to her family's poverty, Abbas took a job as a maid in order to earn money to send to her family. When she arrived in New Delhi to begin her job, she was immediately locked up, beaten savagely and raped. This was the beginning of her imprisonment and forced prostitution. Unfortunately, this is the story of many young women and children.

After many years held in captivity in a brothel in Delhi, beaten and raped repeatedly and without hope of escape from this life, Abbas was finally rescued by the organization known as Prajwala. Because of the shame of the situation, Abbas could not return to her family home. She found rescue and recovery in the shelter of Prajwala. She found a new home, a healthy home, a place where she could be safe, learn job skills and have a new life. To see her as she was in the photo was to see a glowing, healthy, confident woman, no longer a victim. We were ready to learn more about Abbas Be, Prajwala and the stories of other victims.

As often happens in life, the opportunity to understand more, not just through reading, but through experience began to unfold. Our good friend and client, Marty Malley, in his work with Union Pacific, called us with an amazing request.

Union Pacific contracted for several years with the US business, ProKarma, to partner with Marty's staff in developing key IT systems for the Railroad. These systems were critical to the UP future.

ProKarma's US headquarters are in Omaha, NE. They have several US offices and a large office in Hyderabad, India. Marty and two executive leaders of ProKarma, Vivek Kumar and Vijay Iiju, invited the two of us to India to work with key managers in both organizations, Union Pacific and ProKarma, through a common leadership development experience. It was an opportunity for the two companies to have key members from both countries, who had only worked together daily online, now work and learn together face-to-face in India.

What an incredible opportunity for the two of us: to bring our many years of experience, knowledge and skills to serve this important Union Pacific project. And, we would provide this program in India!

The two of us prepared for the ProKarma/UP work for months, working to ensure our program design would support their work. The program was called *New Maps for Leaders* because both the Americans and Indians working on the UP project were discovering new ways to work together. We were very keen to experience India and compare it with our years in Russia and China. Both of us knew there was much to learn and looked forward with great expectations. However, in reality, we had no real idea what was ahead.

We felt blessed, not only with this grand work and life experience, but also with the opportunity to actually expand our own understanding of the realities of sexual slavery. The large ProKarma operation in India was in Hyderabad. The photo of Abbas Be was taken in Hyderabad, close to where she lived within the Prajwala rescue and recovery complex. What an incredible gift the Universe was offering us. There must be an opportunity to visit Prajwala while we were in Hyderabad. We vowed to find a way.

We knew we had to discuss this with both Marty and our ProKarma clients Vivek and Vijay prior to leaving the US. We were, after all, working for them. All three saw it as something quite possible. In fact, Vivek told us we could use ProKarma transportation and travel with a key ProKarma leader to Prajwala.

Both of us were elated with this news, though we did not need to decide more about Prajwala at the time. All of our focus went into designing and preparing for our work with the Union Pacific/ProKarma leaders. We would let the possibilities with Prajwala flow toward us.

There were no pre-trip connections with Prajwala. Our Indian clients said it would be easy to simply give a call to inquire if we were welcome. The support was heart-warming and we continued preparing for all that lay before us.

We felt anticipation and gratitude. That this trip was offered to us at this time, in this location, seemed to be a sign of confirmation that the work to raise awareness about sexual slavery all over the world was ours to accept.

There were really no preparations we could take to be ready for Prajwala, except to read and learn more. We quickly purchased Kristoff and WuDunn's new book, *Half the Sky*. Though the two of us spent many years working together to learn and inform others about the issues of oppression of women, our focus was not geared enough outside the US. The earlier work would be useful, but there was much more to learn. It is never easy to read the stories of the difficult lives so many women and children experience all over the world.

Despite our many trips to Russia and China, nothing could have prepared us for our first flight to Delhi. The lengthy flight was exhausting but our desire to reach India was strong.

Immediately upon our arrival, Vivek began our on-the-ground education about India through marvelous sightseeing and history "lessons." The bright leaders who came from Union Pacific were with us.

Prior to accepting the work with ProKarma, the two of us asked for first-hand travel and cultural experiences in India rather than professional fees for the program we would provide. We could never have imagined just how valuable this would be in our work and in our lives.

Throughout those three weeks, we provided the UP/ProKarma program, but were also given opportunities to spend time in Delhi, Agra, Hyderabad, Kerala, Goa and Mumbai. These trips offered us travel by plane, train, boat, van and elephant!

Without understanding it at the time, the historic sites, the large crowds, the different cultures of the six Indian States, all prepared us for both our work with Union Pacific/ProKarma and with the women and girls of Prajwala. We needed the lessons in culture, in history and our own personal reactions to this huge country. The many books the two of us read about India's history, culture and customs were useful and worthwhile, but nothing matched these first-hand experiences.

As we experienced and learned about both the history of, and present day India, the coming visit to Prajwala was never far away. Today, sometime later, never a week goes by without some aspect of this first experience in India crossing our minds, filling our hearts or entering our conversations.

We were better informed, with our minds and heart fully in India, as we left Delhi and landed at the sparkling new Rajiv Gandhi Airport, Hyderabad. Here we were greeted by Mr. Akula Kumar, a senior leader of ProKarma, India. His friendship quickly became one of the greatest gifts we received in India.

There was an immediate closeness with him and we recognized him as a man of great abilities, wisdom, maturity, honor and experience. Over the three years of our work in Hyderabad, our first impression of Mr. Kumar proved true over and over again. He became a dear, respected friend to both of us and to our work. Though not yet our ages, Mr. Kumar became a marvelous role model.

Our first assignment, and reason for coming to India, was to work with the bright, energetic ProKarma professionals and their UP counterparts. Designing our program for ProKarma was really no different from our work with INFLUENCE and FOCUS in terms of how we approached the design stage. We would be working with bright, young business professionals from India and the US, ready for more focused learning about leadership and how they could become more effective working as a global team.

The Indian women and men came from a variety of states in India, but now all lived and worked in Hyderabad. They were eager to move ahead in the company and enjoyed and valued learning. They were a delight. We gave thanks for such generous and bright clients from ProKarma and the Union Pacific Railroad.

It was fitting that a highlight in the history of FGI took place in the Marco Polo Lounge at the Kakatiya Hotel, Hyderabad India. Hyderabad is arguably the center of the world of the future! The Marco Polo Lounge reminded us not only of the stories of the famous world traveler, Marco Polo, but of the previous seventeen years of our own FGI world travel.

We were observing a group of thirty-two women and men from Argentina, India, Nepal and the United States as they experienced our simulation, *The Global Interaction* (*TGI*). We observed *TGI* many times, both before and after this October 2010 offering. There was just something about watching it in India that made it even more special. We were standing in Asia witnessing talented women and men consider the future of the world.

The results were the same as in every time we have done *TGI* anywhere, with two exceptions. First, the Indian participants had even greater understanding of the world than did Russians and Americans. They were able, therefore, to be much more specific in their negotiating. Second, the tempo of *The Global*

*Interaction* in India was much more animated, rapid, emotional. The participants from India approached the subject with great gusto.

It was an amazing day. We learned just how incredible bright, motivated young leaders could be. Their energy, their commitment to excellence, their willingness to take risks, offer this world so much potential.

The other days of our program in India included a wide variety of processes and tools designed to enable teams from across the world who worked together to be more effective on a daily basis. It seemed that each moment was both reflective and action-packed. The young Indians brought both a brilliance and commitment to the process which made everything work. Additionally, the participants from the US and Argentina were open to the process and had great commitment to the outcomes.

*New Maps for Leaders* was very successful. The day after we finished, Mr. Kumar told us he made a connection with the General Director of Prajwala, Dr. Sunitha Krishnan. She had accepted our request for a visit. This seemed quite amazing. One day we read about Abbas Be and Prajwala in our office in Omaha. Only a few weeks later, we were in India, preparing to meet Dr. Krishnan and others at Prajwala.

Graciously, ProKarma supplied the car and driver. Mr. Kumar himself accompanied us. During the previous week in Hyderabad, we stayed at a lovely, even extravagant hotel, the Kakatiya. The life we experienced at the Kakatiya was not the usual life of most Indians or of most people living in the US. This was luxury and service beyond what we had expected. Soon, it was clear just how extraordinary the life of the Kakatiya was when compared with the lives of ordinary people of India, let alone those who are victims of sexual slavery.

As the car maneuvered the streets of Hyderabad, we were amazed as the vehicle swerved to avoid camels and even elephants. Beside those "exotic" animals, American, European and Indian cars, buses, trucks and fast moving motorcycles swerved to avoid both the animals and each other.

The drive to the Prajwala office felt quite serious to the two of us. As we imagined and discussed what was at stake, we could never have understood in advance all that was possible. We believed we were going to learn and to volunteer. How could we know that when Dr. Krishnan understood our genuine interest in serving the Prajwala mission, our lives would be enriched and forever changed?

We were naïve, having no idea what we would learn. We were being called without knowing fully all that would flow to us.

Looking out from the car it was clear we had moved from the sumptuous neighborhood of the Kakatiya Hotel into the older neighborhood of Charminar. It is an ancient area of town with shops and vendors on all sides. Our driver pulled up next to the Hyderabad Bus Station. Women dressed in Burqas and total head coverings except for narrow slits across their eyes, were walking about, shopping, talking and enjoying the day. A camel walked by lazily, almost as if to say, "You are not in Omaha anymore."

Mr. Kumar got out of the car and the driver came around to open the door for us. We were jolted back from our thoughts and feelings. "Here we are," said Mr. Kumar. "I hope you don't mind climbing a few stairs. We politely said, "Not at all."

The few stairs were several flights, with each individual stair seeming to be a different width and slightly different height from the one before it. The Prajwala offices were on the third floor.

In the outer office, we sat looking at the graphic posters depicting the horrors of sexual slavery, showing women victims and providing statistics that surprised even us. Our emotions were heightened. We felt angry and sad about the many victims; furious and disgusted by the perpetrators. It was time to learn and understand more.

After a short wait, Dr. Sunitha Krishnan came to greet us. This was the woman we came to see. She, along with the late Brother Jose Vetticatil, began Prajwala during the mid- 1990s. The hearing in her right ear is gone, the result of a severe beating by crime bosses when she entered the Red Light District to rescue women and their children held against their will as sexual slaves. As she gestures, we see the misshaped bones in her arm. These, too, are the result of further severe beatings, multiple broken bones and threats to stay away from what organized crime bosses believe belongs to them.

The Mafia never succeeded in stopping her work. Dr. Krishnan believes these women and their children, held as prisoners, have the right to be rescued, not kept and sold for sex. She calls the hundreds of girls and women she has rescued, "My girls, my children."

We had no idea at the time how Sunitha would inform us, how she would challenge us, how she would befriend us and share deeply about her work and her life, how she would change our lives for the better.

Upon first arrival, Dr. Krishnan told us she had only ten minutes to talk. She was very business-like and perhaps still wondering how we ended up in her office. We had many questions, but also told her we desired to become involved in supporting the work of Prajwala.

Sunitha was very polite though somewhat doubtful of us, but perhaps more concerned we may not know what we were getting into. However, she responded to our questions with amazing information, examples and teaching.

When it comes to the women and children of Prajwala, it's as easy to remember the stories Sunitha shared with us now as it was the day we heard them. Early in the history of Prajwala, one of the focal points of the work was saving the lives of those forced into prostitution. One significant and life changing incident for Prajwala came early. Sunitha and Brother Jose asked some women held in prostitution what kind of support/help Prajwala could provide. Our understanding is that these women generally said it was probably too late for them. Their fate had been cast. Their plea was "Please save our children."

These children saved by the two, Brother Jose and Sunitha, became many of the early children of Prajwala, along with the children who had been used for prostitution. The term "second generation prevention" is used to describe how Prajwala worked to save and keep the children born as a result of prostitution from also being forced into prostitution.

Mr. Kumar sat quietly in the room with us, slightly away from where Sunitha and the two of us sat. He heard some of the history upon his earlier visit to the Prajwala office to prepare for our visit. Now, he wanted us to hear and understand what we had come to learn.

Sunitha talked almost non-stop, explaining to us a reality incredibly more horrific than we could have understood or believed. With our deep interest and engagement, apparently she began to understand we were serious students and dedicated to learning more.

Suddenly, at the end of two and a half hours, she stood up and said, "Come, I want you to meet my children!"

There was no hesitation in our response to her offer. The four of us were up and on our way to Astha Nivas! It was beyond our dream to be able to actually go to the main school and work site of Prajwala.

There would have been no way to imagine all we saw and learned that day. It became the day we will never forget.

In the ProKarma car with Mr. Kumar, it was at times difficult to keep up with Sunitha. It seemed a long ride. The different neighborhoods of Hyderabad were visible as our car drove through the crowded city. The two of us wondered where exactly we were going, what we would see, what we would learn?

Finally, the car approached a tall, white stucco wall surrounding a site of about three acres – larger than two American football fields. The only entry was through a huge, solid metal gate about twelve feet high. A uniformed guard opened the gate for both Sunitha's and the ProKarma vehicles. This was the outer view of Astha Nivas.

Astha Nivas was the largest Prajwala site as of 2009. Once inside, we found ourselves in a protective "village." There was a school with grades pre-school through grades six or eight. There were sleeping units by ages. There was a covered outdoor kitchen for meals. There were gardens for growing vegetables and flowers. Most surprising to us were the larger buildings which provided the Employability Training Unit and Prajwala Enterprises.

Sunitha invited us to visit the various classrooms of the school. It became even more touching and impressive. The first classroom we visited was that of four-year olds. They sat cross-legged on the floor with a carpet underneath. Oh my, they were tiny and beautiful, with huge dark eyes and bright minds. They sang for us and our hearts melted. To hear these tiny girls sing to us "Twinkle, Twinkle Little Star" in English remains one of the most touching experiences of our FGI lives.

These little girls, so recently babies, were rescued from the life of sexual slavery. Some of them had been used for sex; others were the daughters of sexual slaves. We admired their beauty and bright minds, and were delighted and happy to hear and meet these precious children.

However, the harsh reality of their lives was evident. Instinctively we wanted to grab each girl, to hold each close to our hearts. To tell her how remarkable she was. The urge to scream and cry out at the perpetrators was overwhelming. Carol blew them a kiss instead. Clearly, our hearts were already handed over and yet, we had many more classrooms to visit.

We moved from room to room.

Each grade level was proud to show us their learning. Some would recite poems, some would speak to us about what they were studying, others would ask us questions about our lives. Each grade from pre-school on wore the same simple but appropriate blue jumpers over white blouses. Each class was amazingly positive and so full of life. We were witnessing and feeling the rehabilitation before our very eyes.

Tim thought about his granddaughters, Alex and Beth, who were in 3rd and 5th grades at the time. How different were their lives in Omaha grade school. And yet, the girls we met in Astha Nivas had the same bright eyes, same smiles, same youthful energy. How could adults have treated the girls of Prajwala this way? Then again, thinking of the US, we know that girls such as Tim's granddaughters, all across our country, are sold into sexual slavery everyday. We must act.

Women above school age were working in such various occupations as welding, carpentry, bookbinding, printing and screen-printing. Today even more businesses have been added. Prajwala actually sold completed wooden desks and tables from their carpentry shop to the local school system. We found the excellence and achievement of Prajwala Enterprises very impressive.

As we moved from the classrooms to the work units and employee training, the positive spirit and bright minds were once again apparent. In the work units, the women were anywhere from 18 – 35. As Carol looked into their eyes, they looked back with confidence and love. Yes, love.

These women and Carol seemed to have some fast recognition at Soul Level. As both of us worked more with the older women and girls, our friendships became deep and real. These were not people to whom we ministered. These were our friends and our teachers, just as we were to them.

However, for these early moments of becoming parts of each others' lives, none of us had any idea what would unfold between us.

While the accomplishments of Prajwala were many, Sunitha had even bigger dreams and goals in mind. We walked along together and she gave us little tidbits of her ideas. Her mind could imagine and project anything. It seemed to us that Astha Nivas was miraculous in all that had been accomplished. However, Sunitha was looking into the future and imagining even more.

As she became clearer on the nature of our FGI work in leadership development, Sunitha believed we could fulfill a significant developmental need within Prajwala. She knew there were leaders inside Prajwala who must be developed further. Some of the very girls she rescued from sexual slavery were now the key leaders and managers of a growing Prajwala. These young women had true leadership responsibility such as managing the Business Enterprises, serving as Security Guards, providing Community Outreach, acting in key roles on the Rescue Teams, day-to-day management of Astha Nivas, supervision and oversight of many of the rescued girls and their rehabilitation.

To make the "dreams" more urgent, the owners of the land where Astha Nivas was located decided to sell to a developer for a shopping center. Prajwala had only a year to move.

The push from the landlords caused "the dream" to immediately move into action. Sunitha dreamed of a large campus in the City. But the Mafia made sure no one would sell her land. She understood she would have to move farther away. As Sunitha turned her sights outside the City, new opportunities also unfolded.

She could imagine large tracts of land for gardens which could supply food. The gardens would provide work for the girls and women, plus the accomplishment of harvesting fresh vegetables and fruits. There would be larger living areas for all ages plus a state of the art school for grades pre-school through high school.

To support all of this and move Sunitha's dreams into the future, Prajwala needed money, lots of money.

Together, Sunitha and the two of us agreed that while we would work to raise money and awareness about Prajwala and sexual slavery in general, we would also serve the work by developing the leadership capacity of the entire organization. A clear agenda was set. We had never before or since been given such meaningful work.

The fact that we were able to be involved with Sunitha and Prajwala was a result of the open-mindedness and generosity of our ProKarma clients and friends. Due to our friend Marty Malley, ProKarma and the Union Pacific Railroad brought us to Hyderabad, India in 2009 and again in 2010. ProKarma continued to support us in our dedication and work with Prajwala. During the first two years of work in Hyderabad, we were working with Sunitha as well as providing leadership development programs for ProKarma and Union Pacific leaders. We were challenged to new levels and felt ourselves growing and learning as we served.

The two of us were eager to return to the States to begin to write and share about our experiences and to engage more fully in supporting and actively fundraising for Prajwala.* Yes, there was some hesitation on our parts as we wondered if our goals were at all feasible. However, things like feasibility have never really held us back at FGI International. Our belief has always been: if you intend it, it will manifest. Yes, as founders of FGI International/FGISpirit, we have never been ones to scale back on a dream . . .

*Please refer to the section of our website, www.fgispirit.org, entitled, "Our Reflections," to read more on our Prajwala work.

## CHAPTER THIRTY-ONE

# From Victims to Wise, Joyful Teachers

The two of us returned to Omaha, full of energy and new information to share. For us, it's a lack of courage, a lack of conscience and consciousness to stay quiet, once we know what we know. We promised to speak out and continue do so. We were ready to ask others to speak out, to serve, to contribute.

Our plans began to grow and build with goals for how much money we would raise to assist Prajwala in relocating its main center. We had no belief that all Sunitha planned would be anything but possible.

The fundraising was quite an undertaking, but we were full of commitment. Those dark, beautiful eyes of the precious Prajwala children and friends remained our beacons of light and fueled our quest to make a difference.

It was Fall 2009. We began our campaign writing regular letters and emails to our substantial client base sharing what we experienced and learned as a result of our work with Prajwala. We did this totally as an educational goal. Our many FGI friends and clients were interested and asked to learn more.

Our writing soon grew into a larger campaign. We shared more complete and detailed information about the work and goals of Prajwala, in order to support the fundraising. Our lives took on new meaning as we added more to the always-full FGI agenda. In spite of this additional work, our positive energy and dogged determination seemed to keep us fueled and in a constant learning/teaching mode. We were more keen and sharp with our messages and clearer on our goals about this work with Prajwala.

Through the generosity of our FGI/FGISpirit donor friends, we were able to raise a significant amount of money to support the Prajwala construction.

The time flew by and we began to imagine the 2010 trip to India. Flowing in a dual-stream was our positive energy and focus on returning to Hyderabad with the leadership program for

ProKarma/Union Pacific friends. We would also have our much desired return to Prajwala to be with Dr. Sunitha Krishnan and her "girls."

Plans also began to take shape for providing a 2010 leadership program for the Supervisors and Managers of the Prajwala businesses. Each one had her own story of having been sold or taken into, and then some years later, having been rescued from sexual slavery. The years in between were full of ugliness, pain and horror.

Their lives of sexual slavery were usually a blur during those years of pain and mistreatment. It was purely a survival existence and even that was difficult from minute to minute. As we thought about how to develop a special leadership program for these women, there were no examples for us to follow. We had to rely on our experiences, intuition and judgment.

Carol's work in women's leadership programs at the University of Nebraska Omaha provided a good place to start. Additionally, the shared work we did at the Union Pacific Railroad in developing programs for women was also relevant in many ways. We read all we could about the issues of sexual slavery, but it was still reading. It was the stories Sunitha told us that inspired us, horrified us, gave us hope and made us believe the kind of approach we would naturally take was right.

Our primary goal was to ensure these women, ages about 20-42, knew and felt our respect and belief in who they were and what was still possible in their lives. They were no longer alone. They were no longer sexual slaves. They were no longer invisible. They were working in ways that served society. To us, they were our valued and worthy students. Our desire was to serve them.

Our understanding grew in terms of how alone their lives must have been as they struggled to survive in a world of pain, degradation and imprisonment. The constant threat of death lived at their doorsteps. We desired to surround them with love, learning and when/if possible, even laughter.

And so design of the October 2010 program for Prajwala began our inspiration to make a positive difference in their lives.

Our determination was strong to provide ways for these women to celebrate, have fun and understand that for centuries of existence, women have been coming together to serve each other, to listen to each other and to share what it means to be a woman.

Our clear goal for ourselves was to find ways to celebrate and have fun with the women as a group. At first, there was some concern because Tim is a man. Would they see him as a symbol of the men who had brutalized and tortured them? Would they shy away? Would they close down?

Our memories remained from that first meeting when Sunitha told us we were naïve. In terms of her work, Sunitha was correct. However, the two of us had been out in the world. We did know how to develop an agenda that would serve the needs of these women in spite of the horrors they had experienced in their lives. All of the concerns were not valid. We were simply Carol and Tim: regardless of audience or location all over the world. It took no time at all before they trusted us as elders, present to serve and celebrate them.

Thirty-five women gathered with us on a hot, rainy day at the Henry Martyn Institute outside of Hyderabad. We began the program with an old favorite saying we have used with other women's programs in the US and China.

It seemed to be as relevant in India as it has been everywhere else:

> *"Every morning, woman rises, kisses the world awake,*
>
> *smoothes out its rough edges, mends its tears, then*
>
> *sends it out to keep on turning until tomorrow."*

This seemed relevant and appropriate for our women students.

It was something they related to and understood. It was not a far-fetched theory, but simply another way to talk about the nature of their lives.

And guess who one of the students was? Abbas Be! When she entered the room, we felt like it was the arrival of a rock star. Of course she was unaware of our attention. What was most remarkable is that within an hour, we had begun to know the other women, all of whom were just as impressive as Abbas Be.

Our goal was to assist their empowerment. It seemed essential to find as many ways as possible to serve these friends in acknowledging who they really were as humans of worth. Sunitha's work had confirmed and taught this for many years. Their lives had taken them through many dark years, but it was clear in the bright sparkle in their eyes they had been renewed and had developed a sense of self.

We knew we wanted to provide them many different healing "mantras" or affirmations to carry with them back out into the world. Carol began the program with one of the mantras she had written for these women. It was larger than we had understood, but it called them toward us and they felt its power.

One of their favorites of these mantras was *"I have a place of worth in this world."* Just thinking of their strong voices saying this aloud, continues to give us positive energy and hope today.

Many options for the agenda were developed, just in case we hit a wall or somehow something did not seem relevant. The agenda gave us the freedom to "bob and weave" as the moment presented itself.

There was one aspect of the agenda that threw us a curve for a short time. We planned a time for self-reflection involving drawing. Drawing was not something these women had done. There had been no time for such activities. Life was survival.

Our goal was always to have them see themselves as we saw

them: strong, bright, beautiful survivors contributing daily to making the world a better place. This of course, requires one to know self deeply. However, both the physical self and the emotional self of each of these women had been injured in many horrific ways. So, when it came time for the drawing, we hit a wall. The suggested task was to draw one's own face.

It suddenly became clear to us: these women had never seen their own faces. There were no mirrors in their lives. They had no idea how to even start the activity. The two of us in no way wanted to cause any pain or hurt for these women. We loved them the moment we met them. However, for a brief moment, less than a minute really, Carol was actually tongue-tied.

And then, as often happens, a Higher Power intervened. Carol was given the insight to suggest to the women they use each other to tell them how they looked. Oh my, what gifts they gave to each other!

They would say with such caring:

"You have the most beautiful, thick, shining hair."

"Your eyes are dark and round and large. They sparkle."

"You have a beautiful nose that looks like the nose of a statue."

"Your smile is so wide and lovely. It makes me smile back without thinking."

It went on like this until each woman had produced a hand-drawn self-portrait. Interestingly, they drew on small tablets, printed by the Prajwala printing presses. It all came together in marvelous ways. While it was not a part of the agenda for us to do so, it seemed only natural for us, the "old teachers," to walk around the room and admire each and every one of those self-portraits.

Each one of the portraits was beautiful and seemed full of life and confidence. Surely, it was one of the most meaningful and touching moments of life either of us has experienced. We did do our best to not just stand there and weep with gratitude and love for these Prajwala women. Though, this would have been easy since we felt it so deeply.

It was important to serve these women in more deeply understanding who they were. What are those little things that help them understand this? We worked with the agenda to make it simple, straightforward and still an opportunity for each woman to go to a deep place of being.

Such simple approaches brought deep responses. Before our eyes, they gathered information about themselves and each other that had never been elicited in their lives. Something so simple as our asking, "What is your favorite color?" took us on a deep and meaningful time of connection.

The idea that it was possible to have the right to choose one's favorite color was totally new. Of course, at some level in a life of survival, one's favorite color is irrelevant. After those times of dealing only with survival, everything that we did together had never had a place in their lives. During our day together, they were simply present to learn, to laugh, to enjoy life with old, safe teachers and experience ways to understand who they really were.

For over thirty years, Carol worked with issues of women's health and women's rights in the United States. It had not always been easy. Even the women, who seem healthy, smart and strong, often struggle with self-worth, self-love and understanding about having rights. From our experiences in 5-6 different countries, this is more often true than not.

Therefore, another important aspect of our Prajwala program was to introduce the concept of having the right to do or be something or someone.

We shared our own belief that genuinely strong, confident women know they have rights. Working together with the

Prajwala women allowed some possible ideas to surface. They delighted in understanding and discussing these.

Imagine having been held in locked, often dark rooms, unable to have the right to go to the bathroom, to eat or drink, to make any life choices at all. Imagine being misused and injured sexually over and over again, year after year by strangers who hurt and maim you physically and emotionally so that you begin to believe you are worthless.

We did not ask them to develop their own sense of Rights at this time; nor did we put the Rights in any order of hierarchy. Instead, a list of Rights was simply offered for discussion. The Rights shared were these:

1. I have the right to go to school.

2. I have the right to play.

3. I have the right to have friends.

4. I have the right to be safe.

5. I have the right to feel strong.

6. I have the right to laugh.

As a group, we repeated them over and over. Then the women gathered in small groups for discussion of what each one really meant to the individuals present. It was deep. It was real.

Then, it was time for some fun. We decided in advance to focus on the Right, "I have the right to laugh." We know from other work that genuine laughter is rejuvenating, healing and good for the body, mind and spirit.

Using laughter can sometimes feel frivolous or even unhealthy, but the right kind of healthy laughter can be magic and healing for us humans.

Going back to a favorite song she learned at age seven, Carol decided to teach the women a song that since childhood had brought her joy and even laughter. Carol learned this song as a little girl during her time as a Brownie (Girls Scouts of America.)

Together, laughing and singing, the women leaders of Prajwala with Tim and Carol sang over and over about "Kooka Burra" sitting in the old gum tree, kissing monkeys. The song worked it's magic. As a group, we were singing, laughing and thoroughly enjoying ourselves. All were safe. All were happy. All were healthy. All were friends. We were all teachers for each other.

To understand one has rights is to understand one is valuable in this world and can make decisions about one's life. This had never before been a part of these women's lives until their rescue and rehabilitation. Sunitha and the work of Prajwala brought these women and girls back to life one day at a time over many years. They sat before us now, energetic, strong, bright women.

There had never before been such meaningful and significant work for the two of us. That we were asked to return and serve another even larger group of Prajwala women was a gift beyond what we could have imagined.

When our time with the women ended, all of them clustered around us, some were moved to speak up.

"Madame Carol, Mister Tim, our parents sold us or did not find us when we were taken. You have shown us more love in one day than we have felt in our entire lives."

Another woman spoke: "Today I laughed for the first time I can remember and it felt good. Thank you!"

One of the teen girls spoke: "Always I have had that small, dark place deep inside me. Today it is gone. I thank you."

And finally, as we were standing and moving to leave, one woman, somewhat cautiously, walked up to Carol. She was face to face with Carol and she said: "Madame Carol, will you hug me like a Mother hugs her child? I have never felt this." Carol hugged her with deep joy and tears flowing.

The moments of emotion were nearly overwhelming. After all the women were hugged by Carol, about one-third of them approached Tim for a hug. Given their life stories, this was more than we expected. Tim was also overwhelmed by the ways they trusted him and reached out to him. They recognized him as their advocate and friend.

As 2011 began to unfold, it was decided there would not be another ProKarma/Union Pacific program. But we knew we must return to Prajwala. There was so much meaningful work to be done and so much love, learning and joy that flowed into our hearts and souls as a result of this work.

Sunitha was ready for us. She invited many of those we worked with in 2010 plus others whom we had not yet met. The two of us designed a more ambitious and demanding 2011 agenda based on our experiences the past year of the sheer ability to learn and go deep with these women. They were there to learn and pushed themselves into new areas of being and depth.

Plus, it was blatantly clear: the two of us loved these women and girls as if they were our own children. It is perhaps hard for the reader to understand how we could so quickly have deep love for these women who lived 12,000 miles from Omaha. But we truly do. What they experienced in their lives was beyond what most people in the US could ever imagine. Their own ability to learn deeply and make connections was surely a key part of their having been true survivors; survivors of the most horrible and heinous treatment any human could imagine. That they were now able to laugh, to learn, to love, to thrive is more than a miracle!

We returned to the Henry Martyn Institute, but to a much brighter room than in 2010. We were amazed to see so many present. Some of the women had been with us for the 2010 program. With these, we embraced as dear "family friends." We were especially surprised to see that among the thirty-six assembled, two were men. Up until this time, we had only imagined men as the perpetrators of the women and girls. Little had we understood, many young men are also misused in a variety of ways in sexual slavery. This added an entirely new aspect of learning for us. It somewhat changed, but only slightly, the program dynamics. These men with us were not the perpetrators; they were also misused. Every person present clearly understood this, felt comfortable and was ready to jump in.

Our 2011 agenda was more complicated and went deeper into leadership attributes and content. We felt ready to take to India some of the early INFLUENCE agenda content. They were bright, eager-to-learn students and the timing was right.

At first, there was some doubt on our parts due to our having increased the challenges of the content based on the 2010 success. Additionally, seeing that we had so many people we had never worked with before made us wonder, could we develop the group and go as deep as necessary? Our concerns proved groundless. All of the women and men were open and ready to learn and contribute. Their behavior, earnest learning, ability to share their joy and go deep as students certainly added to the positive experience had by all.

We did take some basic INFLUENCE content, believing it would be appropriate for those with whom we had worked in 2010. The specific content on leadership was based on the research done by the two of us over 30 years. But, here we were, sharing it in India with women and men who were not working in corporate or non-profit organizations in the US. We were sharing the content with women and men who were educated as a result of difficult and often horror-filled life stories. Rather than being traumatized, they were hungry for new learning and amazingly able to transfer it into their lives at the moment. Their thoughtful, free minds took each subject and enhanced it.

When we provided them with information about the qualities of leaders, they understood each one and were able to differentiate for themselves which were their strengths and which were the ones to focus on for development. They were able to be specific about their own internal traits and areas of excellence and those areas for improvement and learning. They were able to coach and encourage each other. The work Sunitha was doing in these women's lives was clearly deep and life changing. At the same time, our experiences with these women had the same effects on us. Our lives were changed forever for the better.

No words can adequately describe the depth to which these women, girls and those two young men, have changed and honored our lives. For this, we will forever give thanks. No day goes by when we do not think of them with love and wish we were with them.

This program experience far exceeded our expectations. Many of the women we were with for two years in a row in our programs became dear friends. One of those is Abbas Be.

Our commitment to Prajwala and speaking out against sexual trafficking has not waivered. Our further investigation and research has not stopped. Our work in sharing the information has not stopped, will not stop.

We must not wallow in the heinous crimes these children and women have endured. We must give up feeling sad and hopeless. Our action is required. As adults we must learn to speak out and speak about sexual slavery and sexual trafficking. We must have courage if we are going to change the most complex issues of this global society. Today's reality is that no country borders separate us anymore from the raw truths of life. We know, for example, that one in every five women are sexually assaulted in college and that at least one in every four women in Nebraska will be raped during their lives.

We continue to spread the word in order to take others out of their denial. Tirelessly we continue to raise awareness and ask you to do the same.

# FINAL REFLECTIONS

Those thirty-plus years of challenging, exciting work seemed to fly by. It's only now, at the end of capturing our memories, we more fully realize the many life experiences, learning gifts and global opportunities which blessed us.

The adventures challenged us. The constant learning grew and stretched us. However, within weeks, we were always back on the road again.

Having now had this time to reflect and write, each one of us is even more aware of all that has come from our FGI/FGISpirit work. To have friends we can call upon in many countries is precious. To know deep in our hearts those friends would respond with love and caring is, indeed, a blessing. To know those friends understand they are always welcome into either of our homes simply closes the circle.

Our many years of being international business consultants unfolded in so many ways. Though each one of us began our career in a classroom as a school teacher, our FGI work took us to countless global business experiences never imagined before FGI.

Working in multiple countries has made it possible for us to experience and understand the importance of Spirituality in our lives. There is more than "doing" and it is "being." Learning to be conscious in the world allows the understanding of self and the honoring of others who make it all possible.

The two of us have consciously practiced the discipline of Reflection since our first days of creating FGI. Our work on this book has given us the ultimate Reflection time. No consultant can be successful without clients who are open and able to learn. In most cases, the leaders with whom we were privileged to work were also our teachers, our guides, our forever friends and sometimes, even our caretakers in a foreign environment. Those who lived in other countries opened their lives, their families, their homes and their hearts to us.

Each one of our families, Hunter and Rouse, supported and confirmed us over many years of coming and going. With each return over those 30 years, Terry was there for Carol and Maryanne was there for Tim. This gave the two of us the comfort, strength and love necessary to carry us during those 80-hour weeks, one after the other, in multiple countries.

Along with our two families, our many clients and friends in the US and abroad have made all of this possible. Plus, when we traveled, many talented, dedicated people who have been a part of FGI/FGISpirit, held things together in Omaha. They were the voices of "Tim and Carol" to those who called and came to FGI. Of course, our FGI Team would have been incomplete without Denny Aron, always a key part of FGI travel and success over the years.

Deep gratitude, plus our many stories fill our hearts today.

The book, as you see it here, is also the work of Rebecca Blair. Rebecca turned hundreds of computer pages and many photographs into the actual book. Her excellence is unparalleled.

This is never over 'til it's over. The FGI work continues . . .

# END NOTES

## Chapter 1

1. Union Pacific 2011, Sustainability & Citizenship Report, www.UP.com, 31 May, 2012.

## Chapter 3

2. American Society for Training and Development (ASTD) and Organization Development Network (OD Network)

## Chapter 4

3. Refer to Context 1979-1990.

4. *Creating* INFLUENCE *From the Inside Out: A Report on the* INFLUENCE *Program After Nine Years.* FGI and The Browning Group, May, 1991.

5. Senge, Peter. *The Fifth Discipline: The Art and Practice of The Learning Organization.* New York: Doubleday/Currency, 1990.

## Chapter 8

6. The Virginia Satir Global Network, http://satirglobal.org

## Chapter 9

7. As we reported in our 1993 book, "This first conversation with Gennady exhilarated us. Before us sat a brilliant engineer and gearshift designer who had shared in a major Soviet Prize. His specific challenge was the challenge of the entire Soviet professional community: How to transfer the knowledge and business ability from the great Soviet military-industrial complex into the now private sector."

8. *Reflections on Russia: Friendship, Culture, Business.* FGI, Inc., Omaha, NE. 1993.

9. "Profilaktika" is a Russian word meant to infer something able to prevent illness. During Soviet times, tuberculosis was a serious issue. People were sent to sanitariums to be kept away from general society and to recover and grow stronger. The sanitariums eventually were used for both recovery as well as ways to stay healthy. During 1992 when we arrived in Moscow,

our Russian friends believed this would be a great place to have our first Conference.

Chapter 14

10. Twenty-five states have been the homes of INFLUENCE Participants. These include Nebraska, Colorado, Arizona, California, Georgia, Iowa, Illinois, Kansas, Massachusetts, Minnesota, Oregon, South Dakota, Tennessee, Texas, Washington, Wisconsin, Kentucky, Michigan, Nevada, North Carolina, North Dakota, Ohio, Utah and Virginia, Minnesota, Oregon, South Dakota, Tennessee, Texas, Washington, Wisconsin, and the District of Columbia.

11. Fukuyama, Francis. *The End of History and the Last Man. New York: Penguin*, 1992.

12. *Change Leaders: What Does it Take, Who is Ready?"* FGI, 1997.

The information displayed in this FGI report came from evaluation of over 13,000 co-workers who rated more than 1,100 women and 875 men. Based on the demographics of the organizations where the assessment tools were used, it should be noted that the co-workers were far more often men than women, regardless of the gender of the person being rated.

Data displayed in this report represents co-worker evaluations from 1992 through 1996.

Data displayed in this report comes from a study of 45 behavioral items used regularly in FGI 360° assessment tools.

After averaging the scores for all items, it was found that women received statistically significant higher ratings than men in 28 out of 45 items. Men had higher ratings than women on three items. In 14 cases, there was no significant difference between women and men.

Because the differences in the mean scores for each of the 45 items are not numerically large, FGI used z-testing hypothesis of two independent means. The results displayed in this report are statistically significant at the .01 level of confidence. In other words, the differences have been caused by something other than chance.

The persons rated by co-workers in this study range in age from 22 to 55, were compensated between $30,000 and $500,000 per year, work in for-profit, not-for-profit and government organizations ranging in size from sole proprietorship to over 400,000 employees. They come from all parts of the U.S.

13. Our findings from 1997 were confirmed and strengthened by a much more comprehensive study undertaken by the Caliper organization and published in 2005. That study was entitled *The Qualities That Distinguish Women Leaders* and included in depth interviews of both women and men leaders from some of the top companies in the United Kingdom and the United States. Some highlights from that study will be reported in Chapter 25. There are two more recent books that confirm and expand this research: Gerzema, John and Michael D'Antonio. *The Athena Doctrine: How Women (and the Men Who Think Like Them) Will Rule the Future.* San Francisco: Jossey-Bass, 2013, and Hewlett, Sylvia Ann and Ripa Rashid. *Winning the War for Talent in Emerging Markets: Why Women Are the Solution.* Boston: Harvard Business School of Publishing, 2011.

14. BRIC is an acronym coined by Goldman Sachs, 2001, to label the four fastest growing large economies: Brazil, Russia, India and China.

Chapter 17

15. FGI International is our for-profit corporation. FGISpirit is a 501(c) 3 not-for-profit organization which provides a variety of leadership experiences in both the US and foreign countries.

16. The Commonwealth of Independent States is a quazi-organization of most of the former Soviet Republics. It has had limited successes in trade and investment.

17. Russia parlance to describe the huge, fast acquired wealth of some business men of the former Soviet Republics during privatization in Russia after the dissolution of the Soviet Union in the 1990s.

Chapter 18

18. Robert Bly, poet and author, is often considered the father of the men's movement in the 1990s. He is remembered most for his book: *Iron John: A Book About Men*. New York: Addison-Wesley, 1990. His work and the work of other men of the period greatly expanded the self-definition of many Euro-American males in the US. Even those who never read one of the books or participated in any of the retreats for men were affected. The reality for men was different.

Chapter 20

19. Cousineau, Phil. *The Art of Pilgrimage: The Seekers Guide to Making Travel Sacred*. Berkeley: Conari Press, 1998. Page xxiii.

Chapter 23

20. Gerzema, John and D'Antonio, Michael. *The Athena Doctrine: How Women (and the Men Who Think Like Them) Will Rule the Future*. San Francisco: Jossey-Bass, 2013.
21. Fareed Zakaria, *Newsweek,* 2006.

Chapter 25

22. Abdullah, Sharif. *Creating a World That Works for All*. San Francisco: Berrett Koehler, 1999.
23. Wheatley, Margaret J. *Turning To One Another, simple conversations to restore hope to the future*. San Francisco: Berrett-Koehler, 2002.

Chapter 26

24. News media in the West lead one to believe Tibet has been a recent illegal Chinese takeover. History is more complicated. Tibet came under Chinese influence in the 7th Century C.E. through a royal marriage. At one point, during a time of trouble in China, the British intervened to make Tibet independent of China.

Chapter 29

25. Pew Research Center, Global Attitudes Project, July 13, 2011.
26. In 2003, Geil and we decided to discontinue the Phoenix INFLUENCE program. All three of us were traveling overseas regularly and it became essential to reduce our commitments

at home. In 2006, we discontinued the Denver INFLUENCE program for the same reason. All of INFLUENCE would be consolidated in Omaha. So the past seven groups of INFLUENCE have met in Omaha. Participants come from all over the country. More than twenty states have been represented in the groups since the consolidation.

27. "The Qualities That Distinguish Women Leaders," Research Report, Princeton: Caliper, 2005.

# ABOUT THE AUTHORS

Carol Hunter and Tim Rouse are the founders of the organization/leadership development and management consulting firm, FGI International and the not-for-profit FGISpirit International. Through FGI, Carol and Tim have consulted with over one hundred organizations in areas such as mergers, strategy, culture and leadership development. FGISpirit provides nontraditional leadership development for the world of the future. The two organizations have enabled work with over 5,000 leaders from over 40 countries. Both Carol and Tim served as adjunct faculty at the Center for Creative Leadership for thirty years. Both have also lectured at universities in the US, Russia, Canada, China and New Zealand.

Carol and her husband, Terry, live in Papillion, NE. They have two children and two grandchildren. Carol and Terry lived in Turkey for two years where Terry served in the US Air Force and Carol taught college level mathematics for the US Dept. of Defense. This opened Carol's love for learning and teaching in different cultures. Her bachelor's degree is from Arizona State University and her Masters from University of Nebraska at Omaha. She also studied at Indiana University and the Kellogg School at Northwestern.

Tim and his wife, Maryanne, live in Omaha, Nebraska. They have three children and seven grandchildren. Tim's life was significantly influenced by his love for history and especially that of Russia. A past President of the Omaha City Council and two-term member of the Omaha Board of Education, Tim is a graduate of Creighton University and the University of Nebraska at Omaha. He also studied at the University of Michigan and Stanford University.

Carol and Tim's work together has been focused on creating a world that works for all.